Solitary Pagans

Solitary Pagans

Contemporary Witches, Wiccans, and Others Who Practice Alone

HELEN A. BERGER

THE UNIVERSITY OF
SOUTH CAROLINA PRESS

Published by the University of South Carolina Press
Columbia, South Carolina 29208

uscpress.com

Printed in the United States of America

Library of Congress Cataloging-in-Publication Data can be found at http://catalog.loc.gov/.

ISBN 978-1-64336-008-9 (hardback)
ISBN 978-1-64336-010-2 (ebook)

To Christa Caggiano
and
In memory of Leigh S. Shaffer

Contents

Tables

Preface

This book grew out of two seemingly unrelated events: the publication of an article criticizing contemporary Pagan studies and the appearance of an unexpected finding in my survey data. The survey on which this book is based, "The Pagan Census Revisited" which was conducted with James R. Lewis, was initially conceived as a follow-up to "The Pagan Census," my first survey, completed fifteen years before. I had planned to do something of a longitudinal study by including most of the same questions as were in the first survey and a few new ones. When I started to analyze the data, what was most surprising is how little had changed, except for one thing—the growth of solitary practitioners. Of course as one of the most famous fictional detectives, Sherlock Holmes, points out in the *Hound of the Baskervilles,* the dogs that do not bark in the night are as important a clue as those that do (Doyle 2010). However at about this time Marcus Davidsen (2012) published an article that was critical of all but two scholars of contemporary Paganism—one of which was me—and therefore of the entire subfield. An entire session of the contemporary Pagan Studies section at the American Academy of Religion was dedicated to a response to this article, and as a result I read it more carefully than I might otherwise have. Almost hidden among his criticisms was a concern that so little had been written about solitary practitioners, although they were the majority of the religion. His source for stating that the religion was primarily composed of solitaries was *Voices from the Pagan Census* (H. Berger et al. 2003). I was struck with how prescient this criticism was, as in the first survey just under 51 percent of contemporary Pagans were solitary, a bare majority. In the second I found that over three-quarters now are practicing alone. Truly, solitary practice is the face of contemporary Paganism. I put aside my first aspiration to examine how the religion had changed, or more correctly had hardly changed, over the past fifteen years and decided to focus instead on solitary practitioners.

This book is the first systematic overview of those contemporary Pagans who are solitary. Although the survey was conducted internationally, and received over eight thousand responses from fifty-nine nations, over six thousand of those were from the United States. I therefore decided to focus on the United States, as I felt the other data was less robust. I have throughout the chapters used the other data for comparisons where possible, most particularly the data from Canada and the United Kingdom. The survey was written in English, making the data from non-English-speaking nations more suspect as only those who were fluent would feel comfortable filling out a long survey in a language not their own. The level of response from the United Kingdom and Canada was better than most of the other nations represented in the survey, and for the majority in those countries English is their native language too. To the degree that the data from other, particularly non-English-speaking nations, is representative, solitary practice is the most common way in which the religion is practiced worldwide.

The larger response from U.S. contemporary Pagans than from elsewhere, I suspect, is due in part to my being better known, respected, and trusted in this country than in others. Some of those who responded to the second survey noted in the comment section that they had responded to the first survey as well. I have no way of knowing what percentage of the respondents to the second survey also responded to the first. I was concerned throughout with maintaining respondents' anonymity. In my second survey, as in my first, I had the help of some of the contemporary Pagan leaders who sent out word about the survey. As with my first survey I found that contemporary Pagans, at least in the United States, want to be heard.

Throughout the book I compare solitary and group practitioners to illuminate how those who practice alone are similar and different. As I have done in the analysis of my first survey, where possible I compare the data from "The Pagan Census Revisited" to available data about other Americans. Some of the questions in the survey were taken from the General Social Survey (GSS) with the intent of doing this type of comparison. In other instances I have found data that would permit contemporary Pagans to be compared to other Americans. I believe, in doing research on any group, that it is important to have a comparative group or a baseline. Otherwise one can erroneously attribute what one finds to the group when it is within the normal range of the larger society. In her important book *The Making of a Moonie: Choice or Brainwashing,* Eileen Barker (1984), compared psychological profiles of group members of the Unification Church in the United Kingdom to other British citizens. She discovered that there was less, not more, mental illness in this group than in the society at large.

Having a comparison between solitaries with those contemporary Pagans who practice in groups is particularly important in my study when looking at levels of social and political activity as it provides a point of comparison within the religion. However, it is not enough to compare one set of contemporary Pagans to another. It is essential to have another comparison, one with ordinary Americans, who are not contemporary Pagans. In comparison to group members solitaries are less active—socially, spiritually, and politically—but when compared to other Americans they are not. It is important to understand both those truths as we explore this growing phenomenon.

The growth of solitary practitioners within this religion has parallels within the larger society. More and more people are claiming to be spiritual but not religious or to be religious but not to belong to a church or other religious institution. Some scholars like Robert Putnam (2001), Bryan Wilson (1990), and Steve Bruce (2003) see this as resulting in social and political isolation. Others (for example Bender 2010; Woodhead 2013) have argued this is not a disengagement from the world but a new form of religion and social engagement that is consistent with late modernity, with its emphasis on globalization and instant communication. Contemporary Paganism provides an excellent case study for examining these claims as some of its members belong to groups while others do not. Of course these groups are not the same as churches; they are looser and less long lasting. There is no larger hierarchy or organizational structure to which each coven or group belongs and to which they are obliged to answer. As there is no church building to move into or funds associated with the organization, if enough members leave the group it just dissolves; at times new ones are formed, sometimes under a new name and with some of the same and some new people. Nonetheless contemporary Paganism provides something of a natural experiment, in which we can compare those who are completely outside and those inside a religious group. What I found in doing this comparison is that group participation matters. Those in groups do more, socially, politically, and spiritually. However, solitary practice does not result in a withdrawal from the world. The differences are measurable and real but in most instances not large. What is more important, solitary practitioners are more engaged than the average American. At least among contemporary Pagans, participation in a metaphysical religion, even for those who practice alone, is not resulting in social or political withdrawal.

"The Pagan Census Revisited" was distributed over the Internet. As I discuss in the first chapter, no surveys of this new religion, including mine, have been random surveys. The hidden nature of this religion and, as I found in my first survey, the willingness of contemporary Pagans to distribute surveys among those they know and on the Internet, even without being asked, has made it impossible to do a random survey. This difficulty has increased because of the growth of solitary practitioners who may not be members of any organization. Nonetheless this survey, which is the largest survey yet completed of contemporary Pagans in the United States, like my first survey, which is now online at the Murray Institute at Harvard University, provides the best data available.

This book provides an overview of solitary practitioners—where they live, how they earn their living, whether or not they are married or single. It explores their spiritual practices, their social engagement, and their political activity. My survey permitted the voices of over six thousand contemporary American Pagans, and almost two thousand contemporary Pagans from around the world, most of whom practice alone, to be heard. Their voices provide us with one important example of the new spiritual turn in religion and provide one venue to explore what that means for the development of community and political action.

Acknowledgments

This book is dedicated to two people who stepped in at critical moments to help when crises developed in the research process: Christa Caggiano and Leigh S. Shaffer. Christa was the last of my student scholar partners at the Women's Studies Research Center at Brandeis University to help with the research for this book. We were an odd combination, as she was a biophysics major and my work is sociological. But as she was the only student who applied for the position that semester, I thought I would give her a chance. She was better than good; she was essential. When Survey Monkey, which I had used to distribute my survey, changed their platform so that it became impossible to do most of the data analysis that I required, she figured out how to move my data to SPSS—statistical package for the social sciences—and just did it. I went to bed one night believing all my work was basically lost and woke up in the morning to a text saying the data was all moved and would in short order be ready to be analyzed again. In addition to her ability to do statistical analysis and work on the computer, Christa has an overriding curiosity and interested in almost everything. She and I discussed each finding as we crunched the numbers and celebrated as more and more of the data presented a consistent picture. She read books and articles on the religion to learn more and still sends me materials that she finds online. She is now in the process of getting her Ph.D. in bioinformatics at University of California, Los Angeles. She is a natural researcher.

Leigh S. Shaffer was my colleague at West Chester University and my co-author with Evan Leach of *Voices from the Pagan Census* (2003). Leigh taught methods and statistics in my department and had the office next door to mine. When I learned that my first survey, "The Pagan Census," on which I had worked to make a random sample of members of large umbrella groups, was now being distributed online and hand to hand by contemporary Pagans who wanted their voices heard, he was the one who helped me figure out how best to proceed. He suggested this was a positive development as more people would be surveyed. He then helped me work with this as a snowball sample. As this second survey is based on the first, it was his help with that survey that made this one possible. Leigh died in the summer of 2017 while I was writing this book; he, his insights, his intellect, and most of all his friendship are missed.

In addition to Christa, I had five other student partners who helped me analyze data for this book, John Nunn, Ashely Lynette, Zoe Novic, Rebekah McDowell, and Diana Marte. I owe them each a debt of gratitude for their work and insights. Arya Bourdaie, a student in the Computer Science Department at Brandeis University, created "patches," when SPSS could not do the analysis I needed. The book would be less without the magic he was able to perform, quickly and seemingly effortlessly.

I am grateful for the Women's Studies Research Center of Brandeis University and its founding director, Shulamit Reinharz, for providing me an academic home at which to do my research and write this book. It is a wonderfully supportive, creative, and intellectually stimulating community of scholars. I am particularly grateful to members of my Social Issues Research Study Group who read sections of this book and provided me with valuable feedback, stimulation, and support while I was writing. I would like to particularly thank Janet Freedman, Rhoda Unger, Margaret Morganroth Gullette, Rosalind Barnett, Patricia Palmieri, Phoebe Schnitzer, Smriti Rao, and Stephanie Wasserman. In addition the two anonymous reviewers provided valuable input that has improved the book.

My greatest debt, always, is to my husband, John H. Wolff. He reads all my drafts, lives through all the ups and downs of research, and is there through all the crises. He is always supportive and helpful and when needed just pitches in to do more than his share of housework and even makes runs to the shop to pick up more paper for the printer. A thank-you to him, and to all those who helped along the way, is never sufficient, but it is nonetheless heartfelt.

CHAPTER 1

Contemporary Paganism and the Solitary Practitioner

The most common image of Witches, Wiccans, Druids, and other contemporary Pagans is a group of cloaked practitioners with their faces obscured by hoods standing in a circle, often in the woods, calling on ancient deities and doing magical workings. However, much more common than a group of practitioners is a single person drawing her or his own circle and practicing alone. In "What's Wrong with Pagan Studies," Marcus Davidsen (2012), citing my earlier research (H. Berger et al. 2003), observes that although solitary practitioners are the majority in contemporary Paganism, there is almost nothing known about them. He points to an important lacuna in the research on this religion, which has only increased in significance as the proportion of contemporary Pagans who practice alone has grown in the fifteen years between my first and second surveys. The percentage of contemporary Pagans who are solitary practitioners has jumped from just over 50 percent in "The Pagan Census" to 78 percent in "The Pagan Census Revisited." Among the youngest cohort in my current survey 86 percent are solitaries. This growth is mirrored in changes in the larger society in which an increased number of Americans claim to be spiritual but not religious, or religious but unchurched. Although this book focuses on contemporary Pagans who practice alone, it will provide some insights into the issues that surround all those who are not members of a religious organization but claim to be religious, believers, or spiritual.

Fears have been raised that the withdrawal from religious organizations that is growingly common in the United States and other first world nations is resulting in social isolation with its corollary, political withdrawal (Bellah et al. 1985; Bruce 1996; Lasch 1979; Putnam 2001). Others (see for example Houtman and Aupers 2010; Woodhead 2013; Berghuijs et al. 2013; Bender 2010) to the contrary have argued that new and creative forms of social interaction are being generated that result in individuals remaining politically active, particularly on some issues, like environmentalism, that are of importance to them. What I have discovered about contemporary Pagans is that neither of these views is completely correct. Although it is true that solitary practitioners are not socially isolated, they do tend to have fewer contacts with other contemporary Pagans than those who work in a group. As I found in my first survey, "The Pagan Census" and as confirmed in my second, "The Pagan Census Revisited," contemporary Pagans tend to be much more politically active than other Americans; this is particularly true for the causes that speak directly to their spirituality—environmentalism, gay rights, feminism, and animal rights—but it is also true for all forms of political activity including voting. However, those who practice in groups are somewhat more active than those who are solitaries. Solitaries remain more politically active than most Americans, just not quite as active as those in groups.

Those in groups are somewhat more likely to participate in metaphysical activities, although gender also plays a role, with women being more spiritually active on most counts than men. Beliefs and attitudes are less influenced by whether or not the person is a solitary practitioner than are actions, which suggests that practicing alone influences behavior but not beliefs. The consistency of views on social, political, and spiritual issues suggests homogenization is occurring through members of the religion reading the same authors and visiting the same Internet sites. Although contemporary Paganism is in some ways unique, many of the same phenomena are occurring with other religions as there is a growing trend of many religions in having an online presence and therefore enabling people to connect and maintain their religious identities outside of established religious institutions. Contemporary Paganism, therefore, provides a good case study of the intersection of religious individualism, social engagement, and political activism.

Contemporary Paganism

Contemporary Paganism is a "disorganized" religion—there is no central bureaucracy or group that provides an official doctrine or membership list. This means that it is impossible to state that someone is not a member if they claim to be one, and no one person can speak for everyone. This would suggest utter chaos, but that is not actually what occurs. Most contemporary Pagans learn about the religion from books or online sites, which often results in a fair amount of similarity particularly within spiritual paths as the same sources are relied on in creating rituals and celebrating holidays. In taking the label Wiccan, Druid, or Ásatrú, to name three of the many spiritual paths of contemporary Paganism, individuals look at written works and Internet sites to understand what that means and how to best participate. Although no one can require certain behavior or belief, there is a tendency for a consistency in both views and ritual practices to develop. As I discussed in my first book, *A Community of Witches* (1999), the lack of a central organization and doctrine has the effect of creating greater homogenization. As DiMaggio and Powell (1983) showed, in the business world the decentralization of late modernity does not result in more diversity, as one might expect, but less, as individuals and groups become more reliant on the same sources under conditions of uncertainty. The "disorganization," actual celebration of individual innovation and practice in contemporary Paganism, which has increased with the growth of individual practitioners, has not resulted in each person doing something completely distinct and unrecognizable. Each person faced with creating rituals and defining their relationship to the divine or the otherworld looks for guidance, which results in their practices being similar.

Steve Bruce (2003) prefers to refer to religions like contemporary Paganism as diffuse religions because of their lack any center, authority, or even ability to police their boundaries. This lack of center or authority he believes will ultimately result in the demise of the religion as there is no proselytizing to encourage others to join. For most contemporary Pagans there is also no requirement that their children participate in their religion; to the contrary they believe their children should be free to find their own spiritual expression. Bruce, similarly to Bryan Wilson (1990) and Roy Wallis (1976), further believes that the lack of clear institutional structures will result in the religion lacking in moral authority and ultimately having no or little impact on social and political life.

In referring to this religion as disorganized I hope to capture the contemporary Pagans' sense of their religion as open and creative and one that permits them freedom. I furthermore want to separate my analysis from that of Bruce, Wilson, and Wallis in noting that the lack of central bureaucracy or theology does not result in the religion lacking a moral compass. The celebration of diversity and difference and the focus on interconnectedness provide a moral framework. Unlike more mainstream religions it is not a morality that is based on precepts and rules but instead is a form of radical empathy (H. Berger and Ezzy 2007; York 2016; McGraw 2004) in which practitioners seeks to engage the other in a way that permits all individuals' unique needs to be noted and addressed. It is a form of morality that is akin to the one that Gilligan (1982) attributed to girls, which is based on relationships not on universal laws. For contemporary Pagans who believe they live in a web of relationships with the natural world as well as with other humans, that can result in a call to political action, which has within it a moral aspect—one that calls on people to treat others with respect, including other sentient and nonsentient beings and more generally the natural world.

This provides a more complex view of Wiccan ethics than that seen in the Wiccan Rede, "an it harm none do what ye will," which is cited as the Wiccan and more generally contemporary Pagan moral code (Doyle White 2016:46). The Wiccan Rede is similar to the Golden Rule—"treat others as you would like to be treated"; both are pithy, easy to remember, and provide rule-of-thumb morality but should be understood as shorthands to larger ethical frameworks. The disorganized nature of contemporary Paganism, with its lack of doctrine, makes it more open to the charge of being diffuse and without a moral backbone and prone to narcissism. Speaking more generally about metaphysical religions, which like contemporary Paganism tend to be disproportionately female, Sointu and Woodhead (2008) argue that these spiritualities with their emphasis on the self simultaneously embrace and challenge traditional femininity—celebrating relations and caring but challenging traditional notions of women placing their own needs last. The emphasis on the self does not necessarily result in selfishness or self-absorption. It can result in individuals becoming concerned and involved in social movements, such as environmentalism, gay rights, women's rights, and animal rights, that they view as part of their relationships and sense of self. Indeed these social movements have gained strong support from both solitary and group practitioners, although stronger from those in groups.

Contemporary Paganism is the general term for a number of spiritual paths or forms of the religion. In some ways this is similar to the different denominations of Christianity with some shared elements that make them fall under the same rubric but differences that make them distinct. For example Catholicism, Methodism, and Eastern Orthodoxy would all be forms of Christianity, but each is a distinct denomination or church, and there are some people who would just consider themselves Christian with no subset of a particular type. The lack of central organization within contemporary Paganism complicates this. Without an organizational structure to determine doctrine, liturgy, or membership, the borders between different forms of contemporary Paganism are more open than religions with stronger structures. Contemporary Pagans furthermore often consider themselves part of more than one spiritual path. They will claim to have a unique spirituality that combines several different forms or that is eclectic. Solitary practice has increased this tendency. Nonetheless there are separate spiritual paths, which individual contemporary Pagans see themselves combining, and that can be differentiated. The difference in defining different spiritual paths within contemporary Paganism and what occurs in other religions should not be exaggerated as American Christians and members of other mainstream religions often make decisions about which church they will attend based on geography, how comfortable they feel with other members of the congregation, and even what other, nonreligious services the church provides, like daycare or bowling nights. In other words doctrine and liturgy may be of less importance to practitioners than to the church hierarchy. Nonetheless at least on the organizational level one can make clear distinctions among churches, and most individuals belong to one church or at least one denomination at a time. Among contemporary Pagans it is common for individuals to claim allegiance to more than one form of contemporary Paganism.

Some forms or denominations are closer or more similar to one another than others. Within Christianity there are churches or other organizations that set doctrine. Individual practitioners may be unaware of that doctrine or choose to ignore it while nonetheless attending a particular church and taking the label Methodist, Baptist, or some other form of Christianity, but there is something specific to compare their practice against to determine if they are following the stated doctrine or prescribed behaviors or not. This is not true for contemporary Paganism, which is by definition more amorphous and open. Nonetheless as with Christianity there is a basic similarity of practice and belief that makes it possible to identify contemporary Paganism as a religion and to distinguish among spiritual paths.

When I first began studying the religion in the 1980s the most common designation was Wiccan or Witch (the word *witch* in this discussion is capitalized when referring to a member of the religion and lowercased when speaking of historic, cross-cultural, or fictional witches). Today most contemporary Pagans claim to be eclectic, that is, they practice a form of the religion that is created by each individual or group with no need to claim one particular label or form of practice. This change is linked to the growth of solitary practitioners as it is they who are overwhelmingly eclectic; group members remain more likely to be Wiccan than eclectic. However, as Jorgensen and Russell (1999) and Ronald Hutton (1999) note, eclectic Paganism tends to be heavily influenced by Wicca.

In the 1980s the terms *Wicca* and *Witchcraft* were used interchangeably, but that is no longer true. Wicca is a spiritual path that is based directly or at least loosely on the rituals, practices, and cosmology that were developed by Gerald Gardner in the 1930s and 1940s in the United Kingdom and which migrated to the United States during the 1960s (Hutton 1999). Witchcraft most commonly refers to magical practices, which are an element of, but separate from, Wicca. Some Pagans, however, such as those of the Reclaiming tradition use the term Witch instead of Wiccan to draw a distinction between their practices and those of Wicca, and some Wiccans, both male and female, continue to refer to themselves as Witches. Nonetheless most contemporary Pagans make a distinction between the two.

Wicca was adopted and transformed in the United States by a number of social movements that were in ascendency during the time that the religion spread. Feminists were drawn to the religion because of its celebration of the female as well as the male divine. Some feminists borrowed elements of ritual and mythology and language to create a variation of the religion in which the Goddess was celebrated to the exclusion of the God. Miriam Simos, a Californian who writes under her magical name, Starhawk, was both initiated into a Wiccan coven and trained by one of the founders of feminist Witchcraft, Zuzanna Budapest. Starhawk's book *The Spiral Dance* (1979) was one of the earliest published on Wicca; it is also one of the most popular, with over three hundred thousand copies sold (Salomonsen 2002). In this book and her subsequent ones

Starhawk (1982, 1994) helped to forge a link between feminism and Wicca that has influenced the contemporary Pagan movement. This is not to suggest that all forms of Paganism are feminist or incorporate Starhawk's notion of political activity. However, the popularity of her ideas has informed the movement, even if at times it is because they have stimulated disagreement and dialogue.

Environmentalists have also been drawn to the religion because of the images of Mother Earth as sacred. Most Pagans self-define as practicing an earth-based religion or spirituality. What this means can vary, although it normally refers to the various forms of the religion viewing the earth as sacred and using images of Mother Nature in rituals and mythology. The religion has also been influenced by other social movements that were active in the 1960s, particularly the questioning of the place of social institutions and authority and the sexual revolution. All forms of sexuality are celebrated within contemporary Paganism as acts of the Goddess or acts of love. This has made the religion a comfortable home for those who have nontraditional sexual orientations, although like most Americans, most contemporary Pagans are heterosexual.

Still a minority within the religion, but nonetheless of growing interest and importance, are those forms of contemporary Paganism that focus on one national or regional tradition, such as Hellenic Pagans, Druids, or Ásatrú (who worship the northern European deities). These religions attempt to re-create historic religious practices, often based on archeological research and existing texts of myths and poetry that are available. Most practitioners of ethnic or regionally specific Paganism acknowledge that their practices are a re-creation of ancient religions and not an unbroken continuation of the older religions. Many practitioners read archeology, anthropology, mythology, and history texts to better understand how their spiritual ancestors practiced the indigenous religion. However, there are some who believe that their religion is not just a re-creation but is a continuously practiced old religion.

When contemporary Paganism first took hold in the United States it was customary for members to state that theirs was an old religion and for members to claim a continuous line to an ancient Pan-European fertility religion that venerated the Goddess and God, and which had survived underground among the rural poor during the ascent of Christianity in Europe. In my initial interviews with contemporary Pagans in the 1980s I met a number of people who claimed that they were carrying on their family religion, which had been passed in secret to them. Interestingly when I met some of those same people years later they had no memory of making those claims—which were on taped interviews—as their thinking had changed with the majority of other contemporary Pagans accepting and even celebrating theirs as a new or at least a re-creation of the old religion.

More commonly today most contemporary Pagans contend that they are looking to the past for inspiration or as an alternative to what they view as the shallowness of contemporary society and religion. But there remain some who still argue for a continuous nature of their religion (Doyle White 2016; Heselton 2000). The desire for new religions to appear old is typical as age is seen as providing legitimacy. New religions are often dismissed as "made up" or less real than older ones and therefore claim greater authority by creating a link to the past or claiming to be really older than other religions.

Margot Adler (1978) suggests that the histories of the various forms of contemporary Paganism be treated as sacred histories or myths, which provide a foundation for the religion and an indication of what is important in their self-conception, but not as historical truths. The sacred history of contemporary Pagans provides practitioners with a sense of a shared past, which serves as a basis for their contemporary moral and social life and helps to forge a sense of community. For Witches and Wiccans the shared past is one in which their spiritual forbearers were the magical people who were healers, midwives, and magical workers among the peasantry. They were respected and loved. It provides not only a noble past but an image of magic being used for good and a group with knowledge of herbal healing. These healers, spiritual leaders, and magic workers, the myth relates, were the target of the witch trials in early modern Europe. This myth grew out of the work of scholars, most notably Margaret Murray (1971 [1921]), but was picked up by a number of other more contemporary scholars such Barbara Ehrenreich and Deidre English (1973), who placed the trials firmly within feminist thinking. This sacred history has served as a basis of group identity based on a shared spiritual history and as a sense of being survivors of an ancient, noble, but denigrated past. Witches and Goddess worshippers have absorbed this sacred mythology emphasizing the fact that the majority of those persecuted as witches were women. Other groups such as the Druids or Heathens have histories that tie them to a particular historical land; the Druids to the Celtic past and Heathens to northern Europe.

Although most contemporary Pagans now refer to their religion as earth based, this was not always the case. When I began my research it was more common for the religion to be referred to as a magical religion. The focus on the religion as magical flowed from the sacred history of Witches being the "magical folk" who healed, helped, and found lost objects. Magic, mysticism, and having a direct experience of the divine were central to how people spoke about the religion. The change in nomenclature is a reflection of the growing interest in environmentalism among contemporary Pagans and more generally among educated Americans. The focus on it being an earth-based religion has not eliminated its continued connection with magic and metaphysics. Magic continues to be practiced and to be an important element of the religion. The religion in part differentiates itself from other metaphysical religions, most particularly the New Age, by its combination of viewing itself simultaneously as earth based and magical and combining this with a set of ritual practices and mythology.

Sarah Pike (2004), Michael York (1995), and Paul Heelas (1996) all note that the metaphysical or magical aspects of contemporary Paganism create links with it and what is commonly called the New Age. Many of the same techniques, such as channeling, meditation, and alternative healing techniques as well as a view of the world as alive and interconnected are shared by both. As Pike further demonstrates many of these same occult beliefs have been waxing and waning throughout American history. Colonial Americans brought occult beliefs from Europe when they emigrated, and although at odds with the prevailing Puritan norms, occult beliefs and practices were common. Divination of various types, including horoscopes, was quite common in the colonies and served to precipitate the Salem witch trials (Boyer and Nissenbaum 1976).

Transcendentalism, Spiritualism, New Thought, and Mesmerism, which grew in popularity in the nineteenth century, are all the most immediate predecessors of contemporary Paganism and the New Age. All these movements share an interest in the spiritual world and in an alternative reality with a belief that in exploring these the individual can change him- or herself and in so doing transform the world. They have all incorporated alternative medical and health practices into their spiritual teachings. James Beckford (1984, 1992a, 1992b) referred to these religions as new religious and healing movements, and Courtney Bender (2010) has dubbed them the "New Metaphysicals." All these religions believe that through healing the self, often by using nontraditional methods, one will be able to heal the world. All change is believed to begin with the individual. As one opens one's consciousness and alters one's own behavior the world becomes a better place. It is this emphasis on the self that has resulted in accusations of the religion resulting in both narcissism and the withdrawal from politics. As I will show throughout this book that is not the case as the focus on the self, when embedded in an interconnected web of relationships, can result in social activity and serve as the basis for a moral system.

Pike and York both contend that the New Age, unlike contemporary Paganism, tends to focus on the future and less on the past and are "sunnier," that is, they provide a more positive view of both the current state of the world and of things to come. For contemporary Pagans their sacred history, even if that history is religious myth, connects them with the past and provides a different worldview from other New Metaphysicals. Although magical and mystical practices are part of contemporary Paganism and the New Age as well as Theosophy, New Thought, and other spiritual and religious movements, contemporary Paganism distinguishes itself through its emphasis on nature; rituals that celebrate the natural cycles; an acceptance of the existence of evil, destruction, and death; a celebration of community; an emphasis on and celebration of difference as opposed to oneness; and the incorporation of a mythology of a "return" to pre-Christian practices (H. Berger 1999; York 1995; Woodhead 2010). At the edges contemporary Paganism shades into the New Age or other forms of the New Metaphysicals, as practitioners of both often participate in the same classes, workshops, and practices, such as Reiki, astral projections, and learning to create horoscopes.

Ritual, particularly for wheel of the year, that is, the celebration of the yearly changes in the natural world, tends to have particular importance in contemporary Paganism. The most common wheel of the year is the Wiccan one, in which the beginning and the height of each season—fall, winter, spring, and summer—are celebrated. But there are other wheels of the year, some with more or fewer celebrations or *sabbats*. Typically at these celebrations a circle is formed and consecrated before deities are invited in. For some contemporary Pagans the deities are viewed as a metaphor and not taken literally; for others the deities are divine beings, or aspects of the one divine force. On the whole contemporary Pagans state that it is less a matter of belief in divinity than experience. The notion of the divine being something that is experienced is not unique to contemporary Pagans. Evangelicals similarly speak of having a direct relationship with Christ, who they experience and even converse with in their daily lives (Luhrmann 2012). In addition to these yearly sabbats most contemporary Pagans also celebrate the new and full moon, and have rituals for life passages—birth, coming of age, old age, and death.

It is the celebration of the wheel of the year that for many contemporary Pagans is the link between nature and their religious practices. The yearly sabbats make one aware of the changing seasons, what they mean in nature, and how that is meaningful to the individual. If possible most contemporary Pagans celebrate these sabbats in nature. When I was doing participant observation in my earlier work, I realized that my attendance at often more than one sabbat ritual, as I tried to attend as many different covens' celebrations as possible per holiday, made me more aware of the season I was entering or in and made me focus on the changes in nature around me. Each holiday has rituals in which the changes in nature are commemorated and their connection to changes in the individuals' lives are noted. In the spring, for example, there is a celebration of fertility, in nature, in the world, and in people's lives. The notion of fertility is used in its broadest sense to include fertility in each person's endeavor, in the same way that in the fall death, which is celebrated as a natural part of life, is linked to not only each of our impending deaths, and the death of loved ones, but also the death of bad habits or the ending of bad relationships. Within Wicca, each sabbat is linked to a mythology of the changing relationship between the Goddess and the God, as the God is born to the Goddess at the winter solstice, becomes her consort at Beltaine (May 1) and dies at Samhain (October 31) to ensure future fertility to be born again in the following winter. Other spiritual paths have different mythologies that are connected to the sabbats, but they all celebrate the seasons and connect them to a larger mythology. For many the divine is seen in nature itself—trees, plants, and animals are all part of a sacred interconnected web.

Does seeing the divine in nature, celebrating the cycles of the year, and viewing the world as magical mean that one is participating in an earth-based religion, or must one participate in direct environmental action? Questions have been raised about whether celebration of Mother Earth translates into political action for the environment or if contemporary Pagans are environmentalists in name only. This is a question that is often debated among practitioners and scholars of contemporary Paganism (Davy 2005; Harvey 1997; Letcher 2000). Particularly for those who came to contemporary Paganism because of their commitment to environmentalism, there is a sense that the religion is earth based in name only as they would hope for a larger commitment to political action from their coreligious.

Chas Clifton (2006) contends that in part the debate is the result of the term "earth-based" being vague and used by practitioners in three distinct ways: (1) as the "natural," although still unknown, laws that explain the working of magic, (2) as the view of the natural world as a living organism that is interconnected, alive, and in need of protection, and (3) as embodied, in which the divine is in each of us and is seen in the natural functions of the body, most importantly in sexuality. Each of these has a different emphasis. The first focuses on magic, the second most clearly is linked to environmentalism, and the last is one that resonates with feminism, particularly as women's monthly cycles are viewed as connected to the earth, to nature, and to fertility. As all forms of sexuality are celebrated this concept of nature also relates to lesbian, gay, bisexual, and transgender people and rights. Clifton is correct that what it means to be a nature religion or even what is meant by natural is often vague and ambiguous, but a further issue is that some contemporary Pagans joined the religion as a reflection of their commitment to environmentalism. They believe it is consistent with their commitment to the cause and are disappointed that others, the majority of contemporary Pagans, as I will show later in the book, are not members of an environmental group. This creates some tensions and unrealistic expectations when they compare their coreligious with members of a political action group. Throughout the book, when I speak of political activities of contemporary Pagans, my comparison is either between solitary and group practitioners or between members of this religion and other Americans.

Solitary Practitioners

Initially Wicca and other forms of contemporary Paganism were learned through participation in a group that trained initiates. Groups were found through word of mouth or from signs in metaphysical bookstores or other venues where individuals interested in occult knowledge congregated. The groups often met in people's homes or in a room in a metaphysical bookstore. Many were teaching groups and trained interested individuals in a particular spiritual path, such as Wicca. Others were a group of equals who did rituals, practiced magic, and participated in discussing and studying their spiritual path together. The centrality of groups changed, first with the publication of books and journals, and ultimately with the growth of Pagan Internet sites. Although in *The Spiral Dance* Starhawk (1979) emphasized the importance of working in a group, the information she provided about ritual practice, initiation, and mythology made it possible for readers to either start their own groups or to practice alone. This trend was expanded by Scott Cunningham, whose books on solitary practice—*Wicca: A Guide for the Solitary Practitioner* (1988) and *Living Wicca: A Further Guide for the Solitary Practitioner* (1994)—were, as I found in "The Pagan Census Revisited," the most popular of all books on the religion among contemporary Pagans. Cunningham advocated for solitary practice as well as provided information about how to practice alone, from initiating oneself to doing the major sabbats and other rituals. Silver RavenWolf, also a popular author, has written books geared to the young and was noted by many of those who joined as teenagers at the end of the twentieth or beginning twenty-first century as an important initial source about the religion.

Llewellyn, a Minnesota-based publisher who published Cunningham's and RavenWolf's books, has subsequently published many authors who provide spiritual and magical information for those practicing alone. Some claim this has "watered down" the religion, referring to it as Llwellynization of Wicca or of contemporary Paganism in general; nonetheless the books remain popular and serve as an entrance portal to the religion for many. The popularity of Cunningham, Starhawk, and RavenWolf all add to the homogenization of the religion. Even those who claim that they have never read one of these authors are aware of much that they have written as it is often cut and pasted on websites and is part of the larger dialogue. All three have been important in helping to spread the religion to those that practice alone.

At first glance the term *solitary* or *solo practitioner* appears to be self-evident—individuals who practice a form of contemporary Paganism separate from anyone else. The reality is more complex, with this definition fitting some who take the label and not others. Very few are completely isolated; they have friends or family who are members of the religion, or they attend public celebration of sabbats or go to festivals—a type of religious retreat. A small percentage, however, self-define as solitary but nonetheless also regularly participate in a group. I first became aware of this phenomenon when a student at West Chester University of Pennsylvania, where I was a faculty member, informed me that although he was a solitary practitioner he was also a member of a local group, which was composed completely of solitaries. Knowing of my interest in contemporary Paganism he introduced me to one of the leaders of the group who seemed amused by my bewilderment at the possibility of there being a group of solitary practitioners. What struck me as an oxymoron was for her and my student a matter of my misunderstanding of what it means to be a solitary. According to them their group, which gathered together to celebrate holidays and share their spiritual knowledge, was an assembly of distinct individuals all of whom were practicing their own form of contemporary Paganism. Although two people were acknowledged as the coordinators of the group, they did not consider themselves religious leaders. Furthermore they were not a teaching coven. Each person was responsible for her or his own spiritual practice and was expected to come with one in place or learn about it on her and his own. No one had official authority over dogma, belief, or ritual practice, nor could anyone decide who was to be initiated into a spiritual path or who could move up ranks of noted expertise that exist in Wicca and among Druids and some other spiritual paths.

In the first survey, "The Pagan Census," individuals were permitted to choose only one option to describe their form of practice. To capture the ambiguity of those who self-define both as solitary practitioners and as members of a group, respondents in my second survey, "The Pagan Census Revisited," were permitted to choose more than one option when asked if they practiced alone, with one partner, in a group, or in some other way. Only 10 percent of solitary practitioners claimed to also practice in a group. I initially broke down the data into three categories, those who practiced completely alone, those who practiced in groups, and those who self-defined as solitaries but were also members of a group, but I found that the last category, those who both claimed to be solitary and in a group, were not distinct, at least based on my survey data, from those who were in a group. Throughout this book, therefore, the data comparing solitary and group practitioners compares those who are solitary only to those who are in a group or practice with at least one other person. When analyzing this data I thought again about my former student and the women he introduced me to. At the time I had wondered how much joining a group results in homogenization as one person learns from another and each influences the others. After looking at my data I became even more convinced that group membership changes the individuals' practices and perspectives and that my student and his friend were not as much solitary as they thought themselves.

To a greater degree than in more established religions that have churches, synagogues, temples, or mosques for gathering, which are lacking in contemporary Paganism, groups tend to be more prone to disintegration. Churches call ministers to them and let them go; congregants join and leave for many of the same reasons that contemporary Pagan groups dissolve: people move or become disillusioned with the religion, or conflict divides the congregation; but with no building to maintain, it is more common for groups to fall apart with some members joining other groups, others practicing alone for a time, and still others forming a new group. Being a solitary practitioner in some instances is temporary, and in others it is lifelong. In chapter 4 I discuss the frequency with which those who are currently solitary practitioners were trained in a group or had at some time practiced in a group. This book provides a snapshot of those who are currently practicing alone.

Methodology

This book is based on a survey I conducted online with James R. Lewis, "The Pagan Census Revisited" (2009–2010), which is a revised, updated, and expanded version of my earlier survey, "The Pagan Census." Although both surveys are called censuses, neither is a real census. When I conducted the first survey with Andras Corban Arthen, the founder and one of the leaders of EarthSpirit Community, a contemporary Pagan umbrella group, he had hoped to do a census of all U.S. Pagans. Although this goal was unattainable, we collected one of the largest and most diversely distributed surveys. It served as the basis of *Voices from the Pagan Census* (H. Berger et al. 2003), and the data from that survey is now online at the Murray Institute at Harvard University (Berger et al. 1993–95). To permit comparisons with the larger American public, "The Pagan Census" included some questions from the General Social Survey (GSS). In addition to questions from the GSS the new survey has questions from other surveys of metaphysical religions, permitting another set of comparisons. Questions have been added to elicit information about routes to joining the religion, magical beliefs and practices, and participation in alternative medical and health regimes like Reiki, and divination practices such as astrology and runes.

I initially planned a comparison between my two surveys, which I anticipated would show how the religion had changed as it moved from being a new religion to one that had become, if not established, no longer new. However, the story I found in the numbers was not the one I had anticipated, as other than the growth of solitary practitioners there were only a few changes. The relative consistency of the religion was in and of itself interesting, but the real story was the growth of solitary practice. This book, therefore, focuses on a comparison of solitary and group practitioners. Throughout the book, where appropriate, I will point out other changes I found, as these add to the story, but the focus remains on how those who practice alone are similar and different from others who are in groups.

The current survey was conducted over the Internet using Survey Monkey. It was distributed internationally but was written in English. There was a much higher response rate from the United States than from elsewhere, with 6,418 respondents from the United States and 1,656 from fifty-eight other countries. The focus of this book, therefore, will be on the United States, although I will do some comparisons with the United Kingdom and Canada, which had respectively 324 and 418 responses each. I have not included other English-speaking nations because there were too few responses from each of them for me to feel they were representative. The data from non-English-speaking nations was still weaker as there were fewer responses per nation and the data was only from those who were fluent enough in English to be able and willing to complete a thirty-page survey in a foreign language. As this is the first truly international large-scale survey, some of that data still provides some insights, and I have included data from non-English-speaking nations in the response to one question but on the whole have excluded it from any discussion in this book.

Online surveys raise concerns about those not included; even in the United States not everyone has equal access to computers. Women, the elderly, and those with less education tend to have a lower rate of online participation. This is even more of an issue internationally, where Internet access is more limited and even more skewed to the wealthy and better educated. The Internet was used in this case as it was the only way to successfully get data from such a wide group of contemporary Pagans and ensure that those who are not associated with contemporary Pagan organizations would also learn about and have access to the survey. As all previous surveys and ethnographic work has shown, members of this religion tend to be better educated and computer literate, making the use of a computer survey less problematic than it might otherwise have been. Responses were solicited by writing to contemporary Pagan leaders and groups to request that they encourage their membership to participate. Notices were put on contemporary Pagan websites on Facebook and a number of online sites, such as Witchvox and the Wild Hunt. Word of mouth was used as well to let contemporary Pagans know about this new survey. As with the first survey, I found that particularly U.S. contemporary Pagans wanted to be heard and were eager to respond to the survey. Neither "The Pagan Census" nor "The Pagan Census Revisited" are random samples, nor is any survey that has been done on Pagans (Adler 1978, 1986; Jorgensen and Russell 1999). The lack of a central authority and the fact that some contemporary Pagans are still "in the broom closet," makes it impossible to do a random sample. The current sample, like the original "Pagan Census," is the best available sample of this group possible. "The Pagan Census Revisited" received a larger sample of U.S. Pagans than was received by "The Pagan Census" and to my knowledge is the largest sample of contemporary Pagans yet collected.

In addition to demographic questions about age, occupation, educational level, gender identification, sexual orientation, and place of residence, questions were asked about form of practice and which spiritual path the respondent most identified with. As in my first survey, individuals were permitted to choose more than one option for spiritual path because so many contemporary Pagans are initiated in, or consider themselves part of, more than one spiritual path. This means that throughout when the data for spiritual paths is presented the sums are greater than 100 percent. What is most interesting about this is that there remain clear differences among spiritual paths. This is important as although there is sharing and some contemporary Pagans consider themselves part of more than one spiritual path or what might be called denomination of the religion, there are real and consistent differences, particularly as will be evident throughout the book among ethnically or regionally specific forms of contemporary Paganism. Questions were also asked about political activities and groups, social interactions in person and online, and spiritual and metaphysical beliefs and practices. These questions and their answers form the basis of my chapters. After a discussion of demographics and how individuals came to contemporary Paganism, I turn first to social interaction and isolation, then to metaphysical practices, and politics. Throughout this book the focus is on a comparison between solitary and group practitioners, but I will also be exploring gender and age differences as these are often of importance in understanding the data.

Respondents could choose among twenty-three spiritual paths or list another of which they consider themselves a member. I have chosen six to explore more fully in this book. Three of them—Wicca, Witchcraft, and eclectic Paganism—are the three most popular in the United States, the United Kingdom, and Canada. The other three—Goddess worship, Druids, and Ásatrú—were picked both for consistency, as they were included in *Voices from the Pagan Census* and because they provide an important look at one aspect or another of the religion. As previously noted one of the appeals of the religion when it came to the United States was the worship of the female divine; Goddess worship most strongly emphasizes that. I therefore chose this group for that reason; however, they are also the fourth most popular form of contemporary Paganism. Druids and Ásatrú provide two examples of ethnic or regionally specific contemporary Paganism. Both have in the past been particularly appealing to men, the Ásatrú more than the Druids. Ethnic contemporary Paganism focuses on the connection of individuals to a particular historic land and its deities. Among the Ásatrú, there is a focus on northern Europe, its land, its gods, and what practitioners refer to as the folk—a sense of belonging to an ethnic group.

In the survey two different categories of those who worshipped the Northern European Gods were provided, Ásatrú and Odinist; the former worship the Aesir, which are one of two groups of northern deities; the other are the Vanir. The Aesir consist of warrior gods and fertility goddesses and are the better-known deities of northern mythology. The Vanir are earth deities and tend to focus on the agricultural cycle (Adler 1978). Odinists are followers of Odin, the Nordic god. It is more common now for those who follow the northern gods to refer to themselves as Heathens, although this was not always true. Among those who follow the northern gods there are some who are part of the alt-right. Both Jeffrey Kaplan (1996) and Mattias Gardell (2003) have chronicled these groups. Kaplan was careful to note that the Neo-Nazis or white supremacists are only a small subsection of the larger movement. He has further argued that is more common for those who are part of the alt-right to refer to themselves as Odinists than to call themselves either Heathens or Ásatrú. However in my survey I found no statistical differences between those who self-identified as Odinist and those who claimed to be Ásatrú. In the end I combined the data from the two groups and have referred to them as Heathens.

My data, like other research on Heathens (Adler 1978, 1986; Kaplan 1996, 1997; Snook 2015), indicates that they are more socially and politically conservative than other contemporary Pagans. Heathens are a minority of my sample, and only 1 percent of those are ultraconservative. It would be as wrong to paint all Heathens as racists as it would be to ignore the minority who are part of the white supremacist movement in the United States and in Europe. As Kaplan (1996) describes the Nazis themselves had resurrected the ancient Teutonic gods as a response to what they viewed as the feminizing aspect of Christianity. This literature was used by one group of Odinists as foundational materials when they formed. Many of the members may have been unaware of the origins of the materials but were drawn by the ideology nonetheless. This does not mean that all Odinists are racists, let alone all Heathens, but there is a racialist identity with white northern Europeans that is manifest in the religion. As Jennifer Snook (2015) notes for many Heathens white identity politics is viewed as just another form of ethnic group identity politics. They claim that they have as much right as any other ethnic group to celebrate their ethnicity and heritage. As Snook further discusses they appear to be either unaware or uninterested in the historic context that makes the celebration of whiteness racist.

Witches and Wiccans gather together in covens, Druids in groves; for Heathens the groups are called kindred or hearths. Not all Heathens are part of white racial identity politics; for some the draw is the mythology of land of their ancestors and a connection to the Vikings. Kin and bloodlines tend to be of importance among Heathens. For some it is only those whose bloodline runs back to northern Europe who can claim to be Heathen. This has resulted in African Americans being either excluded or made unwelcome because they do not look like the typical image of the descendants of Vikings, although they may well be. However, as with all doctrines and rituals within contemporary Paganism, there are other Heathens that are more open and view it less as an ethnic affiliation and more as a spiritual one that anyone can be drawn to.

Druids, whose spiritual forbearers were also white, do not have the same racialist aspect and are not known for drawing white supremacists to them. Isaac Bonewits, the founder of the largest Druid organization in the United States, Ár nDraíocht Féin, has noted that "those that consider themselves 'purists' (and a few racists here and there) will insist that the word 'druid' can only be applied to people in religious, magical, or social leadership roles with ancient Celtic cultures. . . . Many of these purists will also insist that only people with Celtic ancestry can become druids today. All other modern druids just laugh at them or simply ignore them" (Bonewits 2006:xx). Adler (1986) confirms that neither racist nor racialist attitudes are accepted in Druidism. Nonetheless it is important to emphasize again that most Heathens are not racist. What Druids and Heathens share is an attempt to return to or re-create an ancient form of religious practice, or as Bonewits phrases it, paleopaganism. As he notes this is an act of reconstruction of the older religion that had existed in Celtic areas of Europe. Bonewits was one of the earlier contemporary Pagan leaders and writers to embrace the notion that there was no unbroken chain to older practices but that contemporary Pagans were reconstructing older religious traditions.

The Druids' wheel of the year—the eight major sabbats—is the same as those in Wicca. Bonewits notes that this is because Gerald Gardner, the founder of modern day Wicca, and Ross Nichols, who was the founder of the Order of Bards, Ovates, and Druids (OBOD), the largest and most influential Druid organization in the United Kingdom, were friends who jointly created the wheel of year (Bonewits 2006:180–81). The celebration of these sabbats is similar in the two spiritual paths, but the language used and the general tenor is different. Wiccan rituals are traditionally led by a High Priestess and High Priest, or just the High Priestess in all women's groups; Druid rituals are led by the Druid and involve the bard who reads poetry or tells about the mythology that is connected to the ritual and an Ovate or soothsayer. Ronald Hutton (1999), Danny Jorgensen and Scott Russell (1999), and Jo Pearson (2003) have all noted that Wiccan rituals serve as a template for other forms of contemporary Paganism. Nonetheless both Druids and Ásatrú are distinct forms of the religion with rituals that differ from those of Wiccans.

Diversity is celebrated in the religion, particularly diversity of sexual expression. For most contemporary Pagans gender is considered fluid—something to be considered and played with both in ritual and in their daily lives. To capture at least some of this fluidity, in addition to male and female my survey provides alternatives for those transitioning between genders and those that consider themselves other. As will be discussed in the next chapter the vast majority indicates that they are female or male, but there is greater gender variety than in the larger American society. The survey question on sexual orientation similarly offered "other" as an alternative to heterosexual, homosexual, and bisexual.

Based on the year of birth provided by respondents I broke the data down into four categories, which I refer to as pre-boomers, boomers, generation X, and the young. Pre-boomers include those born prior to 1946 and make up only 2 percent of the U.S. and U.K. samples and are just under 1 percent of the Canadian sample. The lower participation in general of the elderly on the Internet may have resulted in this age group being underrepresented, but my findings are consistent with other surveys and ethnographic studies of the religion, which emphasis that the religion had its first large expansion in the 1960s and 1970s and was particularly appealing to those in the baby boom generation (Adler 1986; Ezzy and Berger 2009; Orion 1995; Jorgensen and Russell 1999). Those born between 1946 and 1966 are counted in this study as baby boomers. Although 1946 is an agreed-on date for the beginning of the post–World War II baby boom era there is some controversy about which year should be counted as the end of that era. I used the same dates as the U.S. Census Bureau, which is consistent with most, although not all, sociological research. Boomers compose respectively 34 percent of the United States, 32 percent of the Canadian, and 28 percent of the U.K. samples. The young in this study are all those born after 1976, who would have come of age after the witchcraft craze in the media with shows like *Charmed* and *Sabina the Teenage Witch*. They form the largest cohort in my study with respectively 36 percent of U.S., 45 percent of Canadian, and 38 percent of U.K. respondents. Contemporary Paganism, as will be discussed in the next chapter, has increased in popularity since the 1960s. The positive images that appeared in the media at the beginning of this century helped to fuel that increase, but so did a more general trend of online spirituality, increased focus of the self as the locus of authority, and the move away from formal religion among the young. The cohort between the boomers and the young I have called generation X and are those born between 1967 and 1975. In the United States 27 percent of my respondents were born between these years. Respectively in Canada 26 percent and in the United Kingdom 31 percent were born in those years. The lower percentage in this group than among boomers or the young is directly related to this group encompassing fewer years than the young, suggesting that although the positive media portrayals had an effect it was not as important as other cultural factors, most particularly the spiritual turn and the influence of the Internet.

Because the United States is a large and diverse country I have compared and contrasted data from different regions within the country. I have followed the convention that we followed in *Voices from the Pagan Census* and included the nine regions, encompassing the same states in each, as are used in the General

Social Survey (GSS). This permitted me to compare my current data both with the previous survey's and with data from the GSS. The nine regions and the states included are

1. Pacific: Alaska, California, Hawaii, Oregon, Washington
2. South Atlantic: Delaware, Florida, Georgia, Maryland, North Carolina, South Carolina, Virginia, West Virginia, Washington, D.C.
3. East North Central: Illinois, Indiana, Michigan, Ohio, Wisconsin
4. New England: Connecticut, Maine, Massachusetts, New Hampshire, Rhode Island, Vermont
5. Middle Atlantic: New Jersey, New York, Pennsylvania
6. Mountain: Arizona, Colorado, Idaho, Montana, Nevada, New Mexico, Utah, Wyoming
7. West South Central: Arkansas, Louisiana, Oklahoma, Texas
8. West North Central: Iowa, Kansas, Minnesota, Missouri, Nebraska, North Dakota
9. East South Central: Alabama, Kentucky, Mississippi, Tennessee

Throughout this book I refer to practitioners of this religion as contemporary Pagans. In my previous books I used the term "Neo-Pagan." Members of the religion normally refer to themselves as Pagans or as members of a particular spiritual path, such as Wiccans or Witches. There is a need to distinguish practitioners of this religion and those referred to as pagan or nonbelievers when Christianity was itself a new or at least newish religion and was gaining converts throughout Europe. Contemporary Pagans have reclaimed the word as they believe themselves to be re-creating or continuing the practices of those earlier peoples who rejected Christianity and continued to practice their traditional religions. Initially I accepted the convention that was in use at that time by scholars of the religion to refer to this as Neo-Paganism, or new Paganism. I have changed to contemporary Paganism because it is the term used by the American Academy of Religion to define practitioners of this religion. It provides a way to talk about the religion that does not predetermine if there was an old, or as Bonewits phrases it paleo, version of the religion, or if the religion that is being practiced today is separate and new from that which existed in antiquity. All labels carry with them some baggage, but I believe this has the least.

This book compares two forms of contemporary Paganism, those who work in groups, which was the traditional way in which the religion had been learned and practiced, and solitary practitioners. The focus on solitary practitioners provides an initial look at what is now the solid majority of this religion. My primary concern is an exploration of which demographic groups practice alone and how being solitary influences their spiritual practice, interconnection with others, and political commitments. This study, however, also contributes to the growing debate about whether or not the New Metaphysicals, as Bender (2010) refers to them, are participating in a form of narcissism, which is resulting in their being socially and politically disengaged from the larger society. As I will show throughout, solitary practitioners are less engaged socially, spiritually, and politically than those in groups, but neither is completely isolated, and both remain politically engaged.

CHAPTER 2

Solitary and Group Practitioners by the Numbers

Demographics

The face of contemporary Paganism has remained remarkably stable in the fifteen years between my two surveys, but the changes that have occurred are in part the result of the growth and impact of solitary practice. The religion remains disproportionately female, with women making up 71.6 percent of adherents. This is a slightly higher proportion of women than was found in "The Pagan Census," in which 64.8 percent of the participants were women. The focus on, or at least inclusion of, the Goddess or goddesses has from its inception drawn women to this form of spirituality. The increase between surveys is largely due to the greater disparity in the gender ratio among the young—that is, those who were coming of age during the 1990s—among whom the female-to-male ratio is 75.1 percent to 23.5 percent. It was during this period that the media were having a romance with teenage witches—producing television shows such as *Sabrina the Teenage Witch* and movies like *Charmed,* which also became a television show—in which the main characters were witches who were portrayed as interesting, empowered, and likeable. The media's interest in witchcraft resulted in a sharp increase in the numbers of Internet searches about the religion, particularly among young women (Harrington 2007). Most who searched did not become involved, and among those who did become involved a small percentage stayed beyond a few months; nonetheless these converts resulted in an increase of participants, particularly female participants as can be seen in my data (H. Berger and Ezzy 2007).

The increase in female participation in the past fifteen years has even affected Heathens, who in the earlier survey were disproportionately male with a ratio of 65 percent male to 35 percent female. Currently Heathens are almost equally divided between women and men, with 50.8 percent female and 47.8 percent male and the remainder defining themselves as transitioning between genders or as other. This is a major change in this spiritual path, which tends to be more traditional and less liberal than other forms of contemporary Paganism and has never had the appeal of Wicca, Witchcraft, or Goddess worship for women.

It is unclear what effect the increased feminization of contemporary Paganism will have as it has always been disproportionately female in all spiritual paths other than Heathens. I was surprised by the increase in female participants in the religion. Even with the influx of primarily women as a result of the teenage witch craze in the media, I anticipated that the gender disparity would decrease in all forms of contemporary Paganism as more children were born to and remained in the religion, offset somewhat by the influx of women. There is some initial research that suggests that many of the children raised as contemporary Pagans have remained in the religion, but it is too anecdotal to provide certainty (Wildman-Hanlon 2009). Only 10 percent of my survey respondents stated that they were raised as contemporary Pagans, and the gender divide in this group is consistent with that found among the young: 73.5 percent female to 25.1 percent male with the rest transitioning between genders or self-defining as other. The religion remains one primarily of converts, in part because it continues to grow and attract more members.

The exact number and the rate of increase of contemporary Pagans in the last quarter of a century is difficult to determine and often a matter of dispute. The United States does not include questions of religious affiliation on its census forms. Both the American Religious Identification Survey (ARIS) and Pew have provided data on the U.S. population's religious affiliations. Both surveys include the categories of Wiccan, Pagan, and Druid. The last ARIS survey was in 2008, and in it they found 711,000 contemporary Pagans, an increase of 131.6 percent from the 307,000 that were counted in their 2001 survey (Lewis 2012). In their 2014 survey Pew found 0.3 percent of the U.S. population self-defined as one of these three categories, which would be just under a million Americans. Although extrapolating from one poll to the other is problematic, if the percentage of increase seen between ARIS surveys was applied to the data between the last ARIS and the Pew study the data would have a consistent rate of increase.

Based on book sales, Internet traffic on websites, and other data, most scholars of contemporary Paganism believe that both ARIS and Pew's numbers are low. The hidden nature of the religion would result in some contemporary Pagans lying, or refusing to answer question about their religious affiliation, or picking a less controversial affiliation, such as Unitarian Universalist, which enough contemporary Pagans have joined to create a group, CUUPS—the Covenant of Unitarian Universalist Pagans. Phone interviews, which are how both ARIS and Pew conduct their surveys, would be particularly prone to having individuals wary of stating that they are adherents of a minority religion, particularly one that is often maligned. Furthermore I suspect these numbers might be higher if other forms of Paganism were included as options. Some contemporary Pagans might state that they are Heathen or Hellenic but not accept the general label Pagan. Estimates of how many contemporary Pagans live in the United States vary widely, but I would estimate there are about a million and a half based largely on adjusting Pew's numbers for the other factors I described.

There are also people who would not claim the identity of contemporary Pagan or any of its forms but do participate in rituals, buy the books, and join with others who are contemporary Pagans for some sabbats. However, just as with those who attend a church sporadically and might give money at Sunday services to maintain the church, but have not actually joined and hence are not on the churches' membership rolls, I would say these individuals are not members. There are always individuals who are at the edge of any group, who appear to be members or might eventually become members, but are not yet actually members and may never join. This is probably more true for contemporary Paganism with its amorphous borders than for more traditional religions, and if these individuals were included the count would be higher.

Between the end of the twentieth and beginning of the twenty-first centuries there was a large increase in the number of contemporary Pagans throughout the English-speaking world. In comparing ARIS surveys between 1990 and 2001 James Lewis (2007) concludes that there has been a massive increase during that time. He notes some problems in determining the exact extent of the increase because the categories changed between surveys. In the first the only contemporary Pagan category included was Wiccan; in the second Druids and Pagans were also included. He calculates that there was a seventeenfold increase if one looks only at those who claimed to be Wiccans and a much greater increase if one includes all contemporary Pagan categories in the second survey versus those who claimed to be Wiccans in the first.

One must be cautious in taking these numbers at face value, as during that time Wicca, and more generally contemporary Paganism, became somewhat more acceptable and less hidden so the numbers may appear to have increased as more practitioners were open about their religious practice. Furthermore some who joined as youths had grown up and were now able to answer for themselves instead of having their parents answer for the family. Some of the increase between surveys therefore is undoubtedly a result of more people being willing and able to come out of the "broom closet" and be counted. Nonetheless there was during this time a real increase, even if it is hard to gauge exactly how large it was. This increase slowed down during the first decade of the twenty-first century as documented by James Lewis (2012) and Douglas Ezzy and Helen A. Berger (2009). Lewis attributes this slower level of growth to the decline of the media's interest in witchcraft, which certainly explains part of the decrease. Attrition is another factor. The large influx of then teenagers and young adults interested in Witchcraft in the late twentieth century would probably result in a larger rate of attrition than normally occurs. Currently there is renewed media interest in Witchcraft and Wicca. For example the Olsen twins have come out with an expensive line of Wiccan ritual equipment for beginners (Mania 2018). If this follows the same pattern as the media "witch craze" of the 1990s there should be an increase in the rate of growth in the near future.

Most contemporary Pagans in my sample have been practicing for two or more years. A minority, 11.8 percent, state that they joined the religion a year ago or less. The majority (65.2 percent) have been practicing for ten to twenty years, and only 2.4 percent have been contemporary Pagans for more than twenty years. The fact that very few have been members of the religion for more than twenty years is consistent with most individuals being converts. The religion continues to grow and like all religions loses some of its members every year, but there is a core membership that remains within the religion and have raised their children in or at least around the religion. About 10 percent of my sample is composed of individuals who have a parent who is also a contemporary Pagan.

Contemporary Paganism continues to be primarily an urban and suburban religion, although the proportion of those living outside of greater metropolitan areas has increased from 16.6 percent in "The Pagan Census" to 19.3 percent in "The Pagan Census Revisited." This has occurred at the same time there has been a decrease in the national average of Americans living in rural areas. Data from the U.S. census indicates that the percentage of Americans living in rural areas has declined from 17.3 percent in 2000 to 16.4 percent in 2008. It has been suggested that contemporary Pagans self-define as practicing a nature religion while avoiding nature by living in urban areas (see for example Letcher 2000). To the contrary contemporary Pagans today are slightly less likely to live in urban areas than the typical American. Furthermore contrary to the trend for Americans on the whole, which indicates a decrease in the proportion living in rural areas, there has been an increase in the proportion of contemporary Pagans living in rural areas between my surveys. This suggests that contemporary Pagans are not avoiding living close to nature but are following a national trend of urbanization and suburbanization.

As can be seen in table 2.1 solitary practitioners have a higher rate of living in rural areas and towns than group practitioners. The majority (55.3 percent) of group practitioners live in urban or suburban neighborhoods. Although solitaries are more likely to live in suburban or urban neighborhoods than any other, the majority of solo practitioners do not live in suburban or urban areas. The growth of solitary practitioners has helped to fuel the increase in the numbers of rural contemporary Pagans. In turn the factors that have made it possible for individuals to avoid joining a group to train and learn about the religion—books and the Internet—have also increased solitary practice and the ability of those in rural areas and small towns to learn about the religion and practice it in areas where there are few if any other contemporary Pagans.

TABLE 2.1. *Percentage of Residential Type for Solo and Group Practitioners*

	SOLO	GROUP
Secluded rural	5.9	5.6
Rural community	13.7	11.2
Small town	19.9	16.6
Large town	14.3	11.3
Metro area	21.9	28.2
Suburb	24.3	27.1

Not only do contemporary Pagans live in a variety of areas from secluded and rural to the center of urban areas; they also live throughout the United States. In "The Pagan Census" we found that most contemporary Pagans lived on the coasts, with the largest concentration in the Pacific regions followed by the South Atlantic. Although the Pacific and South Atlantic regions remain the most popular areas for contemporary Pagans to live in, the distribution throughout the country is less skewed than was found in "The Pagan Census," as can be seen in table 2.2. Most regions have not changed their rank order by more than one number other than New England, which dropped from being the fourth most popular region to almost the least popular for contemporary Pagans to live in. It is possible that contemporary Pagans in New England were oversampled in the first survey as I conducted it with Andras Corban Arthen, one of the founders of EarthSpirit Community, a large New England contemporary Pagan association. It is also possible that the rate of increase has been greater in other areas of the country.

TABLE 2.2. *Percentage of Pagans in Each Region with Comparison to Pagan Census*

PCR* RANK	REGION	PERCENT IN PCR	PERCENT IN PC**	PC RANK
1	South Atlantic	19.1	16.7	2
2	Pacific	15.9	22.8	1
3	East North Central	14.1	14.6	3
4	Mid-Atlantic	11.7	12.8	5
5	Mountain	9.6	7.8	6
6	West South Central	8.5	5.8	7

TABLE 2.2. (*continued*)

PCR* RANK	REGION	PERCENT IN PCR	PERCENT IN PC**	PC RANK
7	West North Central	8.4	3.9	8
8	New England	8.0	13.5	4
9	East South Central	5.0	2.3	9

*PCR stands for Pagan Census Revisited.

**PC stands for Pagan Census.

The current regional distribution of contemporary Pagans is more consistent with American population patterns than was the distribution in the earlier survey. The percentage of contemporary Pagans found in each region in "The Pagan Census Revisited" is within two percentage points of the number of respondents in each of these regions in the GSS with the exception of the South Atlantic region. Although this region has the highest percentage of contemporary Pagans in my survey, it is nonetheless four percentage points below that listed in the GSS for the general American public. The more even distribution of contemporary Pagans throughout the United States and in rural as well as urban and suburban areas is in part the result of added online sources and the distribution of books not only in bookstores but from online venues. It also suggests a move toward normalization of the religion as it becomes spread more evenly throughout the country.

TABLE 2.3. *Ages of Solitaries and Group Members*

	PERCENT IN SAMPLE	PERCENT SOLO	PERCENT GROUP
Pre-boomer	2	1.8	2.9
Boomer	34	32.1	40.0
Gen X	27	26.0	29.0
Young	36	40.1	28.1

Table 2.3 indicates that the young are more likely to be solitary practitioners than are their elders. Baby boomers are most likely to be in group practice. Although age is a predictor of who will be a solitary practitioner, the majority is not young, as the young make up 40.1 percent of solitary practitioners, but they are disproportionately represented, as only 36 percent of my sample is young. Women too are disproportionately represented among solitary practitioners. In

part this is because the young are even more disproportionately female than the other age groups.

As can be seen in table 2.4 the younger the participant the more likely they are to be female. This is occurring at the same time that there is a growth in popularity of ethnic or regional Paganism, which tends to have a higher percentage of men than other spiritual paths of contemporary Paganism. The pre-boomers are the smallest cohort of contemporary Pagans, and the only ones with an almost equal number of men and women. This is in part because those who stayed in the religion until old age have formed romantic relationships within the group or converted with their romantic partner. It is also in part because Wicca, which was the most popular form of contemporary Paganism until recently, in its earliest manifestations was not influenced by feminism (Neitz 1991). The religion changed in the late 1960s and 1970s, as feminists joined the religion to celebrate the female divine. As can be seen in table 2.4 there are about twice as many women as men in the baby boomer generation, many of whom would have joined the religion after it was influenced by feminism. The youngest cohort has an even larger proportion of women than the other age groups; they would have joined after the media's romance with Witches, who were all portrayed as female.

TABLE 2.4 *Gender Distribution in the Four Age Groups (in percentages)*

	MALE	FEMALE	TRANS
Pre-boomer	41.7	57.7	0.6
Boomer	29.5	69.4	1.8
Gen X	28.4	70.6	0.9
Young	23.6	75.2	1.3

The disproportionate number of young people among solitary practitioners helps to explain the lower rate of committed relationships in this cohort. Among solitary practitioners 22.3 percent state that they are single never married as compared to only 11.7 percent of group practitioners. Group practitioners are more likely to be married than solitaries (45 percent versus 32 percent) but are also somewhat more likely to state that they are divorced. Nonetheless the majority of both forms of practice are in some form of committed relationship if one considers not only legally but ritually married, divorced or widowed and remarried, living with life partner, and in a committed relationship. The difference then between solitary and group practitioners is not that large: 71.7 percent of solitary and 76.5 percent of group practitioners are in some form of committed relationship.

TABLE 2.5. *Percentage for Form of Practice, Gender, and Relationships*

	FEMALE	MALE	SOLO	GROUP
Single never married	15.7	22.8	22.3	11.7
Live with life partner	7.6	9.8	11.9	9.9
Committed relationship	14.3	12.4	17.8	11.7
Married legally	41.7	36.4	32.0	45.0
Married ritually but not legally	4.4	5.2	3.7	7.2
Group marriage	0.6	0.6	0.4	0.9
Divorced	12.7	10.5	5.6	10.8
Separated	2.2	1.9	4.5	1.8
Widowed	1.3	0.9	0.7	0
Divorced and remarried	7.2	8.7	5.6	2.7
Widowed and remarried	0.4	0.2	0.7	0
Other	6.4	4.9	8.2	12.6

The general trend in contemporary Paganism is an increase in the percentage of those legally married from 33.3 percent in "The Pagan Census" to 40.1 percent in the more recent survey. In the first survey we found that contemporary Pagans in the South and Midwest were more likely to be married than those on the coasts. We conjectured that in areas that were more culturally and religiously conservative, contemporary Pagans were more likely to try and fit into the larger communities in which they were embedded by marrying instead of living together (H. Berger et al. 2003). The increase between surveys of those legally married, even with the influx of more young people, is suggestive of contemporary Pagans, at least in this way, decreasing areas of conflict with the larger society.

TABLE 2.6 *Percent of Each Sexual Orientation for Solo, Group, Female, Male, and Youth*

	SOLO	GROUP	FEMALE	MALE	YOUNG
Other	3.5	2.7	3.5	2.0	3.1
Heterosexual	68.0	63.5	65.9	69.5	43.5
Lesbian	2.5	3.4	3.7	0.2	2.6
Gay	4.2	6.6	0.1	16.7	7.8
Bisexual	21.8	23.8	26.8	11.6	43.0

One place in which contemporary Pagans do stand out clearly from other Americans is that the majority of the young self-define as nonheterosexual;

almost as many of the young claim to be bisexual as claim to heterosexual. More of the young also claim to be gay than do either solitaries or group members. More interestingly solitaries are slightly more likely to be heterosexual than group members even though a disproportionate percentage of solitaries are young. The difference is not large; 68 percent of solitaires and 63.5 percent of group practitioners are heterosexual, but particularly given the larger proportion of the young who are solitaries, it is suggestive that at least in this way solitaries are more conventional than those in groups. It should however also be noted that although most contemporary Pagans are heterosexual, they are nonetheless more likely than the typical American to be queer.

Just over 1 percent of contemporary Pagans either have transitioned or are transitioning to a gender different from the one they were assigned at birth, which is about twice as many as in the general American public (Hoffman 2016). Contemporary Paganism on the whole celebrates difference, particularly sexual differences. In general within the contemporary Pagan community there is an acceptance of all forms of sexuality as a celebration of the Goddess or the spirit. This is reflected in the higher level of nonheterosexual and trans people within the community, which although minorities within the religion, are a higher percentage than in the general American population. This has made the religion a comfortable place for nonheteronormative people and has resulted in more joining.

Contemporary Pagans remain more educated than their neighbors, but the difference has decreased between surveys. This is largely because Americans on the whole are attaining a higher educational level. When "The Pagan Census" was completed only about half of all Americans had a high school degree. In the 2010 census 87.1 percent of American adults reported having a high school degree or higher. Contemporary Pagans remain better educated with only 2 percent reporting that they do not have a high school degree. Some of the difference may be a factor of age. Younger Americans have more years of education on average than older Americans. The contemporary Pagan movement has a small proportion of people who are older than seventy. Furthermore there are still very few minorities in the contemporary Pagan movement. United States census data from 2010 indicate that among Caucasians 87.6 percent have received at least a high school degree. Nonetheless even with those caveats, contemporary Pagans remain better educated than non-Pagans. Among contemporary Pagans 45 percent have bachelor's degrees or more. This can be compared to the general American public, in which 29.9 percent of all Americans and 30.3 percent of white Americans have a college degree or more.

As in the first survey there are only small regional differences in educational attainment among contemporary Pagans, who are consistently well educated regardless of the region of the United States in which they live. In contrast educational attainment of the non-Pagan American population varies significantly by region. On the whole new religions tend to draw their converts from among the better educated. It has been postulated that this is because all these religions require that individuals read and understand esoteric texts and that the more educated tend to be more open to new realities and possibilities. Furthermore two major ways in which contemporary Pagans learn about their religion is through books and the Internet, both forms of learning that are more appealing and more available to the well educated. Although at this point the religion is no longer new, as it has been in the United States since at least the 1960s, it nonetheless relies on written materials to transmit its teachings and on the Internet as a source of its community building.

TABLE 2.7. *Educational Levels for Solitary and Group Practitioners (in percentages)*

	SOLO	GROUP
Doctoral/law	3.2	5.3
Master's	10.9	16.7
Bachelor's	24.5	31.7
Technical/associate's	13.5	13.4
One to three years college	31.5	26.1
High school diploma	14.7	7.8
Less than high school	2.4	0.7

As can be seen in table 2.7 contemporary Pagans who practice in groups are better educated than those who are solitaries, although both are better educated than the average American. In part this is because solitaries are somewhat younger. Only 9.8 percent of group members are currently university students as compared to 16.5 percent of solitary practitioners. This is in part why solitaries have a higher percentage of their number with one to three years of college. But it does not completely explain the slightly lower educational level. The larger proportion of solitaries who live in rural areas would also help to explain some of the difference. Americans who live in rural areas tend to have lower educational attainments than urbanites. In turn the lower education level of solitaries explains their somewhat lower income.

The 2015 U.S. census found that 33 percent of women and 32 percent of men had college degrees or more (Ryan and Bauman 2016). Among contemporary Pagans 42.9 percent of women and 41.6 percent of men have a college degree or more. Although as previously noted contemporary Pagans are more educated on the whole than their neighbors, the difference between the genders remains consistent in the contemporary Pagan community with other Americans. This, however, is not true for graduate degrees. According to the same census report 12 percent of both men and women have a postgraduate degree; among contemporary Pagans 16.1 percent of women and 17.2 percent of men have a postgraduate degree. This difference is the result of more contemporary Pagan men having doctoral or law degrees than contemporary Pagan women. Only 3.3 percent of contemporary Pagan women and 5.7 percent of contemporary Pagan men have doctoral or law degrees. More contemporary Pagan women than men have master's degrees (12.8 percent versus 11.5 percent). Although fewer contemporary Pagan men complete their bachelor's degrees than contemporary Pagan women, more contemporary Pagan men have completed their doctoral or professional degrees. Contemporary Pagans have a higher rate than other Americans of receiving doctorates or professional degrees, but like other Americans contemporary Pagan men are more likely to reach the top educational levels than their female counterpart.

TABLE 2.8. *Income by Form of Practice and Gender (in percentages)*

	SOLO	GROUP	FEMALE	MALE
$10,000 or less	18.5	9.8	16.9	14.0
$10,001–$40,000	46.9	42.9	47.5	42.1
$40,001–$70,000	21.9	29.4	23.5	25.5
Above $70,000	12.6	17.8	12.1	18.5

Contemporary Pagans on the whole earn less than would be anticipated by their education level. This is consistent between my two surveys. The inequity of incomes between men and women in the United States, even those who have earned a bachelor's degrees or higher and the high proportion of women in this religion, explains most of that lower income. As can be seen in table 2.8 contemporary Pagan women, like other American women, tend to earn less than men. Group practitioners, who tend to be somewhat older and better educated, earn more than solitary practitioners.

In "The Pagan Census" we found, as did Adler (1986) and Jorgensen and Russell (1999) in surveys they conducted, that the most typical occupation for contemporary Pagans after student and homemaker was computer scientist. It was conjectured that this may have been because of the links between the science fiction community and both the contemporary Pagan and computer science communities, or because computer science, like magic, requires conceptualizing a realm that cannot be seen but is experienced. Whatever that link may have been, it is clear that it no longer exists. The most common designations, excluding student and homemaker, for both solitary and group practitioners, is self-employed or business owner, followed by health care professional. Computer science professional is not even in the top nine occupations of group practitioners and is fourth among solitary practitioners if student and homemaker are excluded. Among those who are students, computer science is the seventh most popular major of both those in groups and solitary practice. The humanities, social sciences, natural sciences, and fine arts all rank higher as majors than computer science. There are currently more liberal arts majors than there are computer science, other science, or math majors. There is some variation among contemporary Pagans within the United States. For instance computer science is the second most common major in the South Atlantic with 8.5 percent majoring in this field, but on the whole more contemporary Pagans are small business owners and in the caring professions than in computer science. We did not ask small business owners what type of business they were involved in. It is possible that most of them are working in fields that are directly allied with their religion, such as running a metaphysical store. Nonetheless contemporary Pagans regardless of whether they practice alone or in a group are starting to resemble the typical college graduate if not the typical American, although natural sciences do rank fourth among majors for contemporary Pagan students, which is still a higher percentage than the national average.

TABLE 2.9. *Top Nine Occupations for Solo and Group Practitioners in Rank Order*

	SOLO	GROUP
1	Student	Student
2	Homemaker	Self-employed/business owner
3	Self-employed/business owner	Health professional
4	Health professional	Admin./manager
5	Admin./manager	Teacher/professor
6	Computer science professional	Administrative assistant/ secretary
7	Technician	Sale personnel
8	Teacher/professor	Homemaker
9	Administrative assistant/ secretary	Technician

Women are slightly more likely to be solitary practitioners than are men. Women make up 73.7 percent of solitary and 67.6 percent of group practitioners as compared to men, who make up 25.2 percent of solitary practitioners and 31.4 percent of group practitioners. As women make up the largest percentage of the religion, they are therefore the majority in both solitary and group practices. However, a larger percentage of women than men are solitary practitioners, although the majority of both men and women practice alone. As can be seen in table 2.4 a larger percentage of contemporary Pagan women are young, consistent with their having joined during the media witch craze. Men on the whole are only slightly more likely to have found contemporary Paganism through social networks; 46.6 percent of men and 44.5 percent of women stated that they were introduced to the religion by someone they knew. Women were more likely to cite a relative and men more likely to state that it was a friend or romantic partner who introduced them to the religion.

As can be seen in table 2.5 contemporary Pagan women are more likely to be married or in a committed relationship than contemporary Pagan men are. Among women 68.0 percent are legally or ritually married, in a committed relationship, or living with their life partner as compared to 63.8 percent of men. More women are legally married than are men. As with other Americans divorced men are more likely to be remarried than divorced women. Contemporary Pagan men are more likely than their female counterparts to be single never married. The difference between solitary and group practitioners is larger with 22.3 percent single never married as compared to those who practice in a group, in which only 11.7 percent have never been married. Men are slightly more likely to self-describe as heterosexual (69.5 percent of men and 65.9 percent of women), but as previously noted the majority of contemporary Pagans regardless of their gender are heterosexual, although a larger percentage of both men and women are queer than in the general American population. Interestingly female contemporary Pagans are much more likely to claim that they are bisexual than their male counterparts (26.8 percent of women and 11.6 percent of men). Men are more likely to claim that they are homosexual—16.7 percent of male contemporary Pagans claim they are gay compared to only 3.7 percent of women claiming to be lesbians. It is interesting that among contemporary Pagans more women than men see their sexuality as flexible. This may be part of a commitment to feminism or to a view of gender and sexuality as fluid on the part of contemporary Pagan women.

Demographically contemporary Paganism has changed very little between my two surveys. Contemporary Pagans are still more educated than the average American, although the gap is closing; there are now fewer engineers and computer scientists than in the past. Contemporary Pagans are now fairly similar to the typical American college graduate. They continue to reside throughout the United States, and in fact they are more evenly distributed than in the past. They live primarily in greater metropolitan areas but are more likely than other Americans to live in a rural area. Most contemporary Pagans are in committed relationships. Although most contemporary Pagans self-define as heterosexual there is a larger proportion of gay, lesbian, bisexual, and transsexual members within the religion than is reported in the general American population, which is consistent with contemporary Pagans' support of diversity, particularly of sexual diversity, and celebration of difference.

Solitary practitioners are slightly younger, less educated, poorer, more likely to be single, more likely to be female, and more likely to live in rural areas than group practitioners, although it must be emphasized on the whole these differences are small. Most solitary practitioners like most group practitioners are female, in college, or college educated and live in an urban or suburban setting. Solitary practitioners are more educated than the typical American, just less than those in group practice.

Spiritual Paths

In "The Pagan Census" the two most common spiritual paths were Wiccan and Witch; that is no longer the case as Eclectic is now the most common spiritual path. Wicca remains the most common designation for those in groups, in which half claim to be Wiccan. However, eclectic is the most common designation for solitaries, who make up the majority of the religion now. Eclectic is now the second most common designation for group members. In the earlier survey Eclectic was not even offered as an alternative as it was not a term regularly used. The growth of eclectic Paganism has been aided by books and websites that provide both the tools and encouragement for individuals to create their own form of the religion. Because contemporary Pagans often mix together several traditions respondents were permitted to include all they considered primary identifications, and most did choose more than one; the numbers therefore add up to more than 100 percent.

For solitary practitioners the four most popular spiritual paths after eclectic are Witch, Wiccan, Goddess worshipper, and spiritual but dislikes labels. Only a third of solitary practitioners claim to be Wiccan. Traditionally Wicca was taught and practiced in covens. Books such as those by Scott Cunningham (1988, 1994), which provided information on how to practice Wicca alone, had made the religion available to people outside of the coven tradition. But the tradition of Wicca being practiced in groups has nonetheless survived. Witch is a more common designation than Wiccan for solitary practitioners. For those who work in groups Witch, Goddess worshipper, and magic worker are the next most popular designations after Wiccan and eclectic. On the one hand, four of the top five designations, in slightly different orders, are the same for both solitary and group practitioners, suggesting that those who practice alone share much with those who practice in a group. On the other hand, the order is indicative of some differences between the two forms of practice. Those who practice in a group are less likely to see themselves as being spiritual but disliking labels. They are more likely to be Wiccans than eclectic. As noted in the first chapter eclectic Paganism has been strongly influenced by Wicca. Possibly as Wicca becomes a less popular spiritual path for solitary practitioners it will have less of an influence on eclectic Paganism, and ethnic or regional forms of Paganism will grow in influence. For many solitaries being an eclectic is part of spiritually "doing their own thing." This of course does not necessarily mean that each person's spiritual path is unique as they rely on the same readings and Internet sites to help them formulate their rituals, spiritual language, and even conceptualization of the otherworld. As discussed in the last chapter the amorphousness of practice might actually result in greater similarity as individuals look for guidance to the same authors and Internet sites, and share as their own things they gleaned online. Cowan (2005) has documented the way in which information is cut and pasted on a number of different contemporary Pagan webpages with no attribution of where it originated, resulting in the appearance of a vast number of different voices when in actuality some voices are amplified by their repetition.

TABLE 2.10. *Spiritual Paths for Solitary and Group Practitioners (in percentages)**

	SOLO	GROUP
Agnostic	9.2	6.0
Atheist	2.4	1.7
Buddhist	7.2	6.3
Ceremonial magician	5.9	10.8
Christian	3.8	2.0
Druid	10.2	14.8
Eclectic Pagan	56.3	45.5
Goddess Worshipper	29.9	35.0
Heathen	7.9	11.0
Hellenic Pagan	4.7	4.7
Jewish	1.7	2.4
Magic worker	21.8	27.8
New Age	13.4	11.9
Satanist	0.9	0.7
Santaria	1.3	1.7
Shaman	12.8	16.0
Spiritual no labels	24.3	14.4
Thelemite	1.5	3.2
Unitarian Universalist	9.5	12.2
Vodun	1.9	1.7
Wiccan	33.2	50.2
Witch (not Wiccan)	35.7	37.0

*The totals add up to more than 100 percent because respondents were permitted to indicate all spiritual paths they believe are primary.

As noted in the first chapter, I will be focusing on six spiritual paths of contemporary Paganism; the four most popular, Wicca, Witchcraft, Eclectic, and Goddess worshippers; and two ethnic forms, Druidism and Heathenism. The majority of all these spiritual paths consist of solitary practitioners, although Wiccans have only 59 percent of their members who are solitary practitioners, which is the lowest of all the spiritual paths. Druids and Heathens also have a lower rate of solitary practitioners than average with only 60 percent of their members being solitaries. Witches and Goddess worshippers respectively have 66 percent and 64 percent of their members who are solitary. Eclectics have the highest percentage of solitaries, with 71 percent claiming that they practice completely alone.

TABLE 2.11. *Gender and Age Distribution of Spiritual Paths (in percentages)*

	FEMALE	MALE	PRE-BOOMER	BOOMER	GEN X	YOUNG
Wicca solo	76.3	23.1	2.8	33.7	27.1	36.8
Wicca group	69.3	29.9	3.1	44.4	28.8	23.6
Witch solo	81.1	17.9	0.8	29.8	26.8	42.2
Witch group	71.5	27.5	1.9	34.4	27.2	36.5
Eclectic solo	76.9	22.1	1.6	27.7	26.1	44.4
Eclectic group	71.5	27.5	1.9	34.4	27.2	36.5
Druid solo	56.3	42.8	1.4	30.1	27.9	41.1
Druid group	56.0	42.6	1.2	37.9	32.5	28.2
Heathen solo	49.7	48.4	0.2	20.5	29.5	49.7
Heathen group	46.4	53.1	0	26.5	31.6	42.7
Goddess solo	80.9	18.1	2.3	36.4	26.1	35.1
Goddess group	71.5	27.5	1.9	34.4	27.2	36.5

As the majority of contemporary Pagans are women, they make up the majority of almost all forms of contemporary Paganism, although not equally. Solitary Witches and Goddess Worshipers have a higher percentage of women as members than any of the denominations of contemporary Paganism that are being examined. The very term *witch* is associated in most people's minds with women, although both men and women are practicing Witches. As the data indicates, women are much more likely to self-define as Witches than men are. Goddess Worship, with its focus on the female deity or aspect of the deity appears on the face of it more likely to appeal to women. However there is little difference in the gender distribution of group members of these two spiritual paths and those in Wicca and eclectic groups. This is suggestive that media images are of greater importance among solitary practitioners, resulting in men who practice alone being less likely to become part of a spiritual path that is associated primarily with women.

Druids and Heathens have a larger proportion of men than the other spiritual paths. Among solitary practitioners Heathens have an almost equal gender distribution; among group practitioners there are a higher percentage of men than women, but it is lower than was found in the first survey. The greater gender equity in the second survey compared to the first among Heathens suggests that the religion, which emphasizes warrior gods and fertility goddesses, has modified its masculine focus to at least some extent—particularly in their online message—and has therefore been able to attract more women to its numbers. Although Druids do not emphasize warrior gods, the image of the Druid is masculine, just as the image of the Witch is feminine. On their website the Ár nDraíocht Féin, the largest American Druid organization, lists as one of their frequently asked questions: "do you have to be a man to be a Druid," which they answer in the negative, stating that half their membership is female. I found that more than half of those claiming to be Druids are women, but it is still fewer than in the more popular forms of contemporary Paganism. Not all Druids are members of the Ár nDraíocht, and I am not suggesting that they are wrong about their membership, although it is unclear how often they may update their website.

The gender distribution of the different spiritual paths of contemporary Paganism corresponds to how focused the rituals, mythology, and structure are on women's empowerment and spiritual expression. Women are not as drawn in the same numbers to warrior gods of the land as they are to goddesses that embrace them and celebrate their life cycles and the fecundity of nature. Some of the goddesses celebrated in Goddess Worship, Wicca, and Witchcraft, and among eclectics are of death, destruction, and women fighters, but these are more typically seen as part of the life cycle and are necessary for life or for social justice. These deities, furthermore, are part a larger pantheon that focuses more on the goddesses of life and love than those who are warriors or bearers of death. The differences among the spiritual paths, particularly Heathens, will be most evident in my discussion of politics but can also be seen in their presentation of gender roles. Heathens tend to be more conservative than the typical contemporary Pagan. Although the focus of this book is on solitary practitioners, gender, age, and spiritual path also influence behaviors and attitudes and are therefore important to consider when understanding solitary practitioners.

Heathens have many fewer members than Eclectic, Wiccans, or Witches, but interestingly they have a higher percentage of their membership that is young than any other group, including Druids, which has even fewer members and is also a form of ethnic or regional Paganism. The percentage of young among

Heathens is highest for solitary practitioners; 49.7 percent of solitary Heathens are young. Although not as high as among solitaries, there is a higher proportion—42.7 percent—of the young among Heathen group practitioners than among other spiritual paths. The young and particularly young men are filling the ranks of Heathens. Although this remains one of the smaller spiritual paths, there is a small group of white supremacists among its members. Some of the shields on display during the alt-right march in Charlottesville, Virginia, in August 2017 bore Odinist symbols. Furthermore my data indicates that the young among the Heathens are somewhat more conservative than their elders. Although only 2 percent of young Heathens claim to be far right, that is four times as high as for all young contemporary Pagans and more than four times as high as all other Heathens. As will be discussed in chapter 5, Heathens tend to be less likely to support liberal causes such as women's and gay rights than other contemporary Pagans, and young Heathens are even less likely than their elders to support these movements. What is most striking is that most young contemporary Pagans are even stronger supporters of gay rights than their elders, but this is not true of Heathens. This is not to suggest that that all or even most Heathens are part of the alt-right, but my data is suggestive that this spiritual path is drawing young rightwing men to its numbers.

Heathens, particularly those who work in groups, tend to be the most socially conservative. They are the most likely to identify as heterosexual; 76.5 percent of Heathen group members state they are heterosexual as compared to Wiccan group members, who have the lowest rate of heterosexuality, among whom 62.4 percent are heterosexual. Even the conservative Heathens have a higher rate of queer members than is the norm in the larger American society, so the conservative nature of Heathens should not be exaggerated. However as the young are more likely to be sexually nonconforming it is interesting that among contemporary Pagans, Heathens have a larger percentage of young adherents and at the same time the lowest percentage of bisexual, gay, and lesbian members. Heathens who work in groups are also the most likely to be legally married, with 46.9 percent stating that they are legally married. It is curious that solitary Heathens have the lowest level of those legally married of any of the groups explored, suggesting one area to which the greater social conservatism does not reach. It should be emphasized that although on the whole Heathens are more socially conservative than other contemporary Pagans, they are still less so than the typical American.

Wiccan group practitioners have the highest percentage of members who are baby boomers and the lowest percentage of the young. The percentage of young who are solitary Wiccan practitioners is higher than those in groups, but Wicca tends to have an older demographic than the other spiritual paths I am examining. Not surprisingly as it has become the most popular spiritual path, eclectic solitary practitioners have the second highest percentage of their members who are young after Heathens.

Educationally Wiccans who work in a group are the best educated, with 52.1 percent of them having a bachelor's degree or better. This is a reflection of the higher educational level of baby boomers, who are disproportionately Wiccan group members. Nonetheless Wiccans who are solitary are the least educated among the different spiritual paths, with only 35.2 percent having a college degree or more. Druid and Heathen group practitioners are only slightly less likely than Wiccan group practitioners to have a bachelor's degree or more. Eclectics have the largest percentage (48.6 percent) of solitaries with a college degree or more. The higher completion rate of college or more among group practitioners than solitaries is a reflection of the higher percentage of young among solitaries who are less likely to have completed college. However why solitary Wiccans are less likely than other solitary contemporary Pagans to have a college degree or more is unclear but suggests that those who are more educated and practicing alone are more likely to self-define as eclectic—that is viewing their practice as something that they have put together for themselves.

The United Kingdom and Canada

Canada and the United Kingdom have the same percentage of solitary practitioners as the United States does. The data is less robust in other counties, but it is clear that throughout the world solitary practice is the primary form of practice. As the original "Pagan Census" surveyed only U.S. contemporary Pagans there is no comparative data internationally on the growth of solitary practice. As contemporary Paganism has arrived in many of these other countries later, it is possible that the religion was never primarily practiced in groups. Nonetheless there has probably been a corresponding increase in other countries.

As in the United States, Canada and the United Kingdom experienced increases in the popularity of this religion at the end of the twentieth century, with a slower but nonetheless continued increase at the beginning of this century. Both Canada and the United Kingdom have included religious affiliation in some of their censuses but not in all. Religion was a category in the 1991 and 2001 Canadian censuses but not in the most recently available 2011 census. A voluntary survey was included in the 2011 Canadian census, which included questions about religious affiliation. The voluntary nature of the survey makes it even less reliable than census data, which always underrepresents some groups, particularly the homeless and illegal immigrants. Lewis (2012) found a fourfold increase of Canadian contemporary Pagans between the 1991 and 2001 censuses. According to census data in 2001 just under 0.1 percent of Canadians were contemporary Pagans; this was about half of what was found in the American Religious Identification Survey of U.S. religious affiliations. The 2011

Canadian survey that was included with the census showed a very small increase over the 2001 census. The 2011 survey indicates that there is slightly more than 0.1 percent of the population who are contemporary Pagans. However it is probable that the increase would have been somewhat higher if the question had been included in the census itself and not just in a voluntary and supplemental survey.

The United Kingdom included religious affiliation in their 2001 and 2011 censuses but not earlier ones. In the 2001 survey there was no specific category provided for Pagans. Individuals could indicate "other" and then fill in their religious affiliation. The need to do more than just check a box normally decreases the responses garnered in any survey, and it is reasonable to anticipate it had that effect on this one as well, particularly as answering the question was voluntary. Furthermore there was an online movement in Britain to have people indicate Jedi Knight as their religious affiliation on the census. This resulted in 0.75 percent of respondents to the British census choosing this as their religion. Lewis (2011) believes a disproportionate percentage of these individuals were contemporary Pagans, but it is impossible to determine if he is correct. It is clear this movement further muddied the waters in analyzing the data. The data that was collected when one eliminated "Jedi Knight" and "none" indicate that contemporary Pagans were the seventh most popular religion in the United Kingdom (Crowley 2014) with the same percentage of contemporary Pagans as found in Canada.

For the 2011 U.K. census there was another online movement, this time by some contemporary Pagan organizations to encourage their coreligious to stand up to be counted. This was an attempt to help normalize the religion by showing the extent to which it is practiced in the United Kingdom. The number of contemporary Pagans doubled between censuses while the population of the United Kingdom increased by 7.5 percent. The large increase is clearly in part a reflection of the depression of numbers caused in the 2001 census by the write-in movement for Jedi Knight and effects of the subsequent campaign to get contemporary Pagans counted. It is therefore hard to know how much of an increase there really was between censuses, but the numbers undoubtedly reflect a real increase.

Even with the movement to be counted, not all contemporary Pagans were. Vivianne Crowley (2014) did an online survey to learn why individuals who identified as contemporary Pagans had not indicated their religious affiliation in the 2011 U.K. census. She found this was particularly prevalent in Northern Ireland, where religious identity is tied to political and social identity making it difficult for those from Catholic backgrounds to not identify with that religion, at least as an ethnic, if not religious, identity. Furthermore many were reticent to tell their parents and other family members about their conversion.

Crowley found that among contemporary Pagans who did not register their affiliation on the census, there was apprehension about whether their answers would really be confidential. Concerns were raised about the company who had been hired to do the census and more generally with the issue of security breaches. There was furthermore a countermovement by some left-leaning organizations, such as the Green Party, against answering the religion question at all, that served as a counterweight to the campaign by contemporary Pagan organizations, which advocated for participation.

For some nonresponders religion is a private matter. As one of her respondents stated: "It's none of the Government's business" (Crowley 2014:10). As the census is normally filled out in the United Kingdom, as in the United States, by the head of household, some family members' religious affiliation may have been incorrectly reported. As Crowley notes after the recession this would include not only young people but some middle-aged contemporary Pagans who were forced to move in with their parents for financial reasons. Additionally in Britain as in the United States some felt their religion was a combination of several different ones and refused to check just one box, while others eschew the term religion preferring to see themselves as spiritual and therefore outside religious organizations.

Crowley found that there was about a 15 percent rate of nonresponders among contemporary Pagans to the religion question in the census. Like most researchers of the religion Crowley believes that the census data underrepresented the number of contemporary Pagans in the United Kingdom, which she believes is closer to 240,000. Researchers of contemporary Paganism in all nations believe the general denigration of the religion has resulted in contemporary Pagans remaining in what they refer to as the broom closet, wary of telling others their religious affiliation as it might have negative effects on their work or social relationships, which has resulted in an undercounting of membership. Furthermore people are less likely to answer a voluntary census question if they are required to write in the name of their religion instead of just checking a box, as was possible for more mainstream religions. Relying either directly on survey and census data or on researchers' extrapolations from them results in the finding that the United States has about twice as high a percentage of contemporary Pagans in their population as either England or Canada. On the whole Canada and the United Kingdom have a higher percentage of their population claim to have no religion than in the United States, which would help to explain why contemporary Paganism is less popular in these countries—religion on the whole is less popular (Pew 2018). Nonetheless the combination of the higher percentage and larger population in the United States results in it having a larger number of contemporary Pagans than in other countries and therefore a stronger impact on book sales and Internet sites.

Demographically there is a good deal of consistency, as well as a few differences, among English-speaking nations. The gender gap is larger in Canada than in either the United States or the United Kingdom, with women making up about three-quarters of all Canadian contemporary Pagans. The United Kingdom has a larger percentage of men who practice contemporary Paganism than either the United States or Canada. Religious affiliation in the Canadian census is tabulated by households, not individuals, and therefore there is no data on the gender of participants to compare with that in my survey. The U.K. census did provide a gender division for all religions including contemporary Paganism, which is virtually the same as my data, 66.2 percent female and 33.5 percent male (Crowley 2014: 489). As my data indicates the gender imbalance is lower for group practitioners than it is for solitary practitioners in the United Kingdom; groups have only 9 percent more female than male practitioners.

TABLE 2.12. *Gender of Solitary and Group Practitioners in the United Kingdom and Canada (in percentages)*

	SOLO U.K.	GROUP U.K.	SOLO CANADA	GROUP CANADA
Female	67.0	54.5	74.1	78.4
Male	32.5	45.5	25.7	21.6
Transitioning	0.5	0	0.4	0

In Canada and the United Kingdom, as in the United States, the young are more likely to be solitary practitioners than they are to be in group practice, and baby boomers are most likely to be in group practice than individuals in any other age group. Age distribution of solitary and group members in the United States and the United Kingdom are similar with the exception of generation X, which in the United Kingdom has a slightly stronger preference for group practice than in the United States. Canada has a larger percentage of young than either the United States or the United Kingdom; 44.8 percent of Canadian contemporary Pagans are young as compared to 36.0 percent of U.S. contemporary Pagans and 37.7 percent of U.K. contemporary Pagans. Nonetheless Canada has about the same percentage of solitary practitioners as the United States. The demographic differences among the three English-speaking countries suggest that some cultural differences exist and that the religion has grown somewhat differently in the three countries. These differences need to be kept in mind as other comparisons—particularly social and political comparisons—are discussed later in the book.

TABLE 2.13. *Age of Solitary and Group Practitioners in the United Kingdom and Canada (in percentages)*

	U.K.	U.K. SOLO	U.K. GROUP	CANADA	CANADA SOLO	CANADA GROUP
Pre-boomer	1.9	0.9	3.1	1.0	0.4	1.8
Boomer	28.4	22.6	36.9	31.7	27.6	37.8
Gen X	31.2	26.9	32.3	25.7	23.9	27.9
Young	37.7	42.5	26.2	44.8	48.1	32.4

In Canada and the United Kingdom, as in the United States, there is a larger proportion of group members that have graduated from college than those who practice alone. The pattern in Canada is similar to that in the United States; the majority of group members and slightly more than a third of solitaries have college degrees. In the United Kingdom the difference is not as great with 49.9 percent of group members and 42.9 percent of solitary practitioners having a college degree or more. In all three countries contemporary Pagans are better educated than their peers. Why the United Kingdom has a smaller difference in educational level between group and solitary practitioners is unclear as there is as high a percentage of the young among solitary practitioners there as in the other two nations. It suggests that the difference may only in part be explained by age.

The top major for all contemporary Pagan college graduates in the United Kingdom is the humanities, whether or not the person practices alone or in a group. In Canada solitaries also are most likely to major in humanities, and those who practice in a group in social sciences. Unlike in the United States, where there is a concentration in the helping professions, there appears less of a pattern in the United Kingdom and Canada. The differences in respondents' college majors among the three countries are a reflection of both cultural differences and differences in the job markets and training programs internationally.

At first glance the marriage and commitment patterns in all three countries appear similar, but on closer examination there are a few notable differences. In all three countries solitary practitioners are more likely to be unmarried than are group practitioners. The difference is greatest in the United Kingdom, in which nearly a third of solitary practitioners are single. As in the United States the younger age of solitaries and in the United Kingdom the greater percentage of men, who tend to be less likely than contemporary Pagan women to be married, account for the lower marriage rate. What is more interesting is that group practitioners in the United Kingdom are the most likely to be in some form of committed relationship than in the other countries discussed. Counting legally or ritually married, living with life partner, remarried, and in a committed relationship 83.3 percent of group practitioners in the United Kingdom are in some form of long-term relationship, as compared with 64.1 percent of solitary practitioners in the United Kingdom, and respectively 76.5 percent of group practitioners in Canada and 83.3 percent of group practitioners in the United States. Group members in Canada have the highest percentage of those legally married among the three countries.

TABLE 2.14. *United Kingdom and Canada Relationship Status of Group and Solitary Members (in percentages)*

	U.K. SOLO	U.K. GROUP	CANADA SOLO	CANADA GROUP
Single	31.1	19.1	22.3	11.7
Live with life partner	15.1	9.1	11.9	9.9
Committed relationship	13.7	13.6	17.8	11.7
Legally married	28.3	37.9	32.0	45.0
Ritually married	4.2	18.2	3.7	7.2
Group marriage	0	0	0.4	0.9
Divorced	4.7	3.0	5.6	10.8
Separated	2.8	7.6	4.5	1.8
Widowed	1.4	1.5	0.7	0
Divorced, remarried	2.8	4.5	5.6	2.7
Widowed, remarried	0	0	0.7	0

In all three English-speaking countries most contemporary Pagans are heteronormative. Canada stands out as being more so than the other two countries and being the only one in which group members are less likely to be queer than solitaries. The difference is small among these three countries. As in the United States there are a higher percentage of nonheterosexuals than in the general population. In the United Kingdom, which has a higher percentage of men who are participants, there is a higher percentage of those who self-define as gay and a somewhat smaller number who self-define as lesbians. The religion's celebration of alternative lifestyles and all forms of sexuality makes it appealing to those who are not heteronormative not only in the United States but not surprisingly elsewhere as well.

TABLE 2.15. *United Kingdom and Canadian Sexual Orientations of Group and Solitary Members (in percentages)*

	U.K. SOLO	U.K. GROUP	CANADA SOLO	CANADA GROUP
Heterosexual	66.5	65.2	69.0	71.2
Lesbian	1.4	0	3.0	1.8
Gay	9.0	7.6	3.4	2.7
Bisexual	20.8	25.8	21.3	18.9
Other	2.8	1.5	3.4	5.3

More interesting than the differences that I found are the overriding similarities among contemporary Pagans in all three nations; solitary practitioners tend to be slightly younger, less educated, less likely to be queer, and less likely to be in a long-term relationship than group practitioners. The differences between solitary and group practitioners are not large in any of the countries. The most striking difference among these nations is the larger percentage of men in the United Kingdom and of women in Canada than in the United States.

Spiritual Paths

My data indicates that there is a consistency in the popularity of the spiritual paths in the three English-speaking nations. As table 2.16 shows among solitary practitioners in the United Kingdom and Canada, like in the United States, eclectic is the most popular spiritual path, although unlike in the United States, the majority of contemporary Pagans overall is not eclectic. In all three countries Witch and Wiccan are the two next most popular spiritual paths after eclectic for solitaries. This is followed in Canada, as in the United States, by Goddess worship, which is less popular in the United Kingdom than in either the United States or Canada. In the United Kingdom magic worker is the fourth most popular. This difference is a reflection of the higher percentage of men who are contemporary Pagans in the United Kingdom than in North America. The spiritual path of magic worker tends to be more popular and Goddess worship less popular among men than among women. Among group members in the United Kingdom and Canada, Wicca remains the most popular spiritual path as it is in the United States. Although Wicca has its origins in the United Kingdom, even there less than half of group members are Wiccans. In Canada, after Wiccan, group members are most likely to be either Witches or eclectics. In the United Kingdom, as in the United States, Witches are the second most popular spiritual path for group members. But eclectics are not in the top four designations for group members in the United Kingdom. In fact, U.K. group members are as likely to be Druids as they are eclectics.

Data from the U.K. census provides a somewhat different picture than my data does. Of those who responded to the question about religious affiliation, 70.9 percent wrote in "Pagan." Wicca was the second most popular designation with 15 percent and Druids the third most popular with 5.3 percent of all contemporary Pagans citing each of those as their religious affiliation. This would suggest that Druidism is more popular in the United Kingdom than my study suggests. This data however is very hard to interpret as the "Stand Up and Be Counted" movement by contemporary Pagan organizations in the United Kingdom requested that respondents use the term "Pagan" in the write-in section provided on the census for all minority religions (Crowley 2014). This undoubtedly resulted in a number of contemporary Pagans choosing that designation instead of possibly another more specific spiritual path within contemporary Paganism as all would consider themselves Pagan even if they were Wiccans, Witches, or Druids. The stated goal of the Stand Up and Be Counted movement was to have contemporary Paganism recognized as a religion worthy of the respect and benefits provided to other religions in the United Kingdom. It is therefore almost certain that many who wrote in Pagan would have otherwise listed a specific form of the religion.

It is interesting to note that at least among Wiccans, Druids, Heathens, and Witches, even with the call for consistency in choosing Pagan some listed their specific spiritual path (in the United Kingdom census 2.5 percent claimed to be Heathen and 1.6 percent Witches). However I am unsure how to interpret this. Was it that at least some members of those spiritual paths feel more strongly about their identity within their specific form of contemporary Paganism than members of other spiritual paths? Were they less tied into the larger umbrella organizations that organized the movement? It is possible that my survey, which has a comparatively small sample in the United Kingdom, underrepresented the popularity of Druids relative to other spiritual paths. However it should be noted that a larger percentage of my sample take this designation than was found in the United Kingdom census, suggesting that it was probably not undersampled. The write-in campaign, which was successful in having most if not all contemporary Pagans counted, distorted the data on spiritual paths making it impossible to use this as a guide to how popular each is in the United Kingdom.

My data clearly indicates an elective affinity between eclecticism and solitary practice. However, as the data in tables 2.16 and 2.10 also indicate, in North America, at least, group practitioners are also drawn to being eclectics, albeit at a lower rate than solitaries. Nonetheless this is something that is particularly appealing to solitary practitioners, who work alone and can easily take pieces from several different spiritual forms and add their own flourishes. My data does not permit me to say how unique each eclectic's rituals and incantations are, nor what elements are most commonly mixed together. In my earlier ethnographic work, I have seen some individuals claim that they are doing their own unique practice, which was clearly derivative of Wiccan rituals. In part this is a reflection of the need in general in the developed world for each of us to see ourselves as unique individuals. Contemporary Paganism and other religions that emphasize individual agency and direct relationship with the divine strongly emphasize individualism. Throughout the survey a substantial percentage when given the option chose "other," even when they then wrote in one of the options available to them. This is an indication of the strong desire of members of this religion to see themselves as different and unique—as individuals first and foremost. However, my perceiving a similarity in practices that participants see as unique may also be informed by my being outsider. I see the underlying similarity of the individual's practices with larger spiritual paths, but as insiders the practitioners may view as important what I see as small differences. For example, a practitioner may feel that a poem written or chosen by them and used in the invocation of the divine is an important innovation in their practice. Researchers may instead focus on the fact that practitioners are creating a circle in the same manner as Wiccans, or invoking deities at the same stage in the ritual, even if the particular deity is different from that which is called in another circle or by another contemporary Pagan.

TABLE 2.16. *Popularity of Spiritual Paths in the United Kingdom and Canada (in percentages)*

	U.K. GROUP	U.K. SOLO	CANADA GROUP	CANADA SOLO
Agnostic	10.6	9.0	5.4	7.8
Atheist	3.0	3.3	1.8	2.6
Buddhist	6.1	3.8	3.6	7.8
Ceremonial magician	22.7	3.3	5.4	4.8
Christian	6.1	2.4	0.9	5.6
Druid	21.2	17.9 (5)	7.2	9.7
Eclectic Pagan	21.2	43.4 (1)	39.6 (2)	49.1 (1)
Goddess Worshipper	30.3 (3)	16.0	30.6 (4)	25.7 (4)
Heathen	13.6	4.7	4.5	11.2
Hellenic Pagan	7.6	3.3	4.5	5.2
Jewish	0.0	0.0	0.0	0.7
Magic worker	27.3 (4)	12.3	22.5	16.0
New Age	1.5	6.6	3.6	10.4
Odinist	4.5	1.4	0.9	2.6

TABLE 2.16. (*continued*)

	U.K. GROUP	U.K. SOLO	CANADA GROUP	CANADA SOLO
Satanist	1.5	0.9	0.0	1.1
Santaria	3.0	0.0	0.0	1.5
Shaman	15.2	10.4	11.7	14.1
Spiritual but dislike labels	9.1	22.6 (4)	15.3	21.6 (5)
Thelemite	13.6	2.4	1.8	1.9
Unitarian Universalist (UU)	6.1	3.8	6.3	4.1
Vodun	6.1	0.0	1.8	1.5
Wiccan	45.5 (1)	24.1 (3)	58.6 (1)	28.6 (3)
Witch	33.3 (2)	32.1 (2)	39.6 (2)	34.6 (2)

Becoming a Pagan

As previously noted most contemporary Pagans come to the religion as adults. Only 10.1 percent of my sample were raised as contemporary Pagans. The low percentage of those who were raised in the religion is the result of a combination of two factors: the relatively large influx into the religion at the beginning of the twenty-first century of primarily teenagers and young adults, and the reticence of contemporary Pagan parents to impose their religion on their offspring (H. Berger 1999; Kermani 2013).

Those not raised in the religion have found it through a variety of means, including books, the Internet, social networks, or flyers, which were most commonly either for a college group meeting or a gathering at a metaphysical bookstore. The majority (53.1 percent) of solitaries note that they have come to solitary practice through books and to a lesser degree websites. Group practitioners are more likely to have found contemporary Paganism through their social contacts, whether that is a friend, partner, coworker, or relative. Just under half (49.6 percent) of group practitioners claim that they have found contemporary Paganism through their social networks. Social networks are the second most common way for solitary practitioners to find the religion; 42.6 percent note that they came to contemporary Paganism through their personal networks. Books and Internet sources are the second most common way for group practitioners to find contemporary Paganism; 44.0 percent state they found the religion either through books or websites. As with solitaries, group practitioners found books to be more important than the Internet as an avenue for discovering the religion. About a fifth of my sample claim that they found the religion in some way other than those listed. However most then list a particular relative, book, or website that introduced them to contemporary Paganism.

TABLE 2.17. *Routes to Contemporary Paganism (in percentages)*

	SOLO	GROUP	WOMEN	MEN	YOUNG
Friend	28.3	34.4	29.3	31.9	35.8
Coworker	2.0	2.4	2.1	2.4	1.6
Partner	4.0	6.3	4.1	6.6	6.7
Relative	8.3	6.5	9.0	5.7	10.4
Website	16.6	14.1	15.3	14.8	22.8
Book	36.5	29.9	34.9	32.7	28.0
TV/movie	2.4	2.2	2.2	2.4	1.0
Flyer/poster	1.1	3.0	1.7	1.7	2.1
Student group	2.2	3.5	2.4	2.6	3.6
In prison	0.3	0.2	0.2	0.6	0.5
Other	20.5	21.7	21.8	19.7	15.0

Over a third of the young state they have come to contemporary Paganism through friendship networks, although the majority are solitaries. The young are less likely to be married and therefore more likely to rely on friendship networks. Furthermore as the religion has moved out of the broom closet, it would be more likely that individuals would learn about the religion from others.

As can be seen in table 2.18 the degree of openness varies very slightly with age and gender, but on the whole the majority of contemporary Pagans—almost three quarters of them—are at least somewhat open, with most people completely open with almost everyone; and about a quarter are completely open to everyone about their religious affiliation. Men are slightly more likely than women to be completely open about their religious affiliation. Group practitioners are less likely than those who practice alone to be in the broom closet, and more likely to be completely open about their religious affiliation than solitaries. Being in a group might provide a sense of normalization of their religion and give individuals more confidence to openly embracing their religious identity. Perhaps not surprisingly those raised as contemporary Pagans are the most open about their religious affiliation, with slightly over a third being completely open.

The path to conversion is often more convoluted than direct and may involve multiple contacts. A person might know someone who is a contemporary Pagan and have their interest piqued and then read some books about the religion and search the Internet prior to self-defining as a contemporary Pagan. Nonetheless those in groups are more likely to see social networks as primary in their finding their religion.

TABLE 2.18. *Degree of Openness about Religion (in percentages)*

	U.S. (ALL)	WOMEN	MEN	YOUNG	BOOMER	RAISED PAGAN	SOLITARY	GROUP
Completely open, I tell everyone	24.5	22.6	29.4	23.1	24.6	34.4	21.1	27.1
Somewhat open, I tell most people but not everyone	45.9	47.3	42.6	47.1	45.2	42.7	44.1	41.9
Open with those I believe will be sympathetic	27.4	27.9	26.2	29.1	26.7	18.2	27.8	23.8
In the broom closet; I have told no one or no one other than other Pagans	5.3	5.5	4.8	5.6	5.2	3.8	6.4	2.6

Although most contemporary Pagans are somewhat open about their religion, the majority is not completely open, and this is even true of those who were raised as contemporary Pagans. Being a member of a minority religion, particularly one that is often denigrated, has resulted in some caution in who most contemporary Pagans share the knowledge of their religious affiliation with. Nonetheless since the majority is open at least to most people, it has become more likely that the religion will be transmitted through interpersonal networks than in the past.

Those who stated that they came from a contemporary Pagan family are as likely to be solitaries as are those who are converts. Contemporary Paganism may be a family religion in that individuals were raised around it, were taken to festivals, and possibly were taught the rudiments of rituals, but it does not result in their joining their parents' spiritual group or any other group. In my first book, *A Community of Witches* (1999), I had predicted that as the religion aged and a second and third generation came of age there would be greater routinization. This may be true in the greater interconnection among contemporary Pagans and in the growing importance of certain authors and websites, but not in the second generation maintaining long-standing groups. This is at least in part because the first generation of American Pagans wanted to free their children from what many of them felt was the forced participation in religion that they had experienced as children in primarily Christian homes. Many remember hating attending church or feeling alienated from it. They wanted their children to be free to find their own spiritual path. This has resulted in the next generation often feeling that they were poorly trained in the religion (Fennell and Wildman-Hanlon 2017). It is also in part that the religion itself emphasizes direct connection with the divine and individual inspiration. My data suggests that girls are more likely than boys to follow in their parents' religion. As previously noted in this chapter the gender distribution of contemporary Pagans who are born into the religion is the same as converts.

Spiritual Paths

In the United States the route to each spiritual path is very similar. Books are the most common way in which all contemporary Pagans, regardless of their spiritual path, claim they come to contemporary Paganism, followed by friends and then websites, as can be seen in table 2.19. There are some small differences. Witches are the least likely to come to the religion through a friend, partner, or spouse. Websites are the least important for Wiccans. But these differences are very small. What is more interesting is the similarity among all the different forms of contemporary Paganism, even those that are a minority within this minority religion—Druids and Heathens. My survey question asked how they came to contemporary Paganism, and it is possible that they joined the religion as an eclectic, Wiccan, or Witch and then joined one of the less popular forms of contemporary Paganism later. The growth of solitary practice within each of these spiritual paths makes it easier to become a member via books or the Internet and without necessarily having personal contact with other members of that spiritual path.

TABLE 2.19. *Spiritual Path and Route to Contemporary Paganism (in percentages)*

	DRUID	WICCA	WITCH	HEATHEN	ECLECTIC	GODDESS WORSHIPPERS
Friend	27.2	30.9	29.9	26.5	30.0	29.2
Coworker	1.7	2.7	1.9	2.2	2.2	1.8
Partner/spouse	5.8	5.2	3.6	4.6	4.9	4.6
Relative	10.6	8.0	9.1	6.8	8.0	8.9
Website	17.6	14.0	15.0	19.0	15.2	14.5
Book	32.0	34.2	36.2	36.1	34.4	35.6
TV or movie	2.4	2.6	2.7	2.4	2.2	2.5
Flyer; poster	1.0	2.1	1.9	2.2	1.7	2.6
Student group	2.9	2.3	2.4	3.6	2.5	2.8

TABLE 2.19. (*continued*)

	DRUID	WICCA	WITCH	HEATHEN	ECLECTIC	GODDESS WORSHIPPERS
In prison	0.2	0.3	0.3	0.4	0.3	0.4
Other	25.5	20.9	23.3	24.6	21.2	24.1

As would be anticipated solitary practitioners are more likely to be self-initiated or not be initiated at all in their spiritual path than those who are members of a group. As there is no one organization that ultimately controls any of these spiritual paths, or has the right to declare who is and who is not a member of the religion, there is a good deal of variation even within those who self-define as members of a particular form or spiritual path of contemporary Paganism. Wicca has traditionally been an initiatory religion, in which each of the three degrees is marked by a ritual. Although this process was at one point a secret, it has been described in several books and has been modified for solitary practice by, among others, Scott Cunningham (1988, 1994) and Silver RavenWolf (1993), and little if any of it is any longer unknown. As can be seen in table 2.20 although group practitioners regardless of spiritual path are more likely to be initiated by an elder or someone else in their tradition, Wiccans in group practice are more likely to do this than any other spiritual path. Given how important initiation is in this tradition, it is more surprising that either self-initiation or initiation by someone else is not universal.

Heathens, particularly those who practice alone, are the most likely to claim that their tradition does not require that they be initiated. Heathens have the lowest rate of initiation of any of the spiritual paths that are being explored with less than half being either group or self-initiated. Some listed in the category of *other* that they were not initiated but had been dedicated, taken an oath, or were called by the gods. However in the comments section members of other spiritual paths also made similar claims, particularly about being called by the gods or goddess(es). Ceremonies of initiation for Heathens are available at many Internet sites, but books on the religion tend not to emphasize them.

About a fifth of Druids, whether they are group or solitary practitioners, similarly claim that their tradition does not have an initiation. Two of the largest Druid organizations, the Order of Bards, Ovates and Druids, which is based in the United Kingdom, and Ár nDraíocht Féin, provide written materials, with examinations for those who want to join the religion. This is in some ways more of an academic model than one of initiation. As in Druidism, Heathenism is based on learning the texts of poetry, ballads, and myths. The focus on study and learning among Druids may be more important than dedication or initiation. Nonetheless the majority has had some form of initiation.

Among group practitioners Goddess worshippers stand out in having the highest percentage that is self-initiated. Most Goddess worshipers have a strong feminist belief in egalitarianism and the lack of hierarchy. Although being initiated by another does not depend on a hierarchy as individuals can initiate one another, doing one's own suggests that one is completely in control and that one does not require another person to provide the legitimacy of one's qualification in a spiritual path.

TABLE 2.20. *Solo versus Group Initiation by Spiritual Paths (in percentages)*

	SELF-INITIATED	INITIATED BY ELDER, ETC	NO INITIATION IN MY TRADITION	TRADITION HAS INITIATION BUT NOT INITIATED	OTHER
Druid solo	46.0	16.7	20.3	5.4	11.6
Druid group	15.3	48.9	20.4	2.6	12.8
Wicca solo	57.9	19.6	7.9	4.3	9.9
Wicca group	13.5	70.2	2.5	3.4	10.4
Witch solo	45.3	18.0	20.0	4.1	12.5
Witch group	17.9	55.7	7.2	6.0	13.2
Eclectic solo	48.3	15.6	20.3	3.7	12.0
Eclectic group	21.9	48.6	10.3	4.5	14.7
Goddess worshipper solo	51.5	18.9	14.8	3.9	10.7
Goddess Worshippers group	41.4	30.6	12.6	4.4	10.9
Heathen solo	38.6	9.8	35.8	3.9	11.9
Heathen group	18.7	32.0	28.0	7.3	14.0

Those who choose the category "other" most commonly noted in the comment column that they had been initiated into one spiritual path, such as Wicca, and then subsequently went on to self-identify with another spiritual path, such as Druids. They therefore had been initiated into a contemporary Pagan path, but not necessarily their current one. It should also be kept in mind that contemporary Pagans often consider themselves part of more than one spiritual path, which they combine. We permitted individuals to state all that they considered their primary spiritual paths or forms of Paganism as a reflection of this. Nonetheless even with this caveat, it is clear that participation in initiation varies by spiritual path, suggesting a difference in how individuals join their particular form of the religion. The clear difference between solitary and group practitioners, while not surprising, does highlight one area in which solitaries have fewer interpersonal interactions than do group practitioners. Solitaries are more likely to have learned about the religion from mediated sources and more likely to self-initiate or not be initiated than those in groups.

United Kingdom and Canada

In Canada and the United Kingdom solitary practitioners, like those in the United States, are more likely than group practitioners to learn about the religion from mediated sources—books, the Internet, and movies—and in all three nations books are the most important source of recruitment. Mediated sources are more important in both the United Kingdom and Canada, where respectively 70.8 percent and 64.7 percent of the solitaries claim they were drawn to the religion by them. In the United Kingdom, slightly more group practitioners come to the religion through mediated sources than through their social networks, but it is still just 50 percent unless we include flyers and posters. Furthermore British solitary practitioners cite mediated sources at a higher rate than group practitioners. In Canada the majority of group practitioners have found the religion through their social networks. Friends are the most important means for Canadian group practitioners to find the religion, followed by books. And for Canadian solitaries this is reversed. In the United Kingdom books are the single most important means for recruitment for both solitaries and group practitioners, followed by websites for solitaires and friends for group practitioners.

There are some international differences, but what stands out most is the importance of books and friends for individuals finding the religion both in the United States and in other countries. Differences in how they found the religion exist between solitary and group practitioners, suggesting some differences in the extent of sociability that individuals had prior to joining the religion. But these are small, not large, differences. Of course the question is one that requires individuals to recall how they learned about the religion; people's memories are often imperfect and influenced by their self-image. It is possible that solitaries put slightly less emphasis on the role of social networks than those who work in groups. Although contemporary Pagans are noted readers and purchasers of book, which suggests that books do play a major role in their religious practice and are likely to have played a role in their joining the religion, it might have been overemphasized in people's memories. Nonetheless it does indicate, both in the United States and internationally, that there are differences in how solitary and group members present their route to contemporary Paganism. Social networks play a more important role in the narrative of group practitioners than it does in those of solitaries.

As in the United States, self-initiation is much more common among solitary than group practitioners in the United Kingdom and Canada. On the one hand, this is not surprising, as those who practice alone are less likely to have a

TABLE 2.21. *Learning about the Religion for Solo and Group Practitioners in the United Kingdom and Canada (in percentages)*

	U.K. SOLO	U.K GROUP	CANADA SOLO	CANADA GROUP
Friend	23.6	27.3	30.9	37.8
Coworker	2.4	-	0.7	1.8
Partner	1.9	6.1	3.7	7.2
Relative	6.6	10.6	7.1	8.1
Website	27.4	10.6	22.3	7.2
Book	40.1	36.4	38.7	36.0
TV/movie	3.3	3.0	3.7	-
Flyer/poster	1.4	7.6	1.9	1.8
Student group	2.4	1.5	2.2	-
In prison	-	-	-	0.9
Other	22.6	28.8	18.6	19.8

TABLE 2.22. *Type of Initiations in the United Kingdom and Canada (in percentages)*

	U.K. SOLO	U.K. GROUP	CANADA SOLO	CANADA GROUP
Self-initiated	46.4	12.1	44.7	15.9
Initiated by elder	12.0	50.0	13.6	57.0
No initiation in tradition	23.0	22.7	26.1	11.2
Tradition has initiation but wasn't initiated	3.3	3.0	4.7	7.5
Other	15.3	12.1	12.4	8.4

spiritual elder or other individual available to initiate them. However, the question asked the respondent's current status, and at least some may have been in a group for a time and then become solitaries. On the other hand, what is more interesting is that only about half of those who are in groups have been initiated by others. About a quarter of those in a group stated that that their tradition has no initiation; that leaves another quarter who, although in a group that has an initiation, were not initiated by an elder or others in the group. In looking at the written responses, it can be seen that some stated that although there is an initiation process in their tradition they personally did not feel it was needed or that they were not yet initiated. Many who choose the option of "other" did not provide an explanation, and it is therefore impossible to know why they were uninitiated in a tradition they claim requires an initiation.

The data from the United Kingdom and Canada is useful as it supports the data from the United States, which indicates that solitaries are less likely than those in groups to come to the religion through social networks, and less likely to be initiated by another person. These differences should not be exaggerated. Friends and books are the two most common ways that people claim they found the religion regardless of whether individuals practice alone or with others. But those who practice alone note that books are a more important route to contemporary Paganism than group practitioners do.

Conclusion

Demographically contemporary Pagans have changed only slightly between my surveys. They remain disproportionately female. In fact there has been an increase in the proportion of women in the religion primarily because of the influx of the young during the media romance with teenage Witches. Contemporary Pagans remain more educated than the typical American, although the difference has decreased somewhat because of the general increase of education in the United States. As in my earlier survey I found that contemporary Pagans are consistently more educated regardless of region of the United States they live in, which makes them stand out more from their neighbors, whose educational level varies by region. Although like most Americans they tend to live in urban areas, they are more likely than other Americans to live in rural areas. In the first survey the most common profession listed was computer scientist; now instead it is a small business person or in one of the helping professions.

Solitary practitioners differ from group practitioners by having a larger proportion of women, being somewhat younger, and being more likely to live in rural areas. Solitaries are less likely to have found the religion through friendship networks and more likely to cite books as their entry point into the religion than are group practitioners. They tend to be slightly less educated than group practitioners and less likely to be married and somewhat less likely to be in a committed relationship. Some of this difference but not all of it is due to their being younger. Solitaries are most likely to be eclectic while group practitioners are most likely to be Wiccan, the spiritual path that had been the most popular at the time of the last survey. The differences are not large but are there and on the whole are consistent internationally.

There are some national differences among American, Canadian, and British contemporary Pagans, particularly differences in gender distribution with the British having more males in the religion than the United States, and Canada more females than the United States. In all three countries the majority of contemporary Pagans are solitary practitioners, and the most common spiritual path for solitaries is eclectic Paganism. Solitaries in all three countries tend to be younger and somewhat less educated than those who work in a group.

Solitary practitioners are not a breed apart from other contemporary Pagans; they share many similarities. Each person in the survey was asked about their current form of practice, and at least some of the solitary practitioners were members of groups in the past and some undoubtedly will be members in the future. Nonetheless real differences exist between those who are solitary and those in groups. These differences are sometimes subtle and sometimes less so.

CHAPTER 3

Circling Alone

Isolation or Community

In *Bowling Alone* Robert Putnam (2001) argues that Americans are becoming increasingly isolated as they are less likely to join voluntary associations such as bowling leagues or social groups. In his subsequent book, *American Grace,* written with David Campbell (Putnam and Campbell 2010) they contend that religious organizations are among the few exceptions to this phenomenon. Although they indicate there is growing bifurcation between the pious and the nonreligious in the United States, they claim that few Americans pray alone. But this claim is contradicted by increased research on lived or personal religion—religion as it is actually practiced by ordinary Americans—which suggests that a growing number of Americans consider themselves spiritual, may read the bible and pray, but may never or only occasionally attend church, synagogue, or other religious institutions (Ammerman 2013; McGuire 2008). Their spiritual and religious identities are maintained outside of the church. Contemporary Pagans are in many ways the quintessential example of those who are practicing a religion outside of institutional structures. As I discussed in the first chapter, contemporary Pagans are much more loosely organized than traditional religions. They infrequently have churches or other buildings dedicated to their religion. Groups meet in more informal forums, such as in people's homes, the backroom of an occult store, or at liberal churches that make their premises available, as Unitarian Universalists churches sometimes do. Contemporary Paganism, therefore, serves as a good case study in social integration and isolation among the unchurched or unaffiliated. The focus on solitary practitioners furthermore provides a lens with which to see those who are the most spiritually isolated.

An initial look at data from "The Pagan Census" and "The Pagan Census Revisited" would suggest that contemporary Pagans fit the image of a population that is growing more and more isolated, as an increasing proportion of contemporary Pagans are self-defining as solitary practitioners. Writing at the beginning of the twentieth century Ernst Troeltsch (1992 [1912]) argued that mysticism with its reliance on individual religious experiences—which he believed were unique to each person and impossible to share with others—was dangerous to collective institutions, including religious collectives such as churches. Although mysticism has gained greater societal acceptance since Troeltsch wrote, it is still viewed as suspect as it is seen as complicit in the creation of radical individualism or to use the term developed by Bellah and his coauthors (1985) "Sheilaism"—a spiritual form that is unique to each person and therefore contradictory to the development of a community as no two people share the same spiritual or religious beliefs and practice and thus lack a shared worldview.

Not all scholars, however, view metaphysical religions as a threat to society, organized religion, or social integration. Bender (2010) is a recent and forceful critic of the notion that metaphysics are either the product or the producer of radical individualism. Based on her fieldwork in Cambridge, Massachusetts, of New Metaphysicals, which include contemporary Pagans, Bender argues that their spirituality is embedded in social institutions. Some of these institutions are religious, and others are secular, associated with the arts and alternative medicine. Mainstream religious organizations have integrated some of these by using meditation as part of their services and by allowing their churches to be used by metaphysical groups for spiritual purposes. One example of this is the churches that permit contemporary Pagan groups to use their space, although not their sanctuaries, for open sabbat rituals. Contemporary Pagans and other metaphysical practitioners are often invited to participate in interfaith retreats or dialogues with the more liberal churches.

To the contrary of being isolated, Bender (2010) contends that the New Metaphysicals are integrated into a social network through their participation in workshops, classes, and other activities that bring them into contact with each other. Many of these include alternative medical practices such as Reiki or artists' groups. Additionally not mentioned by Bender are cultural groups such as science fiction readers who come together at conventions such as the Readercon that occurs yearly in Burlington, Massachusetts, and the Society for Creative Anachronism, which often draw a large number of contemporary Pagans to them. Any of these groups can serve as a conduit for individuals meeting one another, interacting, and reinforcing their worldview that there are alternative realities in which different interactions among and between people, animals, and the rest of the natural world exist, or at least may exist. All these venues have the potential to be places in which community, in some of its forms, is built as people see others they know from similar venues, feel part of a group and lifestyle, and continue to make contacts, some of which can be sustained on the Internet.

Bender reminds us that there are a variety of ways in which community can be created in late modernity, some of which occur in temporary or shifting settings, such as classes, lectures, and open rituals in which individuals recurrently meet one another. As will be seen in this chapter, solitary contemporary Pagans are rarely completely isolated from others in their religion. The image of solitary practitioners as participating in a spirituality that is completely mediated through the mass market or is a product of each individual's own spiritual experiences is clearly not correct.

Bender is dismissive of surveys and interviews, which she claims miss the interconnections among practitioners that become evident in a community study; but community studies by their very nature do not include those who are isolated. The current research permits us to explore a wide variety of individuals, including those whose interactions with others in their religion may be limited to the Internet. My data, therefore, provides a more nuanced view of solitary practitioners than either that presented by Bender, whose methods explore only those involved in the metaphysical community, or that of Bellah and his coauthors (1985), who focus exclusively on the individualistic ethic of metaphysical practitioners.

As will be demonstrated in this chapter there is a small group of contemporary Pagans who are experiencing social isolation, but the majority are participating in a new form of social integration. Among contemporary Pagans this social integration is occurring through those venues mentioned by Bender but is also the product of the Internet. Although isolation is rare, solitaries are, nonetheless, more isolated then those who practice in a group. This isolation is seen in many aspects of their lives, including in the frequency with which they join others spiritually and socially. Although my findings support Bender's that the New Metaphysicals are not on the whole isolated, they do indicate that those who practice alone have fewer social interactions than those who work in a group.

In his review of *Age of Fracture* (Rogers 2011), Richard Sennett (2011:166) notes "on the one hand, life on screen has produced . . . social isolation of a profound sort: on the other hand, the communications revolution has enabled people to bond, and to act, in equally new ways." This new form of communication and bonding is evident in many forms of religious life. In many ways contemporary Paganism is at the forefront of this movement, as it developed during the period of transition where several strands of cultural and technological change intersected. During this period not only were new forms of communication developing, spreading, and becoming more affordable, but there were also the cultural changes of the 1960s and 1970s including the second wave of feminism, the growth of environmentalism, the sexual revolution, renewed interest in metaphysical practices and beliefs, and the questioning of all forms of authority. Even the concept of community was changing and becoming more fluid and began to include those interactions and attachments that were maintained primarily on the Internet.

Although churches abound within Christianity, there is a growing online presence and an increase in the number of individuals who, although unchurched, still consider themselves religious or spiritual, some of whom maintain their spiritual life online or through informal networks. Christian music concerts, some of which are hard rock and hence geared toward the young, have become one venue for unchurched Christians to create a shifting and fluid community similar to that seen in metaphysical religions (McDowell 2018, Martí 2017). A closer look at contemporary Paganism, therefore, will have implications for lived religion or those who are unchurched in general as well as for the growing number of Americans and others in the developed world that are becoming involved in metaphysical practices.

This chapter will focus on the statistical data from the United States comparing solitary to group practitioners. As throughout this book, other English-speaking nations, where the data is not as strong as that for the United States, will be used primarily for comparative purposes. Gender will be considered as will age of the respondents. Data will be provided on frequency of face-to-face and other interactions, including on the Internet and phone for both social and spiritual reasons. When possible data will be compared between "The Pagan Census" and "The Pagan Census Revisited." Participation in alternative medical and health practices will be discussed as they have been described as contributing to community life among the New Metaphysicals (Bender 2010; Heelas et al. 2005). To provide comparative data, some survey questions in "The Pagan Census Revisited" were taken from the Kendal project in England. Data collected on these questions will be compared with the Kendal project findings and with my data from U.K. contemporary Pagans to ensure that the differences that are found are not a matter of national specificity.

Training and Relationships

Although the vast majority of contemporary Pagans claim to be solitary practitioners, most of them have been trained in a group and have integrated the religion into their family practice. On the whole these are not isolates. Nearly three-quarters (74.2 percent) of contemporary Pagans have practiced in a group at some point in their lives. Among those who claim to practice alone, 63.0 percent have at one point worked in a group. The young are even more likely than their elders to claim that they have practiced in a group, with 91.9 percent stating that they have at some point worked with others. This is a somewhat surprising finding, as the young are more likely to be solitaries than their elders. This may be the result of the young using a looser definition of working in a group, defining it as even a onetime ritual, while their elders may have defined the question as participating in an ongoing group for a period of time. Nonetheless what is clear is that solitary practitioners are not completely spiritually isolated.

The majority (56.0 percent) of contemporary Pagans who are in a relationship share or partly share their spiritual orientation with their romantic partner. There is a very slightly lower rate (52.6 percent) of the young who share their spiritual path with their romantic partner. However, the difference between all contemporary Pagans and the young is small and may be due to stage-of-life issues, as fewer of the young state that they have a romantic partner or spouse and those that do may be less likely to be in a long-term relationship than their elders. As table 3.1 illustrates, both age and whether or not the person practices alone influences the percentage of those who share their spiritual path with their romantic partner.

TABLE 3.1. *Percentage of Those Who Share Their Spiritual Path with Their Partners*

	SHARE COMPLETELY	SHARE PARTLY
Boomer solo	22.7	28.2
Boomer group	48.3	22.3
Young solo	17.4	32.5
Young group	27.4	31.3

Baby boomers who practice with others are the most likely, and the young who practice alone the least likely, to share their spiritual path completely with their romantic partners. The young are more likely to state that they share their spiritual path partly with their partner than to say that they share completely, indicating that their partner is also a contemporary Pagan but not in the same spiritual path. This is a reflection of more of the young being eclectics and putting a higher value on individual practice as well as that more of the elderly have had a long-term relationship with their partners and hence more time to influence each other. However, combining those who claim to completely share their spiritual path with their partner with those who do so only partially the difference by age virtually disappears for solitary practitioners; 50.9 percent of baby boomers and 49.9 percent of the young share their spirituality with their partners to some degree. The difference is more pronounced for group practitioners, among whom 70.6 percent of baby boomers and 58.7 percent of the young share their spirituality to some degree with their partners. In both cases, however, what is clear is that those in groups are more likely than solitary practitioners to share their spirituality with their partners.

The percentage of contemporary Pagans sharing their spiritual path with their romantic partner has increased between surveys. In "The Pagan Census" only about a third (36 percent) of those in a relationship shared their spiritual orientation with their romantic partner. There is also a modest increase between surveys among those who have a child or children and who claim they are raising their children as contemporary Pagans; from 70 percent to 77 percent. Although those who practice alone are less likely to raise their children in their spiritual path than those who practice in a group (74.8 percent versus 81.8 percent), even this cohort has a modest increase over the previous survey of those who raise their children in the religion, suggesting a growing integration of the religion into individuals' lives, albeit slightly less so for solitary practitioners.

As the religion has aged, its participants are more likely to make it a family practice. This is not an issue of age of the participants but of changes in the religion itself as in both the original and second surveys only those with children were asked about whether they were raising their children in the religion and only those in a romantic relationship were asked about their partner's spirituality. This is an important change as traditionally religions have depended on individuals being born into them to maintain their membership. Within contemporary Paganism this is particularly important because, as I showed in *A Community of Witches* (1999) and S. Zohreh Kermani similarly found in her book *Pagan Family Values* (2013), contemporary Pagans have been leery of imposing their spiritual beliefs on their children, believing that each person should choose her or his own spiritual path. Bruce (1996, 2003) has contended that this attitude, coupled with their lack of interest in proselytizing, would ultimately result in religions like contemporary Paganism having little impact socially or politically. However, it appears from my data that contemporary Pagans have become less concerned about imposing their religious tradition on their offspring and therefore more open to training their children in their spirituality. Nonetheless only a small percentage of my sample claims to have been raised in contemporary Pagan families. Whether this will change in fifteen or twenty years when this crop of children are adults is still to be seen, particularly since the growth in those claiming to raise their children in the religion is occurring at the same time that there has been a growth of solitary practitioners, who are somewhat less likely to raise their children in their religion than group practitioners.

Gathering Together

Most contemporary Pagans gather with others socially as well as for religious or spiritual events. As the data in table 3.2 indicates, more than two-thirds (67.5 percent) of contemporary Pagans meet with other contemporary Pagans during the year for spiritual purposes, and over half (53.4 percent) meet other contemporary Pagans for spiritual work at least once a month. Again this is somewhat lower for the youngest contemporary Pagans in my sample, among whom 45.8 percent meet for spiritual purposes at least once a month. Not surprisingly this is lower for those who claim to be solitaries; the majority of solitaries either never or only once a year meet others for spiritual reasons. However, more interestingly, over a third of those who claim that they are completely solitary nonetheless meet others for spiritual purposes at least once a month.

TABLE 3.2. *Frequency of Meeting with Other Pagans for Religious/Spiritual/Ritual Purposes (in percentages)*

	ALL PAGANS	ALL YOUNG	SOLO	GROUP
Daily or almost daily	3.7	2.4	2.5	5.7
Weekly	15.9	14.4	7.8	32.9
Monthly	33.8	29.0	25.5	49.8
Yearly	14.2	13.4	18.6	4.7
Never or nearly never	32.5	40.8	45.5	6.8

The relative spiritual isolation of solitaries extends to attendance at festivals and moots or local meetings. As seen in table 3.3 those who are solitary are much less likely to attend a festival than those who practice in a group. The young are slightly less likely than their elders to attend festivals, but it is the form of practice that is the most important factor. Among all contemporary Pagans in my sample, over two-thirds attended a festival, and just about two-thirds had attended a moot. Among the young it is just under two-thirds who state they have attended a festival or moot. This is much lower among solitaries and particularly low for those who are young and solitary. It does not appear that the cost of attending festivals—fees charged for attendance, food, and travel—is keeping the young solitary practitioners from these events as those who work in groups are attending at just a slightly lower rate than their elders. It appears that a combination of age and form of practice is resulting in their not attending. This may be an indication of their greater isolation—they may not know that festivals are occurring—and it may also be a factor in their becoming more isolated. It is also possible that those who work in a group are subsidized to attend, possibly being able to get a ride to the event without paying for gas or have coven mates cover or contribute to some other expenses.

TABLE 3.3. *Percentage Who Have Attended at Least One Festival or Open Circle in the Last Year for Solo, Group, and Young Practitioners*

	GROUP	SOLO	YOUNG GROUP	YOUNG SOLO
Festival	70	49	64	25
Moot	66	45	60	36

The young who are solitaries are the least likely to meet others for spiritual purposes. Although meeting for explicitly spiritual purposes is an important indicator of isolation or integration, it is not the only one. Religious organizations often provide venues for their members to meet for reasons not specifically religious, such as breakfasts, travel, or other social events. These events help to bolster individuals' commitments to the group by providing them with friends who are also members, and even if the conversation is not specifically spiritual or religious, it helps to affirm their worldview. These interactions may be of even greater importance for minority religions or worldviews, helping to confirm and legitimate them. As my own ethnographic work (1999) and that of others (see for example Pike 2001; Kermani 2013) has shown, even when contemporary Pagans meet in nonspiritual or religious settings there are frequently discussions of magic and a sense of the world being enchanted. There becomes a taken-for-granted notion that magic is real. People are believed to magically change their lives and to have direct relationships with the divine, who at times provides guidance and information about the future or guides the person in daily activities.

TABLE 3.4. *Frequency of Meeting Other Contemporary Pagans for Social, Nonspiritual Reasons for Solo, Group, and Young Practitioners (in percentages)*

	ALL PAGANS	ALL YOUNG	SOLO	GROUP
Daily or almost daily	14.0	15.9	11.5	18.2
Weekly	24.9	25.0	19.9	34.6
Monthly	28.1	22.9	25.0	34.6
Yearly	9.8	9.0	11.7	6.3
Never or nearly never	23.3	27.2	31.9	6.4

As contemporary Pagans do not, on the whole, have churches, their social interactions are not organized around a religious institution; nonetheless as seen in table 3.4 the majority of contemporary Pagans socialize with other contemporary Pagans at least once a month. However there is a clear difference between those who are solitary and those who are not. Only 12.7 percent of those who are in a group meet less than once a month socially with other contemporary Pagans. This can be compared with 43.6 percent of those who are solitary and who claim that they never or only yearly meet socially with other contemporary Pagans. The young are slightly less likely to meet other contemporary Pagans for social reasons with 67.0 percent of all contemporary Pagans and 63.8 percent young contemporary Pagans having at least a monthly visit with others in their religion. This is offset somewhat by the fact that younger contemporary Pagans are slightly more likely to get together daily or weekly with contemporary Pagan friends (40.9 percent) than contemporary Pagans in general (38.9 percent). Age is not a major factor in the level of social interaction among contemporary Pagans, but whether or not they practice alone is.

Contemporary Paganism is a minority religion, and it is therefore not surprising that a sizable proportion of contemporary Pagans are not socializing with others in their religion weekly or even monthly as they may not live in an area in which there are many contemporary Pagans, or they may not be aware that other contemporary Pagans live near them as they or their neighbors may not be open about their Paganism. Although as noted in chapter 2 only a small percentage (2.6 percent of group members and 6.4 percent of solitaries) are completely secretive, only about a quarter are completely open about their religious affiliation.

Not surprisingly those who self-describe as living in rural or very rural areas are somewhat less likely to meet with others for either spiritual or nonspiritual reasons with 37.9 percent never meeting others for spiritual reasons and 27.3 percent never meeting with other contemporary Pagans for nonspiritual reasons. As one respondent who claimed that he never attended a public ritual or moot states, "This is Alaska. There ain't much." As contemporary Pagans whether or not they live in rural areas are less likely to meet one another for spiritual than social reasons, it is clear that the issue is not only the availability of other contemporary Pagans but their notion of how they choose to practice their spirituality. Another respondent who also stated that she never attended an open circle simply stated, "I practice alone." Nonetheless availability is one factor in individuals' choices. The major factor, however, is whether or not the person practices in a group; 52.8 percent of those who practice in a group meet at least weekly for social events.

The fact that contemporary Pagans interact more often for social than for spiritual reasons may indicate a strong desire to avoid participating in spiritual activities with others, or it may be that people have difficulty finding others from their particular spiritual path. This will be further discussed when exploring the numbers for different spiritual paths. But this lack of interaction by a healthy minority is even starker when we look at table 3.5, which provides data on the frequency with which contemporary Pagans communicate with one another. In all categories the young communicate with others in their religion less than their elders do. The difference between all contemporary Pagans and the young is smallest for the use of blogs and other public Internet sites. In fact the young are more likely than other contemporary Pagans to have used these sites at least once, which is consistent with generational differences in computer use in general. Nonetheless the young appear to be less connected to other contemporary

Pagans than their seniors. This difference should not be exaggerated as we can see that the majority of contemporary Pagans, including the majority of young contemporary Pagans, are in contact on the Internet (both private and public) at least weekly with their coreligious.

Solitary practitioners are less likely to have social contact with other contemporary Pagans. Comparing all four forms of contact—in person, on the telephone, and public or private Internet—it is clear that solitary practitioners are less connected, although this should not be exaggerated as on the whole all contemporary Pagans remain in contact with others in their religion. About three-quarters of those who work in a group state that they have face-to-face interactions with other contemporary Pagans at least weekly, with just under a third stating they do so daily. Among those who work alone approximately 40 percent have at least weekly and 15 percent daily interactions with other contemporary Pagans. Nonetheless the majority of solitary practitioners meet in person with other contemporary Pagans at least once a month.

More than 70 percent of group practitioners speak on the phone to another contemporary Pagan at least once a week, as compared to solitary practitioners, among whom 36.8 percent speak to others at least weekly. The majority of both group and solitary practitioners use the Internet at least weekly to be in touch with others in their religion. However, group practitioners far exceed solitary practitioners in the use of both the public and private Internet, with 83 percent of group practitioners using the public Internet (for example blogs and message board) at least weekly and 89.1 percent using private Internet (for example, e-mails or messaging) at least weekly. This can be compared with solitary practitioners, among whom 71.2 percent use the former and 64.4 percent the latter at least weekly.

Although the differences in rates of contact between solitary and group practitioners are noteworthy, particularly for face-to-face interchanges and on the telephone, very few U.S. contemporary Pagans are completely isolated; only 145 people or 2.3 percent of my sample claim that they never interacted in person, on the phone, or over the Internet with other contemporary Pagans for social or spiritual reasons. Within that group seven claimed to have attended at least one festival of a day or more within the previous year and three to have attended at least one open circle during the past year, decreasing further those who are really completely isolated. Those who claimed no contact with other contemporary Pagans were no more likely to be either men or women or to be young, but they were more likely to live in small towns or rural areas and of course were all solitary practitioners. These individuals' isolation may in part be the result of there being fewer contemporary Pagans in their area, but it does not account for their being less likely to use the Internet to connect with others. As most of these individuals noted an Internet site that was important to them, they clearly use the Internet as a resource and read others' entries, but they do not participate in online conversations. However, what is more important, the majority of contemporary Pagans, regardless of form of practice, are interacting with others in their religion at least monthly. Furthermore even those who rarely interact over the Internet or in person are reading contemporary Pagan Internet sites and therefore keeping current with issues and concerns of others in their religion.

TABLE 3.5. *Frequency of Communication with Other Contemporary Pagans for Solo, Group, and Young Practitioners (in percentages)*

		DAILY	WEEKLY	MONTHLY	YEARLY	NEVER
In person	All Pagans	20.6	30.5	23.8	10.9	14.3
	Young	30.8	43.4	18.7	3.3	3.8
	Solo	15.1	25.2	24.5	14.7	20.4
	Group	30.4	44.5	22.6	1.8	0.7
By telephone	All Pagans	19.2	29.2	19.4	6.8	25.3
	Young	27.2	36.4	19.0	4.3	13.0
	Solo	12.8	24.0	19.7	8.3	34.6
	Group	31.3	38.8	18.7	3.9	7.3
Public Internet—blog, message boards, etc.						
	All Pagans	52.2	22.6	11.6	3.3	10.3
	Young	54.6	29.2	8.6	1.1	6.5
	Solo	47.5	23.7	13.2	3.7	11.5
	Group	62.6	20.4	7.6	2.0	7.4
Private Internet—e-mails, private messages, etc						
	All Pagans	47.3	25.8	13.0	3.8	10.1
	Young	49.7	30.1	10.4	2.2	7.7
	Solo	38.4	26.2	16.1	5.2	14.0
	Group	64.3	24.8	6.9	1.0	2.9

Although solitary practitioners are not isolated, they are less integrated into contemporary Pagan friendship networks than are group practitioners, as can been seen in table 3.6. When asked how many of their friends are contemporary Pagans, 71 percent of solitary practitioners said none or less than half. This can be compared with group practitioners, among whom 34.9 percent similarly said none or less than half of their friends are contemporary Pagans. Almost one-fifth of solitary practitioners have no friends who are contemporary Pagans. Although the majority of all contemporary Pagans have friends who are also members of the religion there is a clear difference between those who practice alone and those who are part of a group. Friendships are one way in which members of any religion or political group maintain their affiliation and worldview.

TABLE 3.6. *Percentage of Friends Who Are Also Contemporary Pagans for Solitary and Group Practitioners*

	SOLO	GROUP
None that I know of	16.3	2.7
Less than half	54.7	32.2
More than half	23.0	46.5
All or almost all	6.1	18.6

Regional and International Comparisons

REGIONS

There are almost no notable regional differences in social or spiritual integration among U.S. contemporary Pagans. Table 3.7 compares the nine regions of the United States on three criteria: solitary practice, training in a group, and having at some time worked in a group. Comparative data is also provided for solitary practitioners between the two surveys. The data from "The Pagan Census Revisited" indicates the largest difference is between the Pacific region, which has the lowest percentage (72.8 percent) of those who claim to be solitary practitioners, and the East North Central, which has the highest percentage of those who claim to be solitary practitioners (80.6 percent). The Pacific region has the second-largest number of contemporary Pagans, and one may be tempted to suggest that this is the reason there are fewer solitary contemporary Pagans, but the region with the most contemporary Pagans, South Atlantic, is midrange with 79.1 percent of contemporary Pagans in that region who are solitary practitioners. The East North Central region also has the smallest percentage (29.8 percent) of individuals who were trained in a group with the Pacific having the highest percentage (45.8 percent). Although it would be tempting to suggest that there is a correlation between training in a group and whether or not the individual subsequently is a solitary practitioner, there is no correlation in the other regions. Of more interest is the fact that there was a greater difference among regions in the first survey, in which the data ranges from the South Atlantic, in which 46.4 percent had solitary practitioners, to East South Central, where 63.0 percent were solitary practitioners. The normalization of solitary practice is seen not only in the increase of numbers but in its being more evenly distributed throughout the country.

TABLE 3.7. *Regional Differences for Solitary and Group Practices (in percentages)*

	SOLITARIES PC	SOLITARIES PCR	TRAINED IN GROUP (PCR)	WORKED AT SOME TIME IN GROUP (PCR)
East North Central	53.6	80.6	29.8	71.6
East South Central	63.0	80.5	33.7	70.7
Middle Atlantic	46.9	80.5	37.1	67.8
Mountain	47.4	77.3	41.1	75.6
New England	57.7	78.5	39.1	79.2
Pacific	50.6	72.8	45.8	81.1
South Atlantic	46.4	79.1	37.2	74.8
West North Central	51.3	78.5	35.2	72.1
West South Central	52.6	79.0	37.3	72.1

On all other indicators that were examined—training children, sharing spiritual path with partners, and the frequency with which they interact spiritually or socially with other contemporary Pagans—there are only minor regional differences. This suggests that region is not of importance in social integration.

INTERNATIONAL

Although on the whole I have avoided looking at data other than from English-speaking nations, in this instance it is informative to place the U.S. data within the larger international context, where it becomes clear that the movement toward increased solitary practice is an international one. Furthermore internationally as in the United States the young are more likely to self-define as solitary practitioners and are less likely to interact socially or spiritually with other contemporary Pagans. It is important to reiterate that the increased isolation of the young may change with time and age, but it nonetheless is significant, particularly when viewed through the lens of the U.S. data, in which I have documented an increase in solitary practice between my two surveys. Of particular interest is the greater similarity in table 3.8 of social interactions among young contemporary Pagans throughout the world to one another rather than to their elders in their own part of the world. The differences between the young and old are not large, but the young have fewer social interactions regardless of geographic region. Putnam (2001) found a larger generational difference among the general American public.

As in the United States, young contemporary Pagans in other nations are more likely to be solitary practitioners and to have never worked or been trained in a group than are their elders in the same nation. The greater similarity among the young internationally suggests a global effect, fostered by the Internet, websites, and the sharing of seminal books. The data suggests that the trend in the United States toward increased isolation of young contemporary Pagans is a worldwide phenomenon.

TABLE 3.8. *Solitary Practice and Group Training or Work: Internationally (in percentages)*

	PERCENTAGE SOLO		GROUP TRAINING		WORKED AT SOME TIME IN GROUP	
	ALL	*YOUNG*	*ALL*	*YOUNG*	*ALL*	*YOUNG*
U.S.	78.2	86.0	37.6	45.9	74.2	91.9
English speaking (not including U.S.)	81.1	87.2	31.7	19.5	64.4	53.6
Canada	74.0	85.2	35.2	20.4	71.4	57.9
Europe	80.8	86.5	30.8	20.8	64.7	61.7
World (not including U.S.)	77.1	87.0	36.0	19.5	71.3	55.6

Turning to the United Kingdom and Canada, the two English-speaking nations that are being compared to the United States, we see a similar pattern of solitary practitioners being much less likely than those in groups to meet with other contemporary Pagans for religious or spiritual purposes. Consistent with the data from the United States, about one-third of those in solitary practice in Canada and the United Kingdom claim to meet with others for spiritual purposes at least once a month. At least within English-speaking nations solitary practice does not always indicate that the individual is unengaged with others spiritually. Nonetheless as can be seen in table 3.9 solitary practitioners do tend to have fewer social interactions with other contemporary Pagans than those who work in groups. Of the three English-speaking countries I am looking at, Canada has the smallest difference between solitary and group practitioners; 29.9 percent claim to be socially engaged with other contemporary Pagans at least once a week, while for those in groups 39.7 percent meet with other contemporary Pagans at least weekly. This can be compared with the United Kingdom, in which 26.4 percent of solitary practitioners and 61.3 percent of group practitioners meet at least weekly with other contemporary Pagans. On the whole North American contemporary Pagans are less socially engaged with other contemporary Pagans than their British counterparts. It is unclear why this might be. The United Kingdom is a small island, and it would be tempting to attribute the difference to the greater population density than in North America. However if we look at Australian contemporary Pagans, a country that also has a large land mass with a small population, we find that they are about as socially engaged as those in the United Kingdom. This suggests that this is at least in part a manifestation of a cultural difference.

TABLE 3.9. *Frequency of Meeting with Other Contemporary Pagans for Social Purposes (in percentages)**

	DAILY OR ALMOST DAILY		WEEKLY		MONTHLY		YEARLY		NEVER OR ALMOST NEVER	
	GROUP	*SOLO*	*GROUP*	*SOLO*	*GROUP*	*SOLO*	*GROUP*	*SOLO*	*GROUP*	*SOLO*
Canada	16.1	14.2	23.6	15.7	26.7	24.3	9.2	11.6	24.3	34.1
U.K.	18.8	10.8	42.5	15.6	30.0	26.9	0	11.8	8.8	34.9

*In Australia 36.6 percent of solitary practitioners and 57.9 percent of group practitioners meet at least weekly with other contemporary Pagans.

As with American contemporary Pagans, solitary practitioners in other English-speaking nations are not completely socially isolated. The majority interact with other contemporary Pagans at least weekly through both public and private Internet communications. Consistent with the data in table 3.9, table 3.10 indicates that Canadians are less socially engaged with other contemporary Pagans than those in other English-speaking nations. Regardless of country and form of communication, solitary practitioners are more isolated than those who practice in groups. Congruous with the data about frequency of U.S. contemporary Pagans socially or spiritually engaging with others in their religion, approximately one-third of solitary practitioners in all English-speaking nations meet other contemporary Pagans in person at least once a week (in Canada 36.6 percent and in the United Kingdom 35.2 percent claim to have face-to-face interactions with other contemporary Pagans at least weekly). This can be compared to 50.4 percent of Canadian and 74.1 percent of British group practitioners who claim to meet others in person at least weekly. A similar pattern can be seen in the frequency with which individuals talk to other contemporary Pagans on the telephone. In Canada 29.1 percent and in the United Kingdom 32.2 percent of solitary practitioners claim to speak to other contemporary Pagans on the telephone at least weekly. Certainly this does not suggest isolation, although it should be noted that among solitary practitioners in the United Kingdom over 40 percent claim to never speak to another contemporary Pagan on the telephone. This can be compared with group practitioners: in Canada 41.5 percent and in the United Kingdom 71.6 percent speak to other contemporary Pagans at least weekly on the telephone.

Although all contemporary Pagans have greater contact with others on the Internet than in person or on the telephone, the pattern of fewer interactions among solitary practitioners persists except for public Internet use in Canada, where the difference is small; 66.6 percent of Canadian solitary practitioners and 69.5 percent of group practitioners are on the public Internet at least weekly. The percentage of solitary practitioners in the United Kingdom who are on the public Internet at least weekly is similar to that in Canada (67.9 percent of British solitary practitioners are on the public Internet weekly). However over 80 percent of group practitioners in the United Kingdom use the public Internet for contact with other contemporary Pagans. Private Internet use among group practitioners is higher than that among solitary practitioners in both countries. Canada has the smallest difference between solitary and group practitioners with 63.2 percent of solitary practitioners and 72.5 percent of group practitioners interacting with other contemporary Pagans on the private Internet. In the United Kingdom 60.2 percent of solitary practitioners and 93.6 percent of group practitioners interact with other contemporary Pagans on the private Internet at least weekly. The data clearly indicates that, as in the United States, contemporary Pagans in other English-speaking nations are integrated into a loose community, but that those in solitary practice are less integrated than group practitioners.

CONTEMPORARY PAGAN SPIRITUAL PATHS

Solitary practitioners are the majority in all spiritual paths of contemporary Paganism. As seen in table 3.11, eclectics are the most likely and Wiccans the least likely to be solitary practitioners; 82.4 percent of the former and 70.7 percent of the latter are solitary practitioners. Traditionally Wiccans were trained by someone who was knowledgeable, most typically someone who had been awarded a third degree. Currently not only are most Wiccans not practicing in a coven, most are not trained in one. In "The Pagan Census" many of the solitary practitioners who were self-trained and self-initiated complained that they felt they were taken less seriously within their religion by others who had a more traditional spiritual lineage (H. Berger et al. 2003). The stigma of being self-taught appears to have diminished among Wiccans as it has become more common.

Eclectics pride themselves on creating their own form of contemporary Paganism—blending together practices, poetry, and rituals from a number of different sources. It is therefore not surprising that they are the most likely to be solitary practitioners. Nonetheless, as seen in table 3.11, even though eclectics are the least likely to do so, almost three-quarters of their members have worked in a group at some point. Over three-quarters of members of all other spiritual paths have worked in a group at some point. Although there is clearly variation

TABLE 3.10. *Contacts with Other Pagans in the United Kingdom and Canada (in percentages)*

		DAILY		WEEKLY		MONTHLY		YEARLY		NEVER	
		GROUP	*SOLO*	*GROUP*	*SOLO*	*GROUP*	*SOLO*	*GROUP*	*SOLO*	*GROUP*	*SOLO*
In person	Can.	19.0	15.2	31.4	21.4	24.9	27.6	8.5	12.5	16.2	23.3
	U.K.	27.3	12.4	46.8	22.8	18.2	26.7	3.9	14.9	3.9	23.3
By tele.	Can.	14.8	11.2	26.7	17.9	21.6	20.3	6.4	8.0	30.5	42.6
	U.K.	23.0	8.2	48.6	24.0	12.2	16.3	4.1	5.6	12.2	45.9
Public Internet	Can.	46.8	40.8	22.7	25.8	15.3	17.3	5.9	7.3	9.4	8.8
	U.K.	65.0	50.7	17.5	17.2	12.5	15.3	1.3	7.7	3.8	9.1
Private Internet	Can.	44.4	35.2	28.1	28.0	16.6	16.9	4.2	6.5	9.6	13.4
	U.K.	64.1	32.7	29.5	27.5	2.6	19.0	1.3	6.2	2.6	14.7

among the spiritual paths, none has even half their members trained in a group. Training is not the only way in which social norms and practices are shared; however it traditionally has been one of the most important forms of religious education in all religions. The lack of group training may well suggest greater, not less, uniformity of belief and practices as individuals turn to the Internet and the same books for inspiration for their practices. It does, however, suggest some degree of less sociability.

TABLE 3.11. *Group Training and Practice by Spiritual Path (in percentages)*

	SOLITARIES	TRAINED IN GROUP	WORKED AT SOME TIME IN GROUP
Eclectic Pagans	82.4	33.0	73.8
Wiccan	70.7	49.2	76.3
Witch	80.0	40.2	78.2
Goddess worshipper	77.1	42.2	78.8
Druids	73.2	41.4	81.4
Heathen	74.9	29.3	77.6

With the exception of Heathens, contemporary Pagans are more likely to get together for social than for spiritual or religious reasons. Druids tend to be the most integrated into contemporary Pagan networks both socially and spiritually; 71.9 percent meet for social reason least once a month and 62.2 percent for spiritual activities at least once a month with other contemporary Pagans. Eclectics are the least likely to join with others for spiritual reasons, which is consistent with their sense of creating their own form of contemporary Paganism. Eclectics, furthermore, are the most likely to have never worked in a group. The trend is not dramatic but is suggestive of less social integration of this spiritual path. This should not be exaggerated, however, as the majority (52.4 percent) join with others for religious or spiritual reasons at least monthly.

Heathens stand out as the most distinct spiritual path; it is an outlier is many ways. They have a higher proportion of men than any other spiritual path and tend to be more politically conservative. As seen in table 3.11 they are less likely to train in a group than other spiritual paths, although they have at least at some time practiced in one at about the same rate as other spiritual paths. The data suggests that this is a choice about how they want to train more than an issue of geographic isolation as Heathens are the most likely of all spiritual paths that I am reviewing to meet with others at least monthly for religious purposes (68.6 percent), but the least likely to meet at least monthly for social purposes (56.1 percent). Nonetheless it would be wrong to see them as socially isolated from other contemporary Pagans as the majority meets at least monthly with others in their religion.

TABLE 3.12. *Frequency of Contemporary Pagans Gathering for Social or Spiritual Reasons for Spiritual Paths (in percentages)*

SPIRITUAL PATH	PURPOSE	DAILY OR ALMOST DAILY	WEEKLY	MONTHLY	YEARLY	NEVER OR ALMOST NEVER
Eclectic	Social	13.7	24.4	28.8	10.3	22.7
	Spiritual/religious	3.4	15.2	33.8	14.7	32.8
Wiccan	Social	13.5	25.8	29.7	9.9	21.1
	Spiritual/religious	3.5	19.3	36.9	13.2	27.1
Witch	Social	17.0	26.9	27.4	9.0	19.7
	Spiritual/religious	5.0	18.0	34.1	14.3	28.6
Goddess worshipper	Social	15.8	27.7	26.3	9.6	17.6
	Spiritual/religious	4.6	18.7	35.8	13.2	27.6
Druids	Social	17.6	24.6	29.7	9.3	18.9
	Spiritual/religious	5.0	19.9	37.7	12.2	25.3
Heathens	Social	3.2	16.1	36.8	14.9	29.0
	Spiritual/religious	17.4	25.2	26.0	11.4	20.1

Solitary practice is not resulting in isolation as the majority meets with other contemporary Pagans for religious and social interactions. Although as noted there are some differences in sociability, these pale next to the similarities among spiritual paths. This is evident when examining the data on sharing of spiritual paths within families. Regardless of spiritual path all contemporary Pagans who have children are more likely to share their religion with those children than they are to share their religion with their romantic partner. There is no notable difference among spiritual paths in the rates at which they share their spirituality with either their children or romantic partners. The higher rate of sharing with their children than with their romantic partners may be a function of the children being a product of a previous marriage or a belief that their children should learn about their religion as well as others.

GENDER

A debate exists in the literature on friendship on whether or not women are the more social gender. Some studies (Rubin 1985; Johnson 1996) note that women are more integrated into social networks, while others (Duck and Wright 1993) suggest that this may not be true. Data from "The Pagan Census Revisited," as indicated in tables 3.13, 3.14, and 3.15, reveal that male contemporary Pagans are somewhat more socially integrated than women, but on the whole it is the form of practice that determines the extent of social integration not the gender of the participant. As seen in table 3.13 women are slightly more likely to practice alone, to not have trained in a group, and to never have worked in a group than men. Nonetheless 73.5 percent of men are solitary practitioners with the majority (59.5 percent) not having trained in a group. The majority of both women and men have worked at some time in a group (72.8 percent of women and 77.5 percent of men).

TABLE 3.13. *Gender and Solitary Practice and Group Interactions (in percentages)*

	SOLITARIES	TRAINED IN GROUP	WORKED AT SOME TIME IN GROUP
Female	80.1	36.4	72.8
Male	73.5	40.5	77.5

Men are more likely to share their spiritual path with their romantic partner and less likely to share it with their children than women are. Nonetheless the majority of both men and women (51.8 percent of women and 66.9 percent of men) share their spiritual path with their spouses or romantic partners. In my earlier ethnographic work (1999) I found that heterosexual men were often introduced into the religion by their female romantic partners. The gender disparity in the religion makes it more likely that heterosexual and gay men and lesbians or bisexual women will meet a partner within contemporary Pagan social circles than heterosexual woman. Even though a smaller percentage of women share their spiritual path with their spouse or romantic partner, a larger percentage share it with their child or children than men do, as seen in table 3.14. This is not surprising as mothers are more likely to have primary custody and traditionally have been more involved in the day-to-day raising of children.

TABLE 3.14. *Gender and Sharing Spiritual Path with Family Members (in percentages)*

	PERCENTAGE WHO SHARE COMPLETELY OR PARTLY WITH ROMANTIC PARTNER	PERCENTAGE WHO HAVE CHILDREN AND TRAIN CHILDREN IN THEIR SPIRITUAL PATH
Female	51.8	79.5
Male	66.9	69.0

More revealing is the data in table 3.15, which provides the frequency of religious and social interactions by gender and by form of practice. This data indicates that there is virtually no gender difference between male and female solitary practitioners or between male and female group practitioners. As previously noted group practitioners are not surprisingly more likely to gather with others at least once a month for spiritual activities. Over 90 percent of both men and women who practice in a group do meet with others for spiritual purposes at least once a month, and about one-third of those who practice alone also do so, regardless of gender. More telling about social integration is that gender plays no part in the frequency with which people gather with other contemporary Pagans for social reasons. Over 90 percent of men and women who work in a group gather with other contemporary Pagans at least once a month for social reason. Just over 50 percent of solitaries regardless of gender gather with other contemporary Pagans for social reasons.

The most important distinction based on gender is that somewhat more women than men practice alone. This in part may be because men are more likely to join an ethnic or regional form of contemporary Paganism than they are to become Wiccans or Witches—two denominations that have the most how-to books written about their practices.

TABLE 3.15. *Frequency of Female and Male Contemporary Pagans Meeting for Social or Religious/Spiritual Purposes (in percentages)*

	PURPOSE	DAILY OR ALMOST DAILY	WEEKLY	MONTHLY	YEARLY	NEVER OR ALMOST NEVER
All U.S. females	Social	13.3	25.2	27.6	10.0	23.9
	Spiritual/ religious	3.6	15.1	33.4	14.8	33.1
Female solo	Social	11.2	20.4	24.7	11.8	31.8
	Spiritual/ religious	5.5	34.3	54.8	4.2	1.2
Female group	Social	16.3	37.7	36.5	5.5	4.0
	Spiritual/ religious	5.5	34.3	54.8	4.2	1.2
All U.S. males	Social	15.5	23.8	29.2	9.4	22.0
	Spiritual/religious	3.9	17.6	34.5	12.9	31.1
Male solo	Social	12.3	17.9	25.6	11.6	32.5
	Spiritual/ religious	2.1	8.1	25.4	18.0	46.5
Male group	Social	20.1	36.8	35.8	4.4	3.0
	Spiritual/religious	5.5	34.3	54.8	4.2	1.2

Alternative Health Practices

One venue through which Bender (2010) contends that the New Metaphysicals interact with one another is through alternative medical practices. According to Bender otherwise isolated individuals interact with their providers and at times with one another when they seek alternative treatments. In their groundbreaking work *The Spiritual Revolution,* Heelas and his coauthors (2005), found that metaphysical practices were surprisingly commonly used in the general population of a typical English town, Kendal. They saw this as part of a more general move toward metaphysical practices and beliefs becoming integrated into English society, and extrapolating from their data they argued this was true in other Western countries as well. Kendal was picked for the case study because the authors saw it as an unexceptional English town. In constructing our survey we used the same categories of alternative practices as those used in the Kendal project to permit comparisons between the studies. As Heelas and Woodhead have extensive lists of these practices, this provides a good overview of most, if not all, alternative practices that are available.

Table 3.16 compares six sets of data—the percentage of the national population of contemporary Pagans, solitaries and those who practice in groups, in both the United States and the United Kingdom, who have stated that they have ever used any of these techniques—with data from Kendal. While on the whole not surprisingly contemporary Pagans are more likely to participate in all these activities than the general population in Kendal, there are two exceptions—the Alexander Technique and osteopathy. The former is a technique that focuses on body alignment during both movement and stillness, which its advocates believe promotes physical and mental health. The latter is a common alternative health practice in both England and the United States. About a third of the Kendal population (30.6 percent) claimed to have at least at some time tried the Alexander Technique. There is a difference between U.S. and U.K. contemporary Pagans with only 8.2 percent of U.S. contemporary Pagans and 14.6 percent of U.K. contemporary Pagans having used the Alexander Technique at some time. The general population in Kendal is also slightly more likely than either U.K. or U.S. contemporary Pagans to use osteopathy. Although the difference between U.K. contemporary Pagans and the Kendal population is very small, it suggests that this is a practice that is slightly more common among the British than among Americans, and that includes U.S. contemporary Pagans.

Indian head massage, a technique of ayvurvedic healing that has been practiced for centuries in South Asia, has been tried by just under a third (30.2 percent) of U.K. contemporary Pagans and 9.9 percent of Kendal residents but by only 4.2 percent of U.S. contemporary Pagans. This is not surprising as India is a former colony of Britain and there is a larger percentage of people from the subcontinent living in the United Kingdom than in the United States. With these few exceptions it is clear that on the whole contemporary Pagans in both countries are more likely to use almost all the alternative medical practices than the average person in Kendal. Solitary practitioners in both countries are slightly less likely to use most of these alternatives than is the general contemporary Pagan population. The difference is larger when comparing group practitioners to solitary practitioners in each country, which suggests that those already well integrated into social networks are more likely to also be integrated into the alternative medicine networks. Nonetheless these networks would be one way in which solitaries do come in contact with others with a similar metaphysical worldview.

There are some national differences between U.S. and U.K. contemporary Pagans, but what stands out is the similarity of practices between them, suggesting a shared network of interest and knowledge—a community of sorts that has developed through books, websites, and personal interactions. This can be seen most clearly in the percentage who participate in astrology, circle dancing, foot massage, spiritual healing, herbalism, homeopathy, massage, psychotherapy, Reiki, relaxation therapy, tarot card reading, and yoga, all of which are much more likely to be practiced by contemporary Pagans on either side of the Atlantic than by the general population in Kendal (see table 3.16). Other differences in the list are not as stark, but the general trend remains the same; with the few exceptions mentioned above and those in which the differences between contemporary Pagans and non-Pagans are quite small, such as for craniosacral therapy, there is a tendency for British and U.S. contemporary Pagans to favor the same alternative therapies and practices and for those in groups to practice them more than solitaries.

TABLE 3.16. *Alternative Therapies and Practices, Kendal, U.K., and U.S. (in percentages)*

	KENDAL	U.K. PAGAN	U.S. PAGAN SOLO	U.K. PAGAN GROUP	U.S. PAGAN	U.S. PAGAN SOLO	U.S. PAGAN GROUP
Acupressure	4.8	28.2	26.0	30.3	47.3	43.7	53.9
Acupuncture	20.2	25.0	22.7	32.7	25.3	21.6	32.8
Alexander Technique	30.6	14.6	13.2	21.2	8.2	5.1	8.0
Aromatherapy	38.5	78.4	79.8	78.1	81.0	81.2	78.9
Art therapy/group	7.9	30.5	28.8	33.3	36.0	34.2	37.0
Astrology	14.3	63.0	61.0	69.8	76.5	73.9	79.7
Bahai group	5.2	1.4	1.4	1.5	3.3	2.8	4.0
Buddhist group	17.1	20.9	19.4	21.2	19.8	16.5	23.9
A cancer care group	7.5	7.5	5.2	11.5	3.1	3.4	6.6

TABLE 3.16. *(continued)*

	KENDAL	U.K. PAGAN	U.S. PAGAN SOLO	U.K. PAGAN GROUP	U.S. PAGAN	U.S. PAGAN SOLO	U.S. PAGAN GROUP
Chiropractor	14.3	24.2	23.0	28.8	53.5	50.2	61.0
Circle dancing	18.7	41.4	33.0	55.4	57.1	49.0	71.8
Craniosacral therapy	13.5	9.9	6.2	16.7	14.5	11.9	19.0
Energy management workshops	2.8	15.6	13.8	16.7	30.4	25.1	39.7
Flower essences therapy	21.4	35.4	35.4	33.3	31.0	28.5	34.6
Foot massage	19.0	52.6	50.7	57.8	68.8	66.1	73.7
GreenSpirit group	2.0	8.7	6.8	10.6	6.0	5.2	6.5
Healing/spiritual healing	19.0	58.1	51.9	69.2	69.0	63.5	77.8
Herbalism	12.7	74.5	72.7	76.9	82.2	79.6	86.2
Homeopathy	34.9	53.0	55.2	51.5	63.3	61.2	—
Hypnotherapy	9.5	28.9	29.5	19.7	29.9	26.1	37.5
Indian head massage	9.9	30.2	29.0	30.3	4.2	3.7	5.0
Interfaith group	15.1	23.1	18.1	27.3	32.6	27.7	40.1
Kinesiology	5.2	9.8	9.0	12.1	13.7	12.2	17.2
Massage	35.3	77.2	75.4	83.3	84.1	81.6	88.5
Meridian therapy	0.8	6.1	6.7	4.6	8.2	6.9	11.6
Metamorphic technique	3.6	2.9	2.9	3.0	2.9	2.2	3.0
Naturopathy	0.8	8.5	10.5	6.1	28.4	26.5	30.8
Nutritional therapy	2.8	23.6	21.2	32.7	45.7	43.3	49.3
Osteopathy	24.6	22.5	21.4	22.7	14.1	12.5	17.3
Palm readings	15.4	37.5	39.0	27.3	45.1	43.2	48.6
Play therapy	1.2	9.9	8.1	12.1	16.2	13.9	18.7
Psychic consultancy	8.7	18.8	19.7	18.2	34.3	30.9	39.6
Psychotherapy	7.9	30.2	29.5	30.8	41.1	37.5	47.8
Rebirthing	4.8	6.6	6.7	6.2	6.9	4.9	9.7
Reflexology	31.3	32.5	34.8	28.8	29.8	27.6	33.9
Shiatsu	13.9	18.3	17.3	20.3	20.1	16.9	26.2
Spinal touch therapy	1.2	4.5	3.8	4.7	5.8	5.0	7.3
Tai Chi	25.0	38.4	33.0	45.5	34.2	31.2	38.5
Taize singing group	7.5	6.1	4.3	7.6	2.6	2.1	3.2
Tarot card reading	11.9	79.9	77.4	84.8	86.9	85.2	89.7
True Vision group	0.8	2.6	2.4	4.6	1.6	1.2	1.9

TABLE 3.16. *(continued)*

	KENDAL	U.K. PAGAN	U.S. PAGAN SOLO	U.K. PAGAN GROUP	U.S. PAGAN	U.S. PAGAN SOLO	U.S. PAGAN GROUP
Universal Peace dancing (Sufi dancing)	11.9	8.0	5.7	12.3	8.5	5.9	13.2
Vision therapy (not opticians)	2.0	4.5	3.8	6.2	6.3	5.6	7.2
Wild Women group	0.8	5.5	6.2	4.6	8.7	7.3	11.6
Yoga	50.8	56.4	55.6	56.1	62.6	61.0	64.5

The alternative medical practices on the extensive list provided by the Kendal study that are most commonly tried by contemporary Pagans are on the whole not surprising—divination, spiritual healing, circle dancing, Reiki, massage, herbalism, and homeopathy—each has been well documented in the literature about this religion. Divination, particularly the use of astrology and tarot cards, is described in most ethnographies of the religion (Adler 1986; Pike 2004; York 1995; Doyle White 2016). Spiritual healing and circle dancing are frequently part of rituals within many forms of contemporary Paganism. Anyone who has attended a contemporary Pagan festival or been to a contemporary Pagan website knows that Reiki, massage, herbalism, and homeopathy are all popular. My research supports Bender's (2010) contention that alternative medicine is one part of the metaphysical network. Certainly, local contemporary Pagans meet through these networks and have their worldview and beliefs refined and supported. But as the effect can be seen internationally, it is also clear that another process is going on, in which contemporary Paganism is encouraging the participation in these alternative practices. The slightly, but consistently, lower use by solitary practitioners of most of these techniques suggests that direct social interactions with others in groups may influence individuals to try these practices to a small degree. However, the general similarity both between solitary and group practitioners in each country as well as between countries suggests that mediated forms of communication are more significant than personal interactions in determining which alternative practices are used by members of this religion. Alternative medical practices are part of the spiritual world and mythology of Witchcraft—and there is the belief that it is an ancient religion whose early adherents were healers who used herbs, body manipulations, and magic to heal.

Conclusion

From the time that it first was established and flourished on American soil, contemporary Paganism has appealed to those who question authority and explore alternative forms of spirituality in which individual experience is central to practice. It is common, for example, for contemporary Pagans to state that they do not believe in the goddesses or gods but that they experience them. Troeltsch feared that an emphasis on individual experience would result in mystics never developing a collective worldview or becoming politically active. At least in his early work, Durkheim (1964 [1893]) believed that modernity, with its emphasis on the individual, encouraged the development of the "cult of man," in which the basic social glue would disintegrate as each person became focused on his or her uniqueness. Although he revised his position on this in his later work (Durkheim 1965 [1912]), his image of the radical individualism of contemporary society continues to have resonance—as seen in the writings of Putnam (2001), Lasch (1979, 1984), Bellah et al. (1985), and Bruce (1996, 2003). But there are other theorists who argue, as Durkheim did in his later work, that individualism can lead to the celebration of people's joint humanity (see for example Taylor 1989, 1992), generating the development of a new sociability and morality. Houtman and Aupers (2010:15) contend that religions like contemporary Paganism that applaud each individual's unique spiritual quest are not antisocial. To the contrary they produce "a networked form of sociality that celebrates the modern value of individual freedom in a collective fashion."

As the data in this chapter indicates, almost all contemporary Pagans have interchanges with others in their religion, either in person or on the Internet, at least on a monthly basis. Furthermore most contemporary Pagans read widely in many areas, including archeology, mythology, science fiction, and contemporary Pagan practice. When asked to list the books that most influenced their development as contemporary Pagans, some stated that there were too many to list, and others had lists of ten or more books. Although no author was mentioned by everyone, five were mentioned by many of the respondents. These are Starhawk, particularly her first book, *The Spiral Dance* (1979), which was one of the first books to describe Wicca and its mystical history, beliefs, and practices; Scott Cunningham (1988, 1994), who wrote books advocating solitary practice and provided a template for doing it; Silver RavenWolf (1993, 1999), who writes books geared to teenagers and young adults; Margot Adler (1978, 1986), who provided the first overview of contemporary Paganism; and Raymond Buckland (1986), who is credited with bringing Wicca to the United States from the United Kingdom and who was among the first to provide a description of Wiccan rituals that would permit individuals to practice alone. Among those practicing ethnic or regional forms of contemporary Paganism such as Druids and Heathens, texts specific to those practices were mentioned as important as were mythologies and folk tales from the regions associated with those groups. Shared readings provide one avenue through which a shared lifeworld is created and through which a sense of spirituality is formed. Furthermore much like people who may not have read Freud but who nonetheless know about the subconscious, the core ideas of foundational readings, such as Starhawk's *The Spiral Dance* (1979), have entered into a more general discourse about contemporary Pagan practice.

Although contemporary Pagans state that books are more important in their spiritual development and practice than the Internet, Internet sites remain important. As with books, a few people claim there are too many Internet sites to list, but there are very few respondents who listed eight or more. On the whole those who answered the question listed one to three sites. The most frequently mentioned was Witchvox, a large site that contains articles of interest to contemporary Pagans, some of general interest and others for specific spiritual paths of contemporary Paganism, as well as advertisements, and a discussion board. Witchvox provides country-specific pages that encourage online discussions of local issues and targeted advertisements for local businesses and services. The Wild hunt, founded by Jason Pitzl-Waters and currently run by Heather Greene, provides information and analysis of current contemporary Pagan issues and concerns and was the second most mentioned site. Facebook and Yahoo groups were also mentioned as being of importance. Many sites were listed, some by only one or two people. Not surprisingly the young are somewhat more likely to use interactive websites, but even older contemporary Pagans are computer savvy and regularly on the Internet.

Alternative healing practices serve as another way in which contemporary Pagans interact and have their worldview confirmed. As seen in this chapter, contemporary Pagans are more likely than the average person to participate in these services. Contemporary Pagans partake in a form of sociability that combines face-to-face interactions with reading books, viewing websites, and participating in interactions in other milieus. They are tied into a network that helps to inform their worldview and their practices.

Contemporary Paganism in many ways encapsulates contemporary trends that have resonance within more traditional religions, most of which have been experiencing challenges to their traditional forms of authority and community as more individuals claim to be spiritual but not religious. Many Americans are participating in what sociologists have called lived religion—that is, a religious life that while important to them may contradict some of the strictures of the religion they claim to practice, and which takes place largely outside of religious institutions (McGuire 2008). Within contemporary Paganism there is no contradiction as each individual is responsible for her or his own spirituality and practice. Contemporary Paganism is in many ways at the forefront of a more general trend within religion in late modernity in which traditional authority structures and community are being challenged, by both the Internet and changing norms that make it legitimate to be "spiritual," that is, to have a religious practice or belief system, without belonging to a congregation (Ammerman 2013).

Within Wicca, which is the largest of the specific spiritual paths of contemporary Paganism, training was traditionally in covens where the authority over initiation and graduation to higher ranks resided with the High Priestess and High Priest. This authority was greatest when there were few covens in an area, and most of those were hidden, making it more difficult for a neophyte to find a coven in which he or she could be trained. The advent of how-to books and Internet sites has leveled those authority structures. Eileen Barker (2005) has argued that the Internet helps to make authority more horizontal in all religions, with religious leaders and adherents having access to communication venues. This would appear to be even more clearly the case within Wicca and other forms of contemporary Paganism as there are so many Internet sites in which individuals can express their religious knowledge and present themselves as experts. The focus within the religion on feelings, intuition, and each person being responsible for her or his own spirituality has resulted in everyone having a claim to being an authority.

Concerns have been raised among some within the contemporary Pagan community that this could result in a watering down of spiritual and magical practices (H. Berger 2003 et al.; Cowan 2005). But to what extent has there really been a leveling of authority? Certainly within contemporary Paganism there is no authority structure that can exclude anyone or their form of spiritual practice. This does permit innovation, but it also encourages individuals to look for inspiration and guidance from the same sources, resulting in some voices becoming more dominant, as certain books and websites become particularly influential. In his research on contemporary Pagan websites, Cowan (2005) discovered that there a good deal of redundancy among sites as those running them cut and pasted the same text from one another, resulting in the same suggestions and information appearing over and over, albeit allegedly by different authors. While online interactions permit individuals to be in control of their spirituality, they do not result in a completely individual expression as participants are influenced by similar sources (H. Berger 1999; Hammer 2010). This is true among contemporary Pagans and among those participating in more traditional religions online (Howard 2011; Lövheim 2013).

The data in this chapter indicates that contemporary Pagans regularly come together either in person or on the Internet. But does that form a community or, more to the point, a religious community? Does the lack of a central building in which people gather mean that a "real" community is not formed? Campbell (2013), in reviewing the literature on religion online, has suggested a "disembodied congregation" is nonetheless a religious community, meeting many of the same needs as face-to-face communities. In his discussion of online Evangelicals, Howard (2011:11) similarly argues that the notion "that sharing knowledge generates a community is at least as old as the Christian idea of 'church' itself." Both Campbell (2013) and Howard (2011) argue that online communities share many aspects with face-to-face communities. Research indicates that contrary to fears that have been expressed about online use, the Internet does not stifle but instead compliments those interactions (Hampton et al. 2009). Contemporary Pagans have a number of different venues through which they meet and interact such as festivals and open rituals and as Bender (2010) illustrated alternative health practices.

In *The Sacred Canopy* Peter Berger (1967) argues that religious communities provide their participants with plausibility structures, that is, a system of beliefs that helps to make sense of life, death, and suffering. These structures are created and maintained through interactions. Within contemporary Paganism there are core beliefs about the interconnectedness of all living beings, the sacredness of the earth, the existence of an alternative or magical universe, and the celebration of diversity. All these beliefs and the basic practices of magic are maintained within the loose network or community that we have seen within contemporary Paganism, which is based on shared readings, Internet sites, and social interactions at a variety of venues.

This chapter illustrates the complexity of deciphering the importance of face-to-face interactions for social integration. On the one hand, solitary practitioners, as theorists like Putman have predicted, are less socially and spiritually integrated than group practitioners. On the other hand, they are not as isolated as his research would suggest, as most are not withdrawn from the larger community. They have been integrated by reading the same books and through the methods discussed by Campbell (2013), Howard (2011), and Bender (2010), including alternative health practices, music festivals or concerts, science fiction conventions, and Internet sites. This is an international community, as my data indicates. Contemporary Pagans tend to favor the same metaphysical practices and tend read the same books and visit some of the same Websites. Patterns among contemporary Pagans are more similar to one another than to others in their own nation. The next two chapters will explore the degree to which solitary practice affects spiritual and magical practices and beliefs and political engagement. These will test the degree to which the somewhat lesser social integration of solitaries influences their behaviors.

CHAPTER 4

Magic, the Otherworld, and Spiritual Practices

It was the practice of magic by well-educated Westerners, some in fact that were trained in the natural sciences, that first caught my imagination when I began to study contemporary Paganism in the 1980s (H. Berger 1994). I was not alone in this as initially most of the research on contemporary Paganism focused on it as a magical religion (Luhrmann 1989; Lewis 1996). Although it is now more common for contemporary Paganism to be called an earth-based religion, it nonetheless remains also a magical one. As can be seen in table 4.1, most contemporary Pagans practice magic. Only 2.9 percent of group members and 5.6 percent of solo practitioners state that they never practice magic. For most contemporary Pagans, a sense of the world as enchanted, with links to the otherworld, is woven into the rituals and worldview of the religion. It is an essential part of being a contemporary Pagan, although some spiritual paths and some individuals practice it more than others.

TABLE 4.1. *Frequency of Magical Practice for Solo and Group Practitioners (in percentages)*

	SOLO	GROUP
Often	15.5	26.6
Regularly	24.6	35.2
Sometimes	35.1	25.4
Rarely	19.2	9.8
Never	5.6	2.9

Magic and the Otherworld

The anthropologist Susan Greenwood (2000), who studied magical practitioners in the United Kingdom, many of whom are contemporary Pagans, notes that there is a link between the magical practices of modern Western magicians and shamans in traditional societies. For practitioners in both cases, "the cosmos is alive . . . essentially holistic" (Greenwood 2000:23). For contemporary Pagans the universe is often described as a web of interconnecting strings of energy that a trained individual can manipulate, thereby changing the course of events—in other words they can make magic happen.

Contemporary Pagans believe that they use their minds to shift the energy and therefore, through their will, can influence the chain of events. Meditation, rituals, and candles are all ways that help them focus their concentration and therefore perform magic. For most contemporary Pagans, however, even the uninitiated or untrained do magic; they just do not do it as often or as well and may well be unaware of what they are doing. As one solitary practitioner in my study stated, "Everything you do is a [magical] working. Every action you take, word you speak is energy set forth." One example of how this everyday magic may work is when someone is thinking about someone else and then that person either calls the person who was thinking about him or her or bumps into the person while going about daily activities. We tend to think of it as a happy coincidence—but for contemporary Pagans it is an example of making something happen through one's thoughts or words. It is believed by magicians that those who are trained can do more magic and have more control over it. They are less likely, for example, to focus on someone they do not want to see only to find that that person at the same party they are attending.

When asked to describe a particular powerful magical working, one American man who works in a group offers this example:

> The last time I was unemployed I went on an interview and was told I was in contention with one other person for the job. Just after I left the interview I settled my mind and imagined the other person getting a better offer at a company close to home that would make them happy so I could have this job. I took out a token I had been charging with "luck" for quite a while and decided to use it for myself (which I very rarely do; they're almost always for someone else). I put my wish into it and flipped it into a grassy area so someone else could find it and hopefully benefit as well. I felt a strong release of tension and energy when it hit the ground, which is uncommon. I felt like I had done something very effective, and as it turns out I got the job. I don't know what happened to the other person, but given the reaction I got I suspect they're okay.

This example brings together many elements of how magic is used by contemporary Pagans. The writer insists that he normally is more concerned about using his magical prowess for other people's needs, focuses on getting something he really requires and that is not frivolous—he is not for instance doing a magical working to get a fancy car or win the lottery—and attempts to ensure that no one else is injured by his magical working. He believes in the power of magic, and he believes it works, although not consistently. As he notes, this time he could feel the energy when his coin hit the ground, implying that there were other times when he had a weaker, or possibly no, response when he did a magical working. Ethically he is committed to no one else being injured by his actions. The focus on doing good and not evil with one's magical abilities results in the most typical spells being for health and healing (Crowley 2000). Vivianne Crowley has noted that doing a healing ritual, particularly for those who are new to the religion, permits them to express their sense of empowerment while doing something positive. Most contemporary Pagans believe that the energy that one sends out comes back to the person threefold; if one wishes ill on another the negative energy he or she is generating will ultimately hurt the person and conversely that if one sends out positive energy it will come back in the form of blessings.

A woman who is a Hellenic contemporary Pagan states that although she does not normally do magic, as she does not consider it part of her tradition, she did do a magical working when attending a group ritual at a Covenant of Unitarian Universalist Pagans chapter. As she describes it: "we wrote wishes on slips of paper. I felt moved to draw little pictures on mine, too. We then tossed them onto a fire with the poem, 'Goddess silver, goddess bright, grant this wish I wish tonight. From full to dark and back again, grant this wish to me by then.' I had several and they all came true in a month, but not necessarily in the way I expected. (I intentionally left them open.)" The use of a token or paper, which two of the respondents I quoted above state that they use, is a typical way in which magic is practiced. Sometimes, particularly in groups, dancing, singing, and meditation are used to raise energy, which is then flung into the universe with raised arms and hands. But in all these examples the goal is to gain something; a new job, a new home, a new love, or health. When doing love magic contemporary Pagans are normally concerned that they do not violate another's will—that the magic calls love to one, not the love of a particular person. It is also common to interpret wishes being granted as the Hellenic women did by saying that they did come true but not in the way she had expected or possibly wanted. Wishing, for example, for a new car only to be given a toy one as a joke gift is one such example, particularly if one's wish was stated in an ambiguous way, such as, "I want a little sports car." The vagueness of the request may also be intentional, as the Hellenic practitioner stated hers was, to avoid requesting something that would ultimately do someone else harm or leaving the possibility of the divine answering it in a way that ultimately was what one needed even if it was not what one wanted.

Some contemporary Pagans refer to what they do as magick, adding the *k* to distinguish their practice from carnival magicians who take a coin out of one's ear or make a rabbit disappear into a hat. I will use that spelling only when

I am quoting someone who does. Nonetheless my discussion throughout is about magic as a technique of, or belief in, changing reality, and not carnival tricks.

Although much magic, like many prayers, focuses on changing some aspect of the person's or their friends' or family members' life circumstances, there are also magical workings for changing the self. One solitary practitioner notes, "During my Imbolc ritual, I charged myself to achieve certain goals, such as to stop biting my nails. Since then, these goals have been met. The intense magick surrounding this particular goal reminds me of what can truly be achieved. This working has inspired me to better myself further." The example that this woman gave should not be trivialized. Her point is that she felt that she was able to change her behavior for the better, first in a small way by stopping a bad habit but ultimately in other areas of her life too. Another person describes a ritual that his group did to release the anger they felt toward another group with whom they were doing spiritual work. The ritual was focused on helping his group members come to terms with what happened without causing harm to members of the other group. Another person describes "connecting to the universal energy flow, to regulate comfort and (my) mood" and still another of using magical energy to control her blood pressure. In each of these examples magic is used by contemporary Pagans for self-improvement. It is a form of self-therapy, which has gained greater acceptance outside of alternative spiritual groups as meditation and self-affirmation have become mainstream and are recommended by medical professionals for treating a number of medical conditions including high blood pressure.

According to Greenwood both traditional and contemporary magic is based on a connection with the otherworld—the spiritual. However, she argues that the major difference between magic such as that discussed by Evans-Pritchard (1937) among the Azande and the magic practiced among contemporary Pagans is that the latter includes a veneration of the divine. For contemporary Pagans magic is integrated into their concept of the sacred; it is an intrinsic part of their spiritual and religious practice, which is why it is almost universally practiced among contemporary Pagans. As one solitary practitioner phrased it, "Any magick work is meaningful as it connects me with the spiritual realm." Phyllis Curott (2001:29), a feminist Witch and author, spells this out. She contends that "*magic is what happens when you have encountered the Divine.* It is the life-altering experience of connecting to the divinity that is within yourself and in the world. . . . *Real Magic is your relationship with immanent divinity, and it is how you craft yourself as a Witch*" (emphasis in original). She further notes that "because the world is an expression of the Divine, magic has always been used for practical purposes" but when used "only for this purpose it soon ceases to work" (Curott 2001:42–43).

Magic as an element of religious practice has resulted in another difference with traditional magic; there is an emphasis as previously noted on doing positive things with magic and a counterdiction against doing harm. In traditional magic as practiced by shamans harming the enemy is part of the practice (Stoller and Olkes 1987). There is a debate among contemporary Pagans about whether or not it is acceptable for there to be retaliatory magic against those who do evil, for example a rapist. Zuzanna Budapest (1986) has argued that a Witch that cannot curse cannot cure. Some contemporary Pagans explore what is called left-hand magic, participating in curses, but this is the minority.

TABLE 4.2. *Beliefs in How Magic Works for Solo and Group Practitioners (in percentages)*

	SOLO	GROUP
Nothing more than human psychology	8.1	10.2
Magic taps an impersonal force; this force is not supernatural	33.0	35.7
Magic involves tapping "spiritual" energies/entities that in some way transcend the ordinary material world	66.6	68.5

As can be seen in table 4.2, approximately two-thirds of contemporary Pagans contend that "magic involves tapping into spiritual energies or entities that in some way transcend the material world," echoing Greenwood's notion that magic involves interactions with the otherworld. The question permitted individuals to answer all that they believed were relevant, so that the columns add up to slightly more than 100 percent. About a third believe magic is an impersonal force that is not supernatural, and about 10 percent of group members and 8 percent of solitary practitioners describe magic as nothing more than human psychology. My ethnographic research indicates that it is fairly common for contemporary Pagans to hold more than one view of how magic works, sometimes veering among them (H. Berger 1999).

Group and solitary practitioners have very similar views of what magic is and how it works, overwhelmingly seeing it as spiritual; however the frequency with which they practice it is different. As indicated in table 4.1 the majority (61.8 percent) of group practitioners and less than half (40.1 percent) of solitary frequently or often practice magic. This is a striking difference as there is such a small difference in the frequency of magical practice between men and women and among age cohorts. The degree to which individuals practice magic is primarily dependent on whether or not they practice alone.

As magic is a spiritual as well as pragmatic activity for most contemporary

Pagans the question must be asked why solitary practitioners on the whole are less likely to practice magic than those who practice in a group. The answer to this is complex but at least in part is the result of magic being incorporated into rituals at group events. The Hellenic Pagan who said that magic is not part of her own tradition but that she participated and had a powerful experience, when she attended the Covenant of Unitarian Universalist Pagans' ritual, is an example of this. Group rituals often involve at least the release of energy for a working—that is the raising of mental energy through dance, chants, or the focus of thoughts to aid a person or a cause, for example the healing of an ill individual or of the earth. As described by respondents above, rituals may also involve other forms of magic, such as writing one's wishes on a piece of paper and then throwing it into the flames or putting it in a small cloth pouch to wear. It is common for individuals who have a problem or a wish, such as the desire for a new home, new job, or new love, to ask their coven mates or members of their group to do a working for them or with them. Certainly solitary practitioners also receive requests for magical workings, either through e-mails, Facebook, or personal communications, just as those who work in groups do. The group context, however, provides an increased opportunity for these requests.

Those who practice alone may also be more reticent to participate in magic as the threefold law makes some concerned about inadvertently doing harm to another and ultimately to themselves. For those who believe that magic is real it is seen as something that should not be played with. Those in groups may have the comfort of sharing the responsibility as much as the encouragement of others in their groups. When one person has a very powerful magical working at a ritual or on their own and discusses it with others it encourages them to do magic.

Tanya Luhrmann (1989) has suggested that the acceptance of magic is a two-pronged process beginning with individuals having metaphysical experiences that are very meaningful to them. One example is provided in "The Pagan Census Revisited" by a female solitary practitioner who in answering the question "please describe your most important or one of your most important spiritual experiences" wrote:

> almost drowning in [a] Lake . . . as a child of 8. I was drawn out by the undertow far, far into the lake and I struggled for a while, and finally a deep peace came over me and for the first time in my life I felt Her. I felt deeply safe, held in the arms of a watery goddess of blues, stones, shells, stars, moons. And she sent me back up to the shore whole and fine, although I'd been under the water a long time . . . never stopped going to the Lake . . . to feel held in Her arms, to feel the deep sense that I am not alone in the universe. She is always there, ready to teach me lessons, give me gifts (both physical and of the spirit) and welcome me home.

It is worth noting that this meaningful experience happened when the woman was still a child. She did not yet have a framework to explain it or fully understand it, but it remained significant to her, as did the place where it occurred. She subsequently learned about contemporary Paganism, which helped to make sense of her experience; it provided a religious context for what she had experienced as a child. This is the second prong of the process that Luhrmann describes, in which through participation in the larger magical community, through interactions with others, reading the same books, magazines, and I would now include, the same Internet sites, individuals come to frame their experiences within a spiritual context. The frequency and depth of spiritual experiences subsequently increase with training in magical techniques, such as meditation and learning to have lucid dreams—that is the process through which one encourages oneself to dream and to remember the dreams. These experiences are transformative for most individuals who have them. It is common for contemporary Pagans to say that they do not *believe* in magic, rather they *experience* it. Luhrmann refers to this as a cognitive drift—one in which they learn to interpret their experiences through a new lens and through which they come to see magic and magical thinking as normative. Although solitary and group practitioners differ in the extent to which they practice magic, they nonetheless have similar views of how it works. This suggests that they are participating in a shared lifeworld, a shared way of defining their experiences, which is a result of their reading the same authors and websites, and interacting with others who share their experiences and their interpretations at festivals, gatherings, and other venues.

This process of interpretive drift occurs and is necessary because, as Greenwood argues, magic is outside of traditional Western thought. It is more dependent on metaphor than lineal reasoning, which makes it and the religions that integrate it into their theology and practices appear as alien or not a serious or "real" religion. However, magic and metaphysical religions have been part of the Western tradition since at least the Renaissance (Shumaker 1979). Spiritualism and Transcendentalism, for example, were popular in the nineteenth century (Pike 2004). Nonetheless Greenwood is correct that magical religions and magic itself are often seen as suspect, and as lesser than more traditional religions, which have a greater emphasis on faith. Magical religions speak less of faith in, and more of experience of, the divine or otherworld.

One of the strongest and clearest presentations of why magical religions are not seen as "real" religions is provided by Rodney Stark (2001) who claims that the concept of a magical religion is an oxymoron. He argues that although both magic and religion focus on the supernatural, they share little else in common as magic views these supernatural forces as impersonal while religion always involves a deity or deities who are viewed as having some form of consciousness and desires for how their adherents treat them or act in the world. He does allow that some forms of sorcery may deal with somewhat more animate forces, but nonetheless he views these as not equivalent to gods.

His notion of religion, which uses Christianity as a model, focuses on beliefs, instead of on practices or spiritual experiences, which are more common in other religions, particularly Eastern and metaphysical religions. Although he does acknowledge the legitimacy of Eastern religions such as Taoism and Buddhism, which in some forms do not have a deity, he discounts them as constrained to the intellectual elite. The masses, he notes, always deform them to include deities. It is this prejudice of seeing all religions from a Western and Christian perspective that I believe makes it impossible for him and others to see the possibility of magic being part of the spiritual experience of Westerners.

It is true that for most contemporary Pagans magic provides more control and power over the outcome than is normally attributed to prayer. However even that distinction is not consistently true. Robert Orsi (1995) describes the primarily working-class women who worship St. Jude as believing they have a reciprocal relationship with the saint, one in which they are dependent on him to answer their prayers for lost causes and he is dependent on them to venerate him. Some contemporary Pagans view magic as an impersonal source, as Stark suggests, but most do not. There is a relationship with the otherworld, which may or may not involve gods and goddesses but does involve a relationship to the divine or spiritual. As can be seen in table 4.3, contemporary Pagans who believe that magic taps into spiritual energies or entities that in some way transcend the ordinary material world are more likely to do magic and do it more often than those who see magic as nothing more than human psychology or as tapping into an impersonal force that is not supernatural. Only 3.0 percent of those who believe that magic is in some way supernatural never practice magic, which can be compared to 17.1 percent of those who believe that magic is not supernatural who never practice it. The majority (51 percent) of those who believe magic is connected to the otherworld practice magic often or regularly as compared to 28 percent of those who do not see magic as spiritual.

TABLE 4.3. *Frequency of Magical Practice Based on Participants' View of Magic (in percentages)*

	NOT SUPERNATURAL	SUPERNATURAL
Often	12.0	21.3
Regularly	16.0	29.7
Sometimes	29.9	32.2
Rarely	24.7	13.8
Never	17.1	3.0

Stark believes that religion unlike magic provides an ethical framework, however, for contemporary Pagans, magic is integrated into their ethics. The threefold law is one way in which morality is enshrined. One would not do to others what one would not like done to oneself. As noted in chapter 1, this is part of their larger perspective that each of us is in an interconnected web with each other and all nature. This is not the transcendental ethics of Christianity, based on the immutable laws that are believed to emanate from God but a relational ethics, based on empathy with the other (H. Berger and Ezzy 2007; York 2004; McGraw 2004). In *The Spiral Dance,* Starhawk (1979:114) speaks about the way in which magic that affects another individual results in one becoming connected on a magical level with that person. She tells us that in order for magic to work, "you must be at least partly identified with that other person. You become the other, as well as becoming the energy you send. For this reason 'what you send returns to you, three times over'. The energy you project to another affects you even more strongly than the other person because you have generated it. You have become it. By becoming the other you empathize and are connected to them."

The focus of this type of morality is not one of self-sacrifice or self-denial but a celebration of the self. But this is not, Starhawk (1979:110) assures us, a call to selfishness. She contends that "in Witchcraft, the flesh, the material world, are not sundered from the Goddess, they are manifestation of the divine. Union with the Goddess comes through embracing the material world. In Witchcraft we do not fight self-interest; we follow it, but with the awareness that transmutes it into something sacred." That transmutation involves radical empathy and care for the other while caring for the self. In her seminal work, Valerie Saiving-Goldstein (1960) argues that the life experiences and therefore the sins of women and men are different. The seven deadly sins presented in Christian texts are, she believes, good guides to the sins that men commit, which she views as the result of their focus on power and pride. Women's sins, however are different, because their life experience has been different; theirs are sins of distraction and diffusion, of permitting others to define them. Contemporary Paganism, a religion influenced by feminism and disproportionately composed of female adherents, provides a morality that is more consistent with what Saiving-Goldstein views as women's lived experience. Eeva Sointu and Linda Woodhead (2008) in their research on mind and body practices such as Reiki and others listed in chapter 3 note that they are often viewed correctly as focusing on the self. However as these authors further describe, these techniques are normally practiced by the marginalized and particularly by women, to whom they provide a sense of self-worth and self-direction in which the self is embedded in a wider web of obligation to the universe and to others. The focus on the self, therefore, does not result in self-absorption.

Magic as practiced by contemporary Pagans may at times be amoral but does not result in the lack of a moral system as most of it is based on a system of reciprocity that has an ethical element. It is an ethics that in part helps to influence the political causes that contemporary Pagans are most involved in, as will be discussed in the next chapter. Magic is an essential element of the spiritual and religious practice of most although not all contemporary Pagans. It is not only a way of attempting to have one's needs met, or to help others, but permits one to have a direct relationship with the divine, the universe, or the otherworld—in other words to have a spiritual experience in which the practitioner sees themselves as empowered.

Gender

Although whether or not a person is a solitary practitioner has a larger effect on the frequency of magical practice, gender is also a factor as is indicated in table 4.4. As previously noted group practitioners are the most likely to practice magic and to practice it more often, but men who practice alone are more likely than women who practice alone to claim that they never or rarely practice magic (9.0 percent versus 4.4 percent). Women in groups are the least likely to rarely or never practice magic; only 11.1 percent state that they rarely or never practice it as compared to men who work in groups, among whom 15.6 percent rarely or never practice magic. Although fewer women never practice magic than men, the latter are more likely to practice it frequently. Among women 39.5 percent of solitary and 61.4 percent of group participants practice magic often or regularly. This can be compared to men, among whom 42.0 percent of solitary and 63.0 percent of group practitioners practice magic often or regularly. Clearly forms of practice, however, are much more important than gender, although gender also is a factor in frequency of practice.

TABLE 4.4. *Frequency of Magical Practice for Solo and Group Women and Men (in percentages)*

	SOLO WOMEN	WOMEN IN GROUPS	SOLO MEN	MEN IN GROUPS
Often	15.0	26.0	16.7	28.1
Regularly	24.5	35.4	25.3	34.9
Sometimes	37.7	27.4	27.4	21.3
Rarely	18.4	8.9	21.7	11.6
Never	4.4	2.2	9.0	4.0

As can be seen in table 4.5 although men are slightly more likely than women to view magic in nonspiritual terms as either nothing more than human psychology or as an impersonal force that is not supernatural, both men and women, regardless of form of practice, view magic as tapping into spiritual energies or entities and hence see it within a spiritual context. The difference is not large but is consistent with other data that will be discussed in this chapter. Not only are women more likely to view magic as a spiritual or religious practice than men, but they are also less likely to claim that it is nothing more than human psychology. Those who are most likely to view magic as tapping into spiritual energies or entities are also more likely to practice magic.

TABLE 4.5. *How Magic Works According to Women and Men in Solo and Group Practice (in percentages)*

	SOLO WOMEN	GROUP WOMEN	SOLO MEN	GROUP MEN
Nothing more than human psychology	7.4	8.4	10.1	13.5
Impersonal force that is not supernatural	31.2	34.0	38.2	38.5
Taps into spiritual energies or entities	67.5	69.3	63.8	66.7

Scientists or those majoring in the sciences are less likely to have a spiritual view of magic than nonscientists are, as can be seen in table 4.6. However, although women scientists are less likely than nonscientists to view magic as based on a spiritual connection, they are still more likely to do so than are male scientists. Although the study of science influences magical beliefs, making it less likely to be seen as spiritual, gender remains of importance in explaining some of the difference.

TABLE 4.6. *Beliefs in Magic of Female and Male Scientists versus Nonscientists (in percentages)*

	FEMALE SCIENTISTS	MALE SCIENTISTS	NONSCIENTISTS
Nothing more than human psychology	9.0	13.9	7.8
Impersonal force that is not supernatural	35.1	41.0	32.6
Taps into spiritual entities	64.0	60.3	67.3

Interestingly, although on the whole those who view magic as the least spiritual are the least likely to practice it, this is not true for male scientists. As indicated in table 4.7 male scientists who are less likely to see magic as spiritual are also somewhat more likely to often or regularly practice magic than are women scientists. A larger percentage of male scientists than female scientists never or rarely practice magic. There appears to be no relationship in this group between the frequency of magical practice and the belief that magic is spiritual. When I did my original ethnographic research many of the scientists I interviewed told me that they believed that magic relied on a new and still undiscovered science (H. Berger 1994). Many cited Thomas Kuhn's book *The Structure of Scientific Revolutions* (1962), which argues that each scientific revolution is dependent on one individual or set of individuals to dispute the current scientific paradigm. This normally occurs after enough anomalies in the data make it clear that the old paradigm is deficient. Until that happens the data is interpreted within the old paradigm, sometimes in very convoluted ways, much as the earth-centric view of the universe, which required accepting that planets and the sun changed direction. Many of the scientists that I interviewed in my initial research felt that magic ultimately would be shown to have a scientific basis.

TABLE 4.7. *Male and Female Scientists' Frequency of Doing Magic (in percentages)*

	MALE SCIENTISTS	FEMALES SCIENTISTS
Often	19.2	17.0
Regularly	29.8	26.4
Sometimes	23.5	35.0
Rarely	19.9	17.1
Never	7.6	4.5

Magic Internationally

Data on other English-speaking nations indicate that, just as in the United States, group practitioners do more magic than those who are solitary. As can be seen in table 4.8 the difference is even stronger in the United Kingdom than in the United States or Canada. Most striking is that although national differences exist within the contemporary Pagan community, group members consistently practice more magic than do solitary practitioners. As in the United States the group appears both to provide a safe place to perform magic and to encourage members to do more of it.

TABLE 4.8. *Frequency of Magical Practice Internationally (in percentages)*

	U.K. SOLO	U.K. GROUP	CANADA SOLO	CANADA GROUP
Often	9.6	23.1	14.2	16.2
Regularly	13.9	29.2	22.5	33.3
Sometimes	41.6	35.4	28.5	36.0
Rarely	23.4	9.2	22.1	11.7
Never	11.5	3.1	12.7	2.7

There is less of a difference in the views of group and solitary practitioners in the United Kingdom and Canada concerning the manner in which magic works than in the United States, as can be seen in table 4.9. Solitary practitioners in the United Kingdom are the least likely to believe that magic is no more than just human psychology; they are also less likely to view magic as tapping into spiritual entities or energies than contemporary Pagans in the United States or Canada. Nonetheless the majority in all three nations holds that magic has a spiritual basis. This suggests, on the one hand, that there is a clear sharing of ideas both through reading the same books and through the same information being shared on the Internet. On the other hand, national differences are real.

TABLE 4.9. *Views of How Magic Works Internationally (in percentages)*

	U.K. SOLO	U.K. GROUP	CANADA SOLO	CANADA GROUP
Nothing more than human psychology	10.8	13.6	13.4	14.4
Magic taps an impersonal force; this force is not supernatural	39.2	47.0	37.5	41.4
Magic involves tapping "spiritual" energies/entities that in some way transcend the ordinary material world	52.4	62.1	58.0	61.3

Divination, Paranormal Experiences, and the Afterlife

Magic and magical practices are part of a larger worldview for contemporary Pagans in which the universe itself is seen as enchanted. For some contemporary Pagans this includes a notion that goddesses and gods intervene directly in their lives, giving them solace, advice, and hints. For others, who may not believe in actual deities, there is nonetheless a notion that the universe is ordered and that there is a possibility of getting clues about the future and guidance from the universe. There are parallels with Evangelical Christianity, in which Christ is believed have regular and personal interactions with his flock, giving guidance, answering prayers, even sending signs (Luhrmann 2012). There are of course also differences. Magic provides participants with a more powerful role in helping to create their own future. Most Evangelical leaders are opposed to the use of any method of divination, often seeing this as the Devil's work. Both groups nonetheless share a view of the world as enchanted.

As table 4.10 indicates, divination methods are quite popular among contemporary Pagans, particularly the use of tarot. The question asked which of these forms of divination the respondent found useful. With the one exception of palmistry, which only 10 percent of both solitary and group practitioners found useful, those who practice in a group found all forms of divination more useful than solitary practitioners. Only 8 percent of group practitioners and 13.7 percent of solitary practitioners find none of these methods of divination helpful. The difference between group and solitary practitioners is small throughout, but nonetheless those in groups are more likely to view most methods of divination as efficacious. The data does not provide a clear reason, but it is possible that the group encourages each participant to see the tarot reading or other forms of divination as being applicable to their lives—pointing things out that the individual might miss on her or his own. The majority of all contemporary Pagans have altered their behavior based on some method or methods of divination, although those in groups are more likely to have changed their behavior than solitary practitioners.

TABLE 4.10. *Divination for Solo and Group Practitioners (in percentages)*

FORM OF DIVINATION	SOLO	GROUP
Tarot	71.5	77.7
Astrology	38.2	44.9
Runes	35.8	43.2
Palmistry	10.2	10.0
Numerology	16.8	18.7
I-Ching	10.3	12.9
Psychic readings	22.5	29.1
None	13.7	8.0
Altered behavior based on divination	56.7	66.8

Tarot is the most popular form of divination among contemporary Pagans. It is much more popular than astrology, which like tarot is popular within the general U.S. population. This is true for both younger and older participants. The young are slightly more likely than their elders to find all forms of divination more efficacious, but the difference is slight, and they are equally likely to have altered their behavior based on divination.

TABLE 4.11. *Divination and Gender for Solo and Group Practitioners (in percentages)*

FORM OF DIVINATION	SOLO WOMEN	SOLO MEN	GROUP WOMEN	GROUP MEN
Tarot	75.8	58.9	81.8	65.8
Astrology	41.1	29.2	49.2	35.3
Runes	34.6	39.0	40.0	50.6
Palmistry	11.6	6.0	11.1	7.7
Numerology	17.8	14.0	19.4	17.3
I-Ching	8.9	14.3	12.1	14.3
Psychic readings	24.7	16.4	31.0	25.2
None	11.4	20.6	7.2	10.1
Altered behavior based on divination	57.3	55.0	67.5	66.1

As table 4.11 indicates a larger factor in how efficacious an individual finds divination than type of practice or age is the gender of the participant. With the exception of palmistry, which is one of the two least popular forms of divination among contemporary Pagans, women find all forms of divination more helpful than men do. Women in groups find all the forms of divination more efficacious than women in solitary practice, who in turn view it more favorably than men in groups. Solitary men are least likely to find these practices helpful. Nonetheless almost 60 percent of solitary male practitioners find tarot to be helpful. Looking at the two extremes in our sample, one-fifth of male solitary practitioners find none of the forms of divination helpful as compared to only 7 percent of women who work in a group. On the one hand, this does indicate that gender combined with form of practice strongly influences how efficacious contemporary Pagans find divination. On the other hand, most U.S. contemporary Pagans do find some form of divination, most likely tarot, to be helpful in informing their decisions.

Because there is some comparative data in the literature, the survey asked more questions about people's beliefs in astrology than about the other forms of divination listed. In retrospect more should also have been included on tarot, which is such a strong favorite among contemporary Pagans. The data on astrology is nonetheless of interest, particularly as it indicates that many more people have tried astrology than claim they find it useful. This is probably also true for the other forms of divination.

The data shown in table 4.12 provides further evidence for both gender and form of practice having an effect on practices, with women in groups on the whole being the most likely and men who practice alone the least likely to do each of the activities listed. Men in groups were about as likely as women who practice alone to purchase a computerized horoscope. Interestingly, in response to questions that asked whether the respondent had visited an astrologer or had had a friend draw up a chart, the form of practice of the respondents was more important than their gender. Approximately the same percentages of both women and men who work in a group have visited an astrologer, and this is a larger percentage than either men or women who practice alone. Those in a group regardless of gender are more likely to have a friend draw up a free astrology chart. Men in groups are slightly more likely to do this than women in groups, and again both men and women who practice alone are about 20 percent less likely than those in groups to have a friend draw up a chart. Those who work in groups are probably more likely to have a coven mate who creates astrology charts for all interested members in the group than those who practice alone are to know someone who will do that for them. Fewer contemporary Pagans have taken a course on how to do an astrology reading than have purchased a book about doing it. This is in part because contemporary Pagans read; they buy books in many areas of interest and are often proud of their large and varied libraries. The difference is also undoubtedly the result of astrology courses costing more than a how-to book. Solitary male practitioners stand out as the least likely to either take a course or buy a book about astrology.

TABLE 4.12. *Astrology by Form of Practice and Gender (in percentages)*

	SOLO WOMEN	GROUP WOMEN	SOLO MEN	GROUP MEN
Purchased a computerized horoscope reading	29.3	32.6	19.7	29.2
Visited an astrologer	21.0	34.5	19.0	32.7
Had a friend draw up a chart for free	43.2	60.2	42.4	64.7
Drawn up their own astrological chart	37.1	44.6	31.3	40.2
Read a teach-yourself astrology book	56.4	59.5	41.8	50.9
Taken an astrology course in person or online	12.0	22.9	8.3	20.8
Given an astrology reading	15.6	19.5	12.7	20.3

Both Pew and Gallup have found that among the general American public women were more likely than men to believe in the efficacy of astrology. The Pew study found that 28 percent of women and 21 percent of men believed that astrology was true (Pew 2009.) Similarly Gallup found that 23 percent of men and 28 percent of women believed in the efficacy of astrology (Lyons 2005). Not surprisingly more contemporary Pagans believe in the efficacy of astrology than the general American public, but the difference between genders is even greater; 43.0 percent of women and 31.1 percent of men in "The Pagan Census Revisited" claim to find astrology useful. This is a higher bar than the question asked in the Pew or Gallup polls, which asked respondents if they believed in astrology. Probably more contemporary Pagans would have agreed that they believe that astrology works than that they found it useful for themselves. It is interesting, nonetheless, to note that the gender difference in the general public can also been seen in the data for contemporary Pagans. This suggests, as does other data that will be discussed in this chapter, that contemporary Pagans are influenced even in spiritual matters not only by their own religious community but by the larger American culture.

The General Social Survey most recently in 2014 asked how scientific both men and women considered astrology; "The Pagan Census Revisited" asked the same question. The results are presented in table 4.13. The middle two columns represent the percentages of all American men and women's views of how scientific astrology is, ranging from very scientific to not scientific at all. The first two columns provide the same data for women who practice alone or in groups and the last two columns provide that data for men who practice alone or in groups. Form of practice has no influence on how scientific contemporary Pagans find astrology, but gender does. Contemporary Pagan women are more likely to find it scientific than contemporary Pagan men. This gender difference is more pronounced than in the general American public, among whom women are only slightly more likely to believe that astrology is scientific than men. Contemporary Pagans are much more likely than Americans in general to believe that astrology is either scientific or somewhat scientific.

Being in group practice instead of being a solitary practitioner has some effect on how efficacious contemporary Pagans find astrology but not how scientific. However, this pales next to the difference between contemporary Pagans and non-Pagan Americans; contemporary Pagans are more likely to find astrology both useful and scientific than the average American. Women are more likely to find astrology scientific than men in both the general American and contemporary Pagan populations.

One study of Canadian undergraduates found that the gender differences in paranormal beliefs were substantially, but not completely, mitigated by college major (Gray 1990). Males are more likely than females to be science, technology,

TABLE 4.13. *Beliefs in Scientific Foundation of Astrology by Form of Practice and Gender Including Data for General U.S. Population (in percentages)*

	SOLO WOMEN	GROUP WOMEN	U.S. (NON-PAGAN) WOMEN	U.S. (NON-PAGAN) MEN	SOLO MEN	GROUP MEN
Very scientific	16.6	16.4	6.5	5.6	11.2	12.1
Sort of scientific	48.8	48.9	29.6	27.0	42.1	44.5
Not at all scientific	21.1	22.7	60.6	64.0	33.8	33.3
Don't know	13.5	12.0	3.3	3.3	12.9	9.3

engineering, and math (STEM) majors; this is even truer for contemporary Pagans than other Americans. According to the GSS 34 percent of U.S. men and 27 percent of U.S. women major in one of the STEM subjects. Comparatively 38 percent of contemporary Pagan men and 20 percent of contemporary Pagan women major in the sciences, math, or engineering. The larger difference may in part be explained by the much higher rate of college attendance and graduation among contemporary Pagans than other Americans, but it is nonetheless surprising as contemporary Pagan men have a slightly higher rate of majoring in STEM subjects than the typical American male. This is not true for contemporary Pagan women, who have a lower rate of majoring in these subjects than other American women college graduates.

Male science majors are the least likely to believe that astrology is scientific. As the data in table 4.14 indicates, 43.6 percent of male scientists state that astrology is not scientific. This can be compared to 32.9 percent of other male contemporary Pagans who view astrology as not scientific at all. Among contemporary Pagan women 28.8 percent of those who are science majors and 21.4 percent of other women state that astrology is not scientific at all. As in the Canadian study, although majoring in a natural science does affect how scientific one believes astrology is, gender is a more important indicator. However, contemporary Pagans regardless of college major or occupation are more likely to view astrology as scientific than those outside the religion. Even the most skeptical contemporary Pagans—male scientists—are less likely than other Americans be believe that astrology is not scientific at all. The community both online and in person helps to support a greater belief in both the efficacy and scientific basis of this form of divination.

TABLE 4.14. *How Scientific Astrology Is by Major and Gender (in percentages)*

	VERY	SOMEWHAT	NOT AT ALL	DON'T KNOW
Humanities	13	45	28	14
Social sciences	15	46	27	11
Science	11.1	42.7	34.8	11.4
Women science majors	13.1	45.7	28.8	12.4
Men science majors	8.5	38.0	43.6	10.9
All women	16.5	49.1	21.4	13.0
All men	11.7	43.5	32.9	11.9

The influence of gender and form of practice is less clear on other areas of metaphysical belief than it is on astrology. We asked six metaphysical questions, the first five of which also appeared in "The Pagan Census." They were included in the first survey as they permitted us to compare the responses from "The Pagan Census" with those in the GSS. In *Voices from the Pagan Census* (H. Berger et al. 2003:42–43) we found that in all instances, contemporary Pagans had more of these experiences than the general American public. These questions were again included in "The Pagan Census Revisited" as they permitted a comparison between surveys. In table 4.15 the data is broken down by form of practice and gender. The last column provides the data from "The Pagan Census" for all contemporary Pagans. Although there is an increase in the percentage of contemporary Pagans between surveys who have often or several times seen events that happened at a great distance as they were happening, and felt they were in touch with someone who had died, or thought they were someplace they had been before but knew it was impossible, the increase was less clear for those who felt as though they were in touch with someone who was far away. In this last case women regardless of whether or not they practice in a group or alone were more likely to have this experience and to have it more often than those who answered the original survey; men were less likely to often have these experiences. Those who worked in groups regardless of gender were more likely to have felt as though they were very close to a powerful spiritual force than either those who practiced as solitaires or the earlier sample.

The data on divination would suggest that contemporary Pagan women are more involved with occult activities than their male counterparts. However, the data on metaphysical experiences somewhat mitigates this. Although there are some differences between men and women and whether or not they are a solitary practitioner, the picture this data presents is somewhat murky. This may be the result of these questions coming directly from the GSS and therefore neither

TABLE 4.15. *Metaphysical Beliefs by Form of Practice and Gender (in percentages)*

FELT AS THOUGH THEY WERE IN TOUCH WITH SOMEONE WHEN THEY WERE FAR AWAY

	SOLO WOMEN	*GROUP WOMEN*	*SOLO MEN*	*GROUP MEN*	*PC*
Never	6.9	7.1	10.0	8.0	6.9
Once or twice	18.4	19.0	24.1	19.0	22.5
Several times	28.4	30.5	31.4	35.8	34.8
Often	43.0	40.6	32.0	34.4	34.7
Can't answer	3.3	2.8	2.5	2.8	1.1

HAVE SEEN EVENTS THAT HAPPENED AT A GREAT DISTANCE AS THEY WERE HAPPENING

	SOLO WOMEN	*GROUP WOMEN*	*SOLO MEN*	*GROUP MEN*	*PC*
Never	44.1	43.7	42.4	38.4	54.4
Once or twice	25.4	27.3	26.4	24.7	26.7
Several times	13.6	12.5	16.1	18.3	11.3
Often	13.3	13.2	11.5	14.1	6.4
Can't answer	3.6	3.3	3.5	4.6	1.2

FELT AS THOUGH THEY WERE REALLY IN TOUCH WITH SOMEONE WHO HAD DIED

	SOLO WOMEN	*GROUP WOMEN*	*SOLO MEN*	*GROUP MEN*	*PC*
Never	16.8	14.1	23.8	17.8	25.7
Once or twice	27.8	29.5	31.4	30.0	35.7
Several times	23.6	23.7	21.9	22.8	23.0
Often	28.7	29.9	19.6	26.2	14.6
Can't answer	3.1	2.8	3.2	2.6	1.1

THOUGHT THEY WERE SOMEWHERE THEY HAD BEEN BEFORE BUT KNEW THAT IT WAS IMPOSSIBLE

	SOLO WOMEN	*GROUP WOMEN*	*SOLO MEN*	*GROUP MEN*	*PC*
Never	5.3	6.8	6.8	4.8	6.2
Once or twice	19.0	21.1	18.9	21.0	22.1
Several times	31.5	33.9	35.9	34.2	42.5
Often	40.5	35.9	35.6	35.6	28.1
Can't answer	3.7	2.4	2.9	4.4	1.1

FELT AS THOUGH THEY WERE VERY CLOSE TO A POWERFUL SPIRITUAL FORCE

	SOLO WOMEN	*GROUP WOMEN*	*SOLO MEN*	*GROUP MEN*	*PC*
Never	14.1	9.5	12.7	9.2	14.4
Once or twice	23.9	20.3	24.6	21.8	24.1
Several times	26.9	27.7	28.8	27.1	28.2
Often	31.0	38.9	30.0	39.3	32.2
Can't answer	4.0	3.6	3.9	3.2	1.1

RECEIVED PROPHECY, VISIONS, OR MESSAGES FROM THE SPIRIT WORLD

	SOLO WOMEN	*GROUP WOMEN*	*SOLO MEN*	*GROUP MEN*
Never	20.6	15.0	24.2	14.8
Once or twice	25.3	25.3	26.7	27.2
Several times	22.6	24.0	22.6	24.2
Often	25.8	30.7	20.3	29.6
Can't answer	5.7	5.0	6.1	4.2

being worded nor oriented toward the contemporary Pagan experience. The exception to this was the last two questions, only the first of which was from the GSS, but both of which are most closely aligned with contemporary Pagan beliefs and practices. These questions ask: (1) Have you ever felt as though you were very close to a powerful spiritual force? (2) Have you received prophecy, visions, or messages from the spirit world? As previously noted the role of ritual in most forms of contemporary Paganism is to help put the practitioner into an altered state where they are most likely to have these types of spiritual experiences. Group practitioners regardless of gender are more likely to have had both of these experiences and to have them more often than solitary practitioners. There are two possible explanations for this difference: Group practices may work to help create these experiences or may provide a context in which the experiences that people have are interpreted as being spiritually significant. Groups are more consistent in doing rituals for each of the sabbats as it is part of the group practice and expectations. Some solitary practitioners undoubtedly do all the rituals, but some may skip the less important ones, or do a truncated ritual when they are busy. This might make the group experience stronger. However, sociological and anthropological research has shown that all our experiences are mediated through our culture and social framework. Interpretations of spiritual experiences have a strong cultural overlay, with people from the same culture using similar words and images to describe what they have experienced. These two explanations are not mutually exclusive, and it is probable that both have an influence.

Afterlife

Not all contemporary Pagans adhere to the same view of the afterlife. Like all theological issues in the religion there is openness to personal interpretation and differences among spiritual paths. Nonetheless most have a similar view of the afterlife, which typically includes reincarnation. The most common beliefs, particularly among Wiccans, but others as well, is that the souls or essences of the dead enter an alternative place, typically referred to as Summerland, where they have a chance to reflect on their previous life, meet with those who went before them, and then prepare to return as a baby in a new life. Each life provides one with a new learning experience; some believe that people get the life that they require to further develop along their spiritual or moral path. But unlike for Buddhists there is no desire to leave this cycle of birth, death, and reincarnation. The difference between the more Eastern notion that one would like to end the cycle and the contemporary Pagan one may be a reflection of life being easier or more pleasant for what are primarily white, well-educated, middle class Americans than it is for those in poorer nations. Among contemporary Pagans there is a desire to return and again be among those that they love and care about, to have another chance, but another chance more or less in the world that they left.

In "The Pagan Census" we found that three-quarters of contemporary Pagans believe in reincarnation. Interestingly this has decreased somewhat, with 59.8 percent of solitary practitioners and 62.3 percent of group practitioners stating that reincarnation best describes their vision of the afterlife. What makes this particularly interesting is that at the same time there has been an increase of Americans who state that they believe in reincarnation. The GSS did not include a question on reincarnation when "The Pagan Census" was distributed, but Yankelovich Partners found that 25 percent of Americans in 1997 believed in reincarnation, which was a major increase from 9 percent in 1976 (H. Berger et al. 2003: 47). The GSS subsequently did include a question in which they permitted respondents to state if they believed reincarnation was likely or somewhat likely, not likely at all, unlikely, or that they did not know. About a third (33.1 percent) believed it to be likely or somewhat likely. The questions are not exactly the same, making a comparison between the 2004 question by the GSS and the earlier findings by the Yankelovich Partners imperfect. Nonetheless there does appear to be an increase in belief in reincarnation in the general public at the same time there is a decrease among contemporary Pagans, although contemporary Pagans are still more likely than the average American to believe in reincarnation.

Even though there has been a slight decrease in a belief in reincarnation among contemporary Pagans, it is still the most popular belief about the afterlife among members of this religion. About a third of both solitary and group practitioners claim that the soul or a part of consciousness lives on in another realm. About a quarter of the contemporary Pagan population believe that some part of the person survives and merges with the cosmos. The rest of the sample state they have other beliefs. The decrease in the percentage of those who believe in reincarnation suggests that other images of the afterlife are emerging within contemporary Paganism, although this should not be exaggerated as the majority still believes in reincarnation. Interestingly there are no real differences between those who practice in groups and alone, which is consistent with other findings that beliefs among contemporary Pagans are similar regardless of form of practice, but behavior and experiences are not.

What is more significant than form of practice is again the gender identification of the participant. As seen in table 4.16 contemporary Pagan women are more likely to believe in reincarnation than contemporary Pagan men regardless of form of practice. In response to the similar GSS question about belief in reincarnation, American women were more likely to definitely believe in reincarnation than men; 1.6 percent of men in the general public and 15.2 percent of women in the general public stated they definitely believed in reincarnation. The same percentage, 18.0 percent of both men and women in the general American public, thought it was probably true. Overall in the GSS women had a higher belief in reincarnation than men. The difference between men and women in the general American public was greater than the gender difference among contemporary Pagans. Nonetheless the gender differences among contemporary Pagans appear to reflect those in the larger culture. Many more contemporary Pagans believe in reincarnation than does the general American public. Gender in both populations plays an important role in spiritual and metaphysical beliefs, although somewhat less so for reincarnation among contemporary Pagans. This may be because reincarnation is such a strongly held belief among contemporary Pagans that gender is a less important factor.

TABLE 4.16. *Percentage Who Believe in Reincarnation by Form of Practice and Gender (in percentages)*

	FEMALE	MALE
Solo	62.4	52.3
Group	64.6	57.3

The gender differences that have been seen within contemporary Paganism parallel those found in the data from the GSS and the sociological literature on women's spirituality and religion. In the GSS women were more likely to report that they believed in an afterlife (74 percent versus 66 percent of men), more likely to consider themselves very or moderately religious (59 percent versus 48 percent of men), to view themselves as a very or moderately a spiritual person (72 percent versus 56 percent of men), and to believe that their religious outlook changed their lives. Churches normally have more women participating, and on the whole women are more likely to be clients for metaphysical practices (Sointu and Woodhead 2008). Interestingly in their research on who buys what they refer to as New Age materials in Texas, Daniel Mears and Christopher Ellison (2000:306–7) find that there are no significant gender differences. The only two questions that "The Pagan Census Revisited" had about purchasing New Age materials were both related to astrology, and in both cases women were more likely than men to purchase charts and books. The Texas data explored by Mears and Ellison may be an anomaly as it is only in one state. It is also hard to make further comparisons as they do not delineate what they are including in New Age materials. Their research is of a more general population and not of contemporary Pagans or other New Metaphysicals in particular. My data, like Sointu and Woodhead's, suggests that the gender difference extends to purchases as well as practices.

My survey was not designed to tease out theological differences among spiritual paths, but to provide an overview of contemporary Pagans practices, beliefs, and social and political activities within the wider context of non–contemporary Pagans. However, the survey did ask individuals to specify their spiritual path(s), permitting spiritual path to be one factor in interpreting behaviors and beliefs. The questions on metaphysical practices and divination show a good deal of consistency among spiritual paths with a few exceptions. Runes, a form of divination from northern Europe, which is based on the throwing of stones, each of which has a letter from the Old Norse alphabet, is particularly appealing to Heathens (Snook 2015:2). Each of the letters has meaning, and their combination is interpreted to predict the future. The system has some similarity to tarot in that there is a need to interpret each individual card or symbol within the larger context of the others picked or thrown. The Nordic background of the system makes it particularly popular among members of this spiritual path, although it is also practiced by members of other spiritual paths. Even among members of the spiritual path least likely to use runes—Wiccans—more than a third (38.2 percent) find them efficacious.

Heathens are the only group for whom tarot is not the most popular form of divination. Wiccans and Witches have the strongest affinity toward tarot, with respectively 80.6 percent and 81.4 percent noting that they have found it efficacious. Nonetheless just over 50 percent of Heathens find tarot useful. Heathens also stand out as being the least likely to believe in reincarnation; less than half (46.4 percent) believe in it. Consistent with the other data on gender differences Heathen women are more likely than Heathen men to believe in reincarnation—49.1 percent of the former and 43.6 percent of the latter claim to see it as part of their image of the afterlife.

Heathen theology is based on Sagas—tales of the gods, goddesses, and their relationship with one another and with men and women—none of which give a consistent view of the afterlife. The best known of these describe Valhalla, where brave warriors, particularly those who died in battle, go to spend their days fighting and their evenings feasting. For those who do not die a warrior's death there are alternative images of the afterlife. The most common is Hel, which is not equivalent to the Christian Hell. It is neither hot, nor necessarily unpleasant, although one section of it is. Some of the dead return as ghosts, and there is a belief that some will be reincarnated back into their family line (Paxson 2006). The ambiguity of beliefs regarding the afterlife in the Sagas, as well as variations among practitioners, explains the lower rate of belief in reincarnation among this spiritual path.

Heathens are also the least likely spiritual path to practice magic, with under a third (30.6 percent) stating that they practice it often or regularly and 13.4 percent stating they never practice magic. It is unclear why they practice less magic. Heathens have several distinct forms of magic, which are considered part of their practices. Unlike Wiccans, who eschew any magic that harms others, Heathens accept curses as part of magical practice—preferably limited—but not separate from the rest. It might be the acceptance of what is often referred to as left-handed magic that results in Heathens using it less. As described by Diana Paxson (2006) Heathen magic is part of a larger spiritual framework. It often involves meditation and connection with the spirit world, of either the divine or the dead. One Ásatrú man, for instance, responding to "The Pagan Census Revisited" question that asked him to describe a particularly effective or meaningful magical working, describes the process of "Utsetia (Sitting Out as in seeking visions or spiritually traveling)" as an important element of that magical act. An Ásatrú woman describes getting a tattoo of particular runes "because not only did it mean passive protection, it meant beloved of the gods. When I had it tattooed . . . I could feel the truth in it, that i really was loved. To this day i do not worry about my future because i know that i have a shield that will protect me from the worst storms, and the love that i feel every day [quoted material presented unaltered and uncorrected]." In both these instances magic was part of their religious practice. Heathen women's most common magical practice, like that of other contemporary Pagan woman, is healing for others.

There are no regional differences of metaphysical beliefs or in the belief in the efficacy of divination. This is consistent with the data from Gallup, which indicates that region does not influence paranormal beliefs among the general American public (Moore 2005).

United Kingdom and Canada

There are some cultural differences between the United States and both the United Kingdom and Canada, but the general influence of solitary practice and gender on metaphysical practices and beliefs remains consistent in both these countries with the findings in the United States. On the whole gender has a larger influence on metaphysical beliefs; women have more and stronger metaphysical beliefs and practices than men regardless of form of practice in both the United Kingdom and Canada. Nonetheless solitary practice in both of these countries does result in a lower rate of participation in most metaphysical practices

Looking specifically at table 4.17, it is clear that group practitioners in the United Kingdom and Canada, as in the United States, use each of the specified forms of divination more than those who practice alone. There are only two exceptions: palmistry and I-Ching. Solitary practitioners in the United Kingdom use palmistry more than their compatriots in group practice, and there is virtually no difference in the use of this form of divination among American contemporary Pagans regardless of form of practice. I-Ching is practiced slightly more among solitary Canadian contemporary Pagans than those in groups, unlike in the United States and United Kingdom, where, as with the other forms of divination, group practitioners are slightly more likely to practice I-Ching. Both palmistry and I-Ching are among the least popular forms of divination among contemporary Pagans in all three countries, which might explain this deviation from the norm, particularly true in the United Kingdom and Canada, where the sample sizes were significantly smaller than in the United States. In both the United Kingdom and Canada, as in the United States, gender plays a more important role than does form of practice in the extent to which individuals find each form of divination helpful. The only exception is that of runes, which U.K. male contemporary Pagans find more useful than their female counterpart. Runes are, as previously noted, associated with Heathens, which has drawn more men to it than other forms of contemporary Paganism. But, since Heathens are a minor percentage of the contemporary Pagan population in all three countries it would only partially explain the difference.

American contemporary Pagans are more likely to alter their behavior based on divination than contemporary Pagans in the other two countries. American women who practice in groups are more likely to alter their behavior than either their male counterparts or those who practice alone. However, American practitioners in groups, regardless of gender, are more likely to alter their behavior based on divination than those who are solitary. There is basically no gender difference between contemporary Pagan men and women in Canada or the United Kingdom to the degree that they have altered their behavior based on divination, and there is only a small difference between those who practice alone or in groups. More interesting is that in all three countries almost a half or more have altered their behavior based on divination. Among contemporary Pagans in all three countries it is American group practitioners who are the most likely to alter their behavior based on divination.

On the whole there is a consistency among the three nations of which forms of divination are the most popular. Regardless of form of practice or gender, tarot is the most popular form of divination by far, and on the whole they decrease in popularity in the same order. Astrology, however, which is the second most popular form of divination in the United States, is the third most popular in the other two countries. Runes, which are the third most popular in the United States, are second in both the United Kingdom and Canada. American group practitioners are more likely to find runes useful than either solitary or group practitioners in the United Kingdom and at the same rate as Canadian group practitioners. There is a slightly lower interest in the United Kingdom and Canada in astrology than the United States, which accounts for astrology being ranked second in the United States and third in the other two countries.

In both the United Kingdom and Canada, as in the United States, men are more likely to find astrology not at all scientific than are women. Table 4.18 indicates that slightly less than a third of British men (32.5 percent) and over half of British women (52.5 percent) consider astrology very or sort of scientific. More Canadian contemporary Pagans believe that astrology is scientific than do the British, but again there is a large gender difference with less than half of Canadian contemporary Pagan men (45.5 percent) and more than half of women (60.8 percent) stating that astrology is very or sort of scientific. Contemporary American Pagans as seen in table 4.13 are about as likely as their Canadian peers to view astrology as scientific or somewhat scientific, but the gender difference is much more strongly pronounced in both Canada and the United Kingdom than it is in the United States. The United Kingdom also shows a strong

TABLE 4.17. *Divination by Country, Gender, and Form of Practice (in percentages)*

	U.K. SOLO	U.K. GROUP	U.K. FEMALE	U.K. MALE	CANADA SOLO	CANADA GROUP	CANADA FEMALE	CANADA MALE	U.S. SOLO	U.S. GROUP
Tarot	68.9	72.7	74.0	57.7	69.9	78.4	75.6	62.7	71.5	77.7
Astrology	24.1	27.3	27.5	18.7	33.8	36.0	35.9	27.5	38.2	44.9
Runes	37.3	31.8	39.5	31.7	42.3	43.2	41.6	44.1	35.8	43.2
Palmistry	9.0	6.1	8.5	6.5	11.5	12.6	13.3	7.8	10.2	10.0
Numerology	12.7	15.2	13.0	11.4	14.9	19.8	17.1	13.7	16.8	18.7
I-Ching	11.8	13.6	9.0	16.3	9.7	9.0	7.9	13.7	10.3	12.9
Psychic reading	20.3	21.2	24.5	14.6	21.2	24.3	25.1	14.7	22.5	29.1
None	14.2	6.1	8.5	19.5	15.6	16.2	12.7	24.5	13.7	8.0
Altered behavior based on divination	49.8	47.7	48.2	44.9	49.8	51.8	51.0	50.0	56.7	66.8

TABLE 4.18. *Belief in Scientific Basis of Astrology in Canada and the United Kingdom (in percentages)*

	U.K. SOLO	U.K. GROUP	U.K. FEMALE	U.K. MALE	CANADA SOLO	CANADA GROUP	CANADA FEMALE	CANADA MALE
Very scientific	7.1	3.0	7.5	4.9	10.8	10.0	12.1	7.9
Sort of scientific	37.3	50.0	45.0	2 7.6	45.7	50.9	48.7	37.6
Not at all scientific	44.3	34.8	36.0	52.0	27.9	26.4	24.2	40.6
Don't know	11.3	12.1	10.5	15.4	15.6	12.7	15.0	13.9

difference between solitary and group practitioners with those who practice in a group more likely than those who are solitaries to believe that astrology is at least somewhat scientific. These differences are less pronounced in North America. Clearly, although there is a good deal of international consistency among English-speaking contemporary Pagans, there are cultural differences. As in the United States, gender is of greater importance than is form of practice in how scientific astrology is perceived to be.

Considering astrology to be unscientific does not necessarily mean that individuals do not use it. It is possible to believe that, although something is non-scientific, it is nonetheless efficacious or worth considering. In fact prayer works this way at least some of the time. Most people who pray would not suggest that this is based on science; in fact they would most likely see it as a matter of faith as opposed to science. According to Pew 45 percent of Americans use prayer and religious meditation for making major decisions, and the majority of Americans believe that their prayers are answered at least some of the time (Lipka 2016). Similarly contemporary Pagans, even those who do not believe it is scientific, may use astrology or tarot to aid them in making decisions. They may believe it helpful, either because they believe that they are getting divine guidance or because they see it as a way to clarify their own thinking.

Although belief in the scientific basis of astrology is more affected by gender than form of practice, actual behaviors are, on the whole, more consistently affected by form of practice. Just as in the United States, being in a group results in contemporary Pagans in Canada and the United Kingdom doing more activities that involve astrology than those who practice alone. Gender is less clearly a factor. As can be seen in table 4.19, members of groups are more likely to purchase computerized horoscopes, visit an astrologer, have a friend draw up a chart for free, draw up their own chart, teach themselves astrology through reading a book, or take a course than those in solitary practice in either the United Kingdom or Canada. The data in table 4.19 for gender is mixed. For example although Canadian males are less likely than their female counterparts to purchase a computerized horoscope, they are more likely to have a friend draw one up. Male contemporary Pagans in the United Kingdom are more likely than their female counterparts to purchase a computerized horoscope but less likely to either have read a book or taken a course to learn to do horoscopes. This is different than in the United States, in which gender and form of practice both influence the rate at which contemporary Pagans participate in each of the astrology activities listed in tables 4.19 and 4.12. In the United States women who work in groups are the most likely, and men who practice alone the least likely, to participate in each of these activities. Furthermore American contemporary Pagans are more likely than their British or Canadian counterparts to do each of these activities. However there is an overall similarity, with the same activities

TABLE 4.19. *Astrology Practices in the United Kingdom and Canada by Form of Practice and Gender (in percentages)*

	U.K. SOLO	U.K. GROUP	U.K. FEMALE	U.K. MALE	CANADA SOLO	CANADA GROUP	CANADA FEMALE	CANADA MALE
Purchases a computerized horoscope reading	19.1	23.1	19.4	23.9	16.2	20.0	19.4	11.2
Visited an astrologer	11.0	15.6	11.3	15.4	17.8	33.6	22.6	21.0
Had a friend draw up a chart for free	30.6	49.2	32.3	40.2	38.9	48.2	42.1	44.4
Drawn up their own astrological chart	27.3	41.5	31.3	33.1	27.2	43.6	33.0	28.1
Read a teach-yourself astrology book	43.3	50.8	45.6	42.2	48.1	57.7	56.7	38.8
Taken an astrology course in person or online	4.3	16.9	10.2	3.4	8.0	14.7	10.1	10.1
Given an astrology reading	11.0	14.3	10.3	16.2	9.6	17.4	13.4	3.3

being the most popular and others being the least popular in all three nations.

In the United Kingdom and Canada, as in the United States, there is no consistent difference between solitary and group practitioners in how likely they were to have felt as though they were in touch with someone far away, seen events that happened at a great distance, felt as though they were in touch with someone who had died, or thought they were somewhere that they had been before but knew that it was impossible. With the one exception of seeing events at a great distance, most contemporary Pagans in all three countries have had each of these experiences, and with the exception of being in touch with someone who is dead did so at least several times. This suggests an international consistency among contemporary Pagans and one that is affected neither by form of practice nor by gender.

As in the United States, group practitioners in the United Kingdom and Canada are more likely to feel close to a powerful spiritual force or to have received prophecy, visions, or messages from the spirit world than those who practice alone (table 4.20). Nonetheless most contemporary Pagans regardless of form of practice or gender were likely to have both of these experiences, which indicates that these experiences are important to all contemporary Pagans. However, the frequency that individuals have these experiences is greater for group practitioners than for solitaries in all three countries.

In the United Kingdom and Canada as in the United States most contemporary Pagans believe in an afterlife. Only 4.8 percent of solitary practitioners and 4.5 percent of group practitioners in Canada, 4.2 of solitary and 1.5 percent of group practitioners in the United Kingdom, and 2.8 percent of solitary and 2.7 percent of group practitioners in the United States do not believe in an afterlife. On the whole American contemporary Pagans are less likely than those in the other two countries to state that they believe there is not an afterlife. The majority of Canadian contemporary Pagans believe in reincarnation. Group practitioners in the United Kingdom and Canada, like their counterparts in the United States, are more likely to believe in reincarnation; 56.5 percent of solitary and 61.3 percent of group practitioners in Canada and 39.2 percent of solitary and 45.5 percent of group practitioners in the United States believe in reincarnation. The United Kingdom stands out as the only one of the three countries where the majority of contemporary Pagans do not believe in reincarnation. The percentage of contemporary Pagans in the United Kingdom who believe in reincarnation is still higher than that in the general British public, which is 27 percent (BBC News 2009). This is about the same percentage of Americans who believe in reincarnation. The difference is therefore not cultural as belief in reincarnation is no more or less popular in the United Kingdom than it is in North America. However what does differ is that the United Kingdom has a higher percentage of Druids and a lower percentage of Wiccans and eclectics than either

TABLE 4.20. *Metaphysical Experiences for the United Kingdom and Canada by Gender and Form of Practice (in percentages)*

FELT AS THOUGH THEY WERE VERY CLOSE TO A POWERFUL SPIRITUAL FORCE

	U.K. SOLO	U.K. GROUP	U.K. FEMALE	U.K. MALE	CANADA SOLO	CANADA GROUP	CANADA FEMALE	CANADA MALE	U.S. SOLO	U.S. GROUP
Never	10.1	6.2	6.7	11.4	13.6	13.8	11.9	17.2	13.7	9.4
Once or twice	26.9	13.8	26.9	17.9	33.3	21.1	27.1	29.3	24.1	20.8
Several times	31.7	33.8	31.6	30.1	22.0	31.2	24.8	23.2	27.4	27.4
Often	30.3	46.2	32.6	37.4	28.0	30.3	33.5	24.2	30.7	39.1
Can't answer	1.0	-	2.1	3.3	3.0	3.7	2.6	6.1	4.1	3.3

RECEIVED PROPHECY, VISIONS, OR MESSAGES FROM THE SPIRIT WORLD

	U.K. SOLO	U.K. GROUP	U.K. FEMALE	U.K. MALE	CANADA SOLO	CANADA GROUP	CANADA FEMALE	CANADA MALE	U.S. SOLO	U.S. GROUP
Never	27.3	16.2	24.1	26.0	27.5	20.6	22.1	31.6	21.4	14.9
Once or twice	29.7	24.2	28.2	25.2	22.9	27.1	24.1	24.5	25.7	26.0
Several times	17.7	21.2	20.0	17.1	22.9	23.4	23.1	19.4	22.7	24.1
Often	20.1	33.3	23.1	24.4	22.5	23.4	27.0	17.3	24.4	30.0
Can't answer	5.3	4.5	4.6	7.4	4.2	5.6	3.6	7.1	5.8	4.7

of the other two countries. In the United Kingdom 19.1 percent of contemporary Pagans claim to be Druids as compared to the United States, in which 11.5 percent, and Canada, in which 9.1 percent, are Druids. Although Wicca originated in the United Kingdom, only 27.5 percent of British Pagans are Wiccan, which can be compared to 37.1 percent of both Canadian and American contemporary Pagans who claim to be Wiccan. Only 38.3 percent of British contemporary Pagans are eclectic as compared to 45.7 percent in the United States and 52.6 percent in Canada. Druids have a lower rate of acceptance of reincarnation than either Wiccans or eclectics, which accounts for this overall difference.

Ronald Hutton (2009:21), a historian who has tracked Druidism from its earliest forms in the British Isles, found that the early Druids believed in "reincarnation of human beings after death in their familiar bodies and their familiar society in a parallel world," which is clearly a different concept than the reincarnation of a soul into a new and different body and possibly even into a different country or society. Contemporary Druids differ among themselves in their belief in reincarnation (Cooper 2010). According to the Order of Bards, Ovates and Druids, the largest Druid organization in the United Kingdom, there is no inconsistency in the belief in reincarnation and Druidism. Nonetheless in the United Kingdom fewer Druids have come to accept reincarnation than in the United States. This may in fact be the influence of Hutton's scholarship. Although an academic Hutton is a popular writer among contemporary Pagans; he is the sixth most cited writer in my survey. There is, nonetheless, a healthy minority of Druids in the United Kingdom that do believe in reincarnation, and they do adhere to this belief at a higher rate than others in the United Kingdom.

"The Pagan Census" included a number of descriptions of the afterlife that were taken directly from the General Social Survey and were repeated in "The Pagan Census Revisited." Two of them—"a life without many things which make our present life enjoyable, and "a pale shadowy form of life, hardly life at all"—were particularly unpopular among the respondents to "The Pagan Census Revisited" with less than 15 percent in all three nations considering either of these very or somewhat likely. The most popular was "reunion with loved ones." This was believed to be very or somewhat likely by the majority in all three countries. Contemporary Pagans in all three nations tend to have an upbeat notion of this and the afterlife, which may be the effect of their social status as primarily members of the white middle class or an influence of their sense of empowerment provided by their magical practices.

Conclusion

As noted previously, being a group member is associated with greater social activity; it is also associated with an increase in spiritual and metaphysical practices. However, while gender played a minor role in social activities, it plays a more important one for metaphysical beliefs and practices. On the whole women in mainstream religions are also more spiritually engaged; they are more likely to the attend church and to pray than are men. The GSS, for example, in 2014 found that 66 percent of women and 44 percent of men prayed at least once a day. Although the majority of Americans pray at least weekly, women are more likely to pray than men. Contemporary Pagan women are more likely to participate in most divination practices, but interestingly the performance of magic does not have as clear a gender bias. Women are less likely than men to never do magic, but they also tend to do it less frequently than men. Divination and magic as practiced by contemporary Pagans are not that dissimilar to prayer. Like prayer both magic and divination put the person in contact with the divine or otherworld. It provides a means of seeking guidance or changing a bad or unpleasant situation.

Americans are most likely to pray, and contemporary Pagans most likely to do magic, for health for themselves or others (Crowley 2000; Almendrala 2016). Divination is often used to help the person focus on what is happening in their lives and what avenues of activity might help them achieve a favorable outcome. This is not that dissimilar to prayer, in which one relies on the divine to help to guide one through life's hardships and in one's choices. There are clear differences as well; magic provides practitioners a greater sense of power. In prayer one is petitioning either God or a saint to provide help, while magic provides more of a sense of control. But the two at times blur together. In *Thank You, St. Jude,* Robert Orsi (1995) describes how those who pray to the saint of lost causes believe that he needs their prayers almost as much as they require his help. Furthermore, as in magic, in which one gives something in exchange for the wished-for end, Orsi describes a sense that when St. Jude makes a prayer come true, something else will be taken. The child who was prayed for will survive the illness, but the family will lose their home or one parent his or her job. These are larger sacrifices than are normally offered by magicians in exchange for their wishes and, unlike in magic, are not offered by the petitioner but taken. However, magicians do not believe that all their magic works, nor that it necessarily occurs as the person wishes it. The divine never comes completely under their power. The divine or spirits may not do the magic or may twist it in a way that it is almost unrecognizable. Nonetheless it is the greater control that magic provides that may make it more comfortable for men to practice. It is the vagaries of magic that might make it more likely to be practiced in groups than among solitaries. Magic might backfire; it might affect the person who does it more than the object it was directed at. Groups also help provide a venue in which individuals can get a tarot reading or an astrology chart done for free, making it more likely that they will be used.

Beliefs are less affected by form of practice and are more affected by gender. The greater belief that women possess in the scientific basis of astrology is in part mitigated by scientific education but not completely. Women are also more likely to believe in the efficacy of most of the other forms of divination other than runes, which is most closely associated with Heathens, a spiritual path of contemporary Paganism that has more men than any other. There are very few differences either regionally within the United States or between in United States and other English-speaking nations. This suggests a homogenization of beliefs among contemporary Pagans, which is the result of greater reliance on printed matter and the Internet for learning about Paganism as more and more individuals becomes solitary practitioners.

The similarity of beliefs that were found among contemporary Pagans, both those who practice alone and in groups as well as nationally and internationally, belies a notion of contemporary Paganism as a truly private or individualized religion. Although each contemporary Pagan is responsible for her or his own spiritual practices and beliefs, the reliance on the same authors, websites, and sharing of this information at festivals and other in-person sites indicates that these ideas are part of a social world. Contemporary Pagans develop a spiritual language or a way of viewing the metaphysical experiences they have had and that they court through rituals and meditative practices. Descriptions of ritual and meditative practices and the framework for interpreting them are shared both nationally and internationally

Kelly Besecke (2005) has observed that religions, such as contemporary Paganism, that are referred to as private or individualized religions are often viewed as less consequential as they are believed to have little, if any, effect on social life. Theorists such as Putnam and Bellah have argued that private religions will not ultimately provide social cohesion for a society. As Linda Woodhead (2013:36) wrote, spirituality is "stigmatized for being nothing more than an inflated narcissism centered on a 'cosmic self.'" But as I have argued in this chapter, contemporary Pagans have a moral compass. It is one based on radical empathy in which they believe their spirituality and their magical practices connect them intimately with the "other," both human and nonhuman, and that it requires that they act on that empathy. There are no hard-and-fast rules for moral behavior as are found in Christianity or Judaism. However, as with other aspects of contemporary Paganism even for those who practice alone, morality is part of a larger ongoing dialogue within the community. It is simultaneously personal and negotiated. Radical empathy provides a way of connecting to all living things, of wanting for the other what one would want, in fact be willing to have, for oneself.

This type of morality has been associated with women (H. Berger and Ezzy 2007). As Woodhead (2013) highlights, Bellah and his coauthors (1985) describe this type of spirituality as feminized, emotional, and sentimental, viewing it as providing at most a sense of therapeutic well-being for practitioners. My data indicates women are more drawn to this religion than men. The Goddess or goddesses are for most practitioners more central to their worship than the God or gods. It was the image of the divine female that has attracted many of the women to the religion. While Bellah and his coauthors may see feminization negatively these participants see it as a positive change for the world, one in which what is typically labeled as female—caring, for the earth, for the other, for those in need of help—becomes central. Many of the rituals and techniques are used for healing the self both physically and emotionally. In an era of "#metoo" it is clear that there are many wounds inflicted particularly on women that require healing. As Woodhead argues spirituality permits women a venue to care for the self as well as the other. For many women this is a radical act, when culturally they are socialized to always put others first. It is this acceptance of care for the self that has resulted in the religion being labeled narcissistic. However, the self is not the only focus. It is a starting point in which one engages the world and, as will be shown in the next chapter, can result in social engagement and activism.

CHAPTER 5

Politics, Social Engagement, and Disengagement

One reason that social theorists such as Putnam and Campbell (2010) and Bruce (1996, 2003) are concerned about what they perceive as the growth of social isolation is that they believe it results in a decrease of social engagement, particularly political participation. What, however, constitutes political activity? This may at first seem obvious, but current social theory brings it into question. Anthony Giddens (1991) was one of the first to argue that in late modernity a new form of politics, which he called lifestyle politics, emerged. This is the politics of life choices made by individuals that result in changes in policies. An example would be choosing to recycle and to purchase goods that are made from recycled or reclaimed materials, which has helped to fuel the development of curbside recycling programs in many neighborhoods. He distinguishes this form of politics from the older form, which he refers to as emancipatory politics—activities like voting, demonstrating, or signing petitions. He attributes the development of this new form of politics to the growth in globalization, whose hallmarks include the development of the Internet and other forms of instant communication, and the current relative ease and speed of long-distance travel, all of which he argues have transformed human interactions including political actions.

More recently Linda Woodhead (2009b, 2013) has demonstrated that simultaneous with the changes in our conception of what constitutes political actions, there has been a change in our notion of what constitutes religion. These changes, she argues, are linked. Building on Stephen Warner's important (1993) article, "Work in Progress: Toward a New Paradigm for the Sociological Study of Religion in the United States," she suggests that in addition to the two eras or paradigms Warner discusses—the old and the new—there is a third, which she calls the emerging paradigm. As Warner describes, in the old paradigm churches were linked to the state, which they helped to stabilize. Most members of the society were born into the church, which defined national identity and informed the inhabitants' worldview. These churches helped to legitimate monarchs and the state. This was religion as it existed in Europe for over a thousand years. It never existed in the United States, which from its inception followed what Warner calls the new paradigm of congregationalism. Congregations are voluntary associations that acknowledge many forms of religious "truth." Their power exists only to the degree that they can encourage their members to be politically active in voting or supporting particular policies. The religious right in the United States has been notably successful in using this form of politics.

Woodhead contends that although Warner is correct that there has been a growth of congregationalism, not only in the United States but throughout the world, that there have been further changes in late modernity, most important the growth of spirituality, including what in the past has been called the New Age, and of contemporary Paganism. According to Woodhead, the various forms of spirituality that exist in the West are simultaneously local and international as participants interact with others at local venues like metaphysical classes and internationally on the Internet. The impact of spirituality is often hidden but can be discerned in things like meditation or drumming groups that have appeared in business milieus, among other places, or the use of alternative health practices, like those discussed chapter 3, becoming more common and even integrated into more traditional medicine. The political impact of these "emerging" spiritualities or religions often falls below the radar but nonetheless is of importance through what Giddens called life choices and Woodhead refers to as feeder projects such as feminism and environmentalism. They also can influence the political dialogue as was seen in the 99 percent movement, which appeared to have little immediate political impact but has in fact helped to fuel a debate about social inequity.

Contemporary Pagans are involved in life politics and in the feeder projects that Woodhead describes, but possibly more important, they are involved in direct political action—or to use Giddens's term, emancipatory politics. Unlike the religious right or Unitarian Universalists, this political action is not done as members of a congregation but as individuals, which may result in its appearing separate from the participants' religious or spiritual commitments but, nonetheless, may be influenced by it. In my first book, *A Community of Witches* (1999), which is an ethnography, I concluded, as had Margot Adler in her ethnographic work (1978), that contemporary Pagans were not politically active in the traditional way. I argued that contemporary Pagans were participating in life politics as they participated in environmentally friendly practices, questioned traditional gender roles, and celebrated all forms of sexuality, and a sizeable percentage became vegans or vegetarians. But when I changed from ethnographic to quantitative methods to do my first survey, "The Pagan Census," I was surprised to see that contemporary Pagans were politically active in traditional ways, such as voting, protesting, and signing petitions. In fact in *Voices from the Pagan Census* (H. Berger et al. 2003) we compared data collected by the Unitarian Universalist association on their membership and found that contemporary Pagans were as active as that notoriously politically liberal church. Similarly in this survey I find that contemporary Pagans on the whole are politically active in traditional ways, voting, demonstrating, signing petitions, and joining political groups. However, as I will show in this chapter, solitary practitioners, although more politically active than the average American, are less active than group practitioners. My research suggests that being in a regularly assembling religious group increases political activity, but being outside a group does not result in the withdrawal from political activity. To the contrary being a member of this religion, even as a solitary practitioner, is associated with greater political activity than the average American.

Politics and Solitary Practitioners

As was shown in chapter 2, contemporary Pagans are not socially isolated. Although solitary practitioners are less integrated then those practicing in groups, they are in touch with other contemporary Pagans on a regular basis. Similarly when looking at voting patterns and participation in political groups and activities, a difference can be found between solitary and group practitioners. This difference should be neither exaggerated nor brushed aside. As I will demonstrate, solitary practice is associated with lower political participation but not with the lack of political activity. This requires a more subtle understanding of the association between practicing alone and political activity than has dominated the discussion.

Causation is always difficult to determine, and my data do not permit me to determine if the lower political participation of solitary practitioners is due to their form of practice or if the type of person who would practice alone is by nature less politically active. What my data does show, however, is that solitary practice does not result in the withdrawal from national or emancipatory politics—but it is associated with a decreased amount, as the tables in this chapter show.

TABLE 5.1. *Percentage of Solitary and Group Practitioners That Voted in the Last Election*

	SOLO	GROUP
National	82.7	91.7
Local	67.0	79.2

Contemporary Pagans vote at a higher rate than the typical American. The Bipartisan Policy Center estimates that 57.5 percent of Americans voted in the last presidential election, down from the previous one, in which 62.3 percent voted (2015). The rate of voting is lower for local elections and during years between presidential elections. The General Social Survey (GSS) found that 63.9 percent of their respondents claimed to have voted in the last national election. Table 5.1 demonstrates that contemporary Pagans who work in a group vote at a higher rate than solitary practitioners, although even solitary practitioners vote at a higher rate than the typical American. Part of this difference, but not all of it, can be explained by the higher educational level of contemporary Pagans as both "The Pagan Census Revisited" and "The Pagan Census" data indicates that contemporary Pagans are more likely to vote than other educated Americans. Nonetheless working in a group as opposed to being a solitary practitioner is indicative of higher voting rate.

*Table 5.2. Percentage of Solitary and Group Practitioners' Political Affiliations**

	SOLO	GROUP
Nonpolitical	18.2	8.8
Libertarian	8.5	9.6
Green	9.1	10.1
Socialist	4.1	3.0
Left-liberal	32.1	42.1
Independent	25.2	21.5
Right-conservative	3.3	2.8
Far right	0.2	0.1
Other	9.0	11.3

*Columns add to more than 100 percent as multiple responses were allowed.

Consistent with their lower voting rate, solitary practitioners are more likely than group members to self-define as nonpolitical. Although less than one-fifth of the solitary practitioners self-define as nonpolitical, that is still twice as many as those who are group practitioners. Contemporary Pagans' self-perception of political activity appears to be consistent with the data on how politically active they are. Group practitioners are also more likely to self-define as left-liberal than solitary practitioners, but most contemporary Pagans remain progressives as was previously seen in *Voices from the Pagan Census* (H. Berger et al. 2003). The percentage who claim to be right-conservative, far right, or libertarian is small, with the largest percentage in that group being not surprisingly libertarian—a political movement that emphasizes individual rights—both social and economic—with a dislike of government involvement in people's lives.

More interesting is table 5.3, which asks the frequency with which individuals participate in twelve different political activities ranging from donating to a political group to holding public office. So few contemporary Pagans, like other

TABLE 5.3. *Frequency of Political Activities for Solitary and Group Practitioners (in percentages)*

	NEVER		OCCASIONALLY		SOMETIMES		FREQUENTLY		VERY FREQUENTLY	
	SOLO	*GROUP*	*SOLO*	*GROUP*	*SOLO*	*GROUP*	*SOLO*	*GROUP*	*SOLO*	*GROUP*
Vote	8.3	3.7	6.8	3.9	11.7	6.9	25.2	22.8	48.0	62.7
Sign petition	8.2	4.8	21.2	17.8	35.8	34.1	21.5	24.7	13.4	18.6
Participate in special event	40.1	26.9	28.1	30.2	24.4	30.9	5.1	7.9	2.2	4.1
Grassroots organizing	50.5	36.6	26.8	30.3	16.2	22.4	4.5	6.7	2.0	4.1
Participating in town meeting	49.1	37.9	30.8	34.0	14.8	19.5	3.5	6.1	1.8	2.6
Active campaigner	75.3	65.9	15.0	20.7	6.7	8.6	2.1	3.5	0.9	1.3
Active lobbyist	88.2	84.6	7.5	9.2	2.9	4.5	1.0	0.7	0.4	1.1
Active spokesperson	58.9	50.6	19.7	20.8	12.0	16.9	6.3	7.4	3.1	4.3
Elected official	96.8	94.2	1.7	2.8	0.8	2.1	0.4	0.1	0.3	0.8
Contact national official	27.7	17.4	26.4	29.3	24.1	25.9	13.2	14.8	8.5	12.5
Contact local official	31.3	21.5	28.0	30.2	23.2	25.5	10.7	12.7	6.8	10.1
Donate to a political group	63.3	47.0	18.4	26.4	12.1	17.1	4.2	6.0	1.9	3.5

Americans, have held political office that this question has little importance, but the other eleven activities indicate that solitary practitioners are somewhat less politically involved than group practitioners. Among those who practice in groups, 43.3 percent frequently or very frequently sign a petition for a cause they believe in. This can be compared with solitary practitioners, among whom 34.9 percent frequently or very frequently sign petitions. Very few contemporary Pagans frequently or very frequently participate in special events, which in the question were described as marches or demonstrations, although group members are more likely to do so than are solitaries. More telling is that 40.1 percent of solitaries and 26.9 percent of group members claim to never have attended one of these special events. A similar pattern can be seen in grassroots organizing, participation in town meetings, and active campaigning. Although there are variations in each category, solitaries are consistently less likely to have ever done these activities and to do them consistently less often than group practitioners. Solitary practitioners are less likely to donate to a political group, or to contact their national or local leaders about social or political issues. Solitary practitioners are relatively politically active, but not as active as those in groups.

Age

Pundits and political scientists have noted the decreased interest in emancipatory politics among the young. This is true of contemporary Pagans as well, although they still remain more active than their peers. Among the youngest in our sample, 70.7 percent of solitary practitioners and 81.8 percent of group practitioners voted in the last national election. Age is clearly a factor, as the young are somewhat less likely to vote then their elders, but form of practice is also of note—as the young who work in a group are as likely to vote as their elders that are solitary practitioners, although not as much as their elders who practice in a group. Looking at table 5.4, a similar trend is seen in the percentage of the young who claim to be nonpolitical. The young are more likely to claim that they are nonpolitical than their elders, but young group members are less likely to self-define as nonpolitical as are their elders who are solitaries. Like their elders the young tend to be progressives, with the largest percentage of both solo and group practitioners defining as left liberal but with more independents than the older generations.

Young contemporary Pagans in general claim to have not participated in most of the political activities listed in table 5.5. They are clearly less politically active than the older generation of contemporary Pagans. Nonetheless those who practice in a group are more likely to be politically active than solitaries. For example young solitary practitioners are less likely to have ever participated in a march or demonstration than their peers who work in groups. Young solitaries are also less likely to have ever contacted a national or local government

TABLE 5.4. *Political Orientation among Young Solitary and Group Practitioners (in percentages)*

	YOUNG SOLO	YOUNG GROUP
Nonpolitical	21.3	13.0
Libertarian	10.1	10.4
Green	9.9	8.7
Socialist	6.5	7.0
Left-liberal	32.7	39.1
Independent	23.5	20.9
Right-conservative	1.4	4.3
Far-right conservative	0.3	0.0
Other	11.3	10.4

agency for a political reason or to have donated to a political cause. The differences are small with the majority of both group and solitary practitioners having voted, signed petitions, participated in a demonstration or a march, and contacted their elected officials at least once, but nonetheless there is a consistent difference.

Gender

Within the general American population, women are noted for voting more often than men. This is not true for contemporary Pagans, among whom 85.5 percent of women and 86.5 percent of men claimed to have voted in the last national election, and 69.7 percent of women and 75.0 percent of men claim to have voted in the last local election. If anything contemporary Pagan men are slightly more likely to vote than women, although the difference is small. However it is a change from the original survey, in which contemporary Pagan women voted more than their male counterparts. It is unclear why contemporary Pagan men have become somewhat more politically engaged in the fifteen years between surveys. It might have to do with an increased interest in environmentalism within the movement, or less emphasis on women's rights issues.

More contemporary Pagan women claim to be nonpolitical than men, although the difference is again small. Men are more likely to be libertarian or politically right wing than women, but the most common designation is left-liberal for both men and women, with women being slightly more likely to be left-liberal than contemporary Pagan men. Men are more than twice as likely as women to be libertarian.

TABLE 5.5. *Political Activities among the Young Solo and Group Practitioners (in percentages)*

	NEVER		OCCASIONALLY		SOMETIMES		FREQUENTLY		VERY FREQUENTLY	
	SOLO	*GROUP*	*SOLO*	*GROUP*	*SOLO*	*GROUP*	*SOLO*	*GROUP*	*SOLO*	*GROUP*
Vote	17.2	10.5	9.2	11.4	14.9	14.9	28.1	28.1	30.6	35.1
Sign petition	12.1	9.6	25.1	22.8	35.0	36.8	18.2	18.4	9.6	12.3
Participate in special events	42.8	32.5	26.9	36.0	23.5	22.8	4.6	5.3	2.2	3.5
Grassroots organizing	57.8	56.6	21.4	16.8	13.7	16.8	4.7	5.3	2.4	4.4
Town meetings	59.8	55.7	25.8	27.8	10.9	10.4	2.0	4.3	1.5	1.7
Campaigner	80.2	77.2	11.7	13.2	5.9	6.1	1.4	0.9	0.8	2.6
Lobbyist	90.9	89.6	6.5	7.0	2.1	2.6	0.8	0.0	0.5	0.9
Spokesperson	63.7	58.8	16.5	19.3	10.2	14.0	6.2	3.5	3.4	4.4
Public office	98.0	96.5	1.3	2.6	0.3	0.9	0.2	0.0	0.2	0.0
Contact national gov't	44.7	35.7	23.0	29.6	18.9	20.9	8.4	8.7	5.2	5.2
Contact local gov't	46.6	36.8	24.0	32.5	18.0	17.5	6.6	9.6	4.8	3.5
Donate to a political group	74.5	63.5	15.1	20.0	8.0	9.6	1.5	5.2	0.9	1.7

TABLE 5.6. *Gender and Political Party (in percentages)*

	MALE	FEMALE
Nonpolitical	12.2	15.7
Libertarian	14.7	7.1
Green	9.5	10.2
Socialist	5.2	3.5
Left-liberal	31.8	36.3
Independent	24.5	24.3
Right	4.3	2.7
Far-right conservative	0.3	0.1
Other	11.9	10.0

Table 5.7 indicates that there are some small gender differences in the extent of political activity. Contemporary Pagan women are slightly more likely to sign a petition than contemporary Pagan men, but slightly less likely to participate in a march or protest. Gender appears to have even less effect on political activities than does age among contemporary Pagans.

Social Issues

Four social issues stand out as particularly pertinent to contemporary Pagans: environmentalism, women's rights, gay rights, and animal rights. Each of these is related to contemporary Pagans' worldview, theology, and rituals. The commitment to each varies, and there are some differences by age and gender, which will be discussed, but on the whole contemporary Pagans are interested in these four movements and involved to varying degrees in them.

ENVIRONMENTALISM

The religion is often described as earth centered (Clifton 2006:41–44; Pike 2004:146). The earth is referred to as our mother, viewed as the Goddess or her body, sung about in chants, and venerated. The divine is viewed by most contemporary Pagans as residing in nature. As noted in chapter 1, questions have been raised about whether contemporary Pagans are environmentalists in ritual practice alone or if they are also politically engaged in environmental issues (Clifton 2006; Oboler 2004). In part whether or not contemporary Pagans are considered environmentalists depends on the criteria used. Is it sufficient to recycle? Or sign petitions? Consider environmental issues in voting? Or does one have to be an active member of an environmental group? And what percentage of participation at each level is sufficient to consider this an environmental religion? In this section I provide data on many different forms of environmental activity.

TABLE 5.7. *Gender and Political Activities (in percentages)*

	NEVER		OCCASIONALLY		SOMETIMES		FREQUENTLY		VERY FREQUENTLY	
	MALE	*FEMALE*	*MALE*	*FEMALE*	*MALE*	*FEMALE*	*MALE*	*FEMALE*	*MALE*	*FEMALE*
Vote	7.0	7.0	6.2	6.0	8.4	11.1	22.8	24.9	55.6	51.1
Sign a petition	7.8	6.8	22.0	19.4	34.8	35.5	21.0	23.0	14.3	15.2
Special events	33.3	37.3	30.5	27.7	26.6	26.2	6.0	5.9	3.6	2.8
Grassroots organizing	42.9	47.3	29.2	27.3	18.7	17.6	5.8	5.1	3.4	2.6
Town meeting	41.3	47.2	32.7	31.3	18.2	15.6	5.5	3.9	2.4	2.0
Active campaigner	69.2	73.4	18.7	16.1	7.4	7.4	3.2	2.3	1.5	0.9
Lobbyist	86.3	87.4	7.4	8.2	4.3	3.0	1.1	0.9	0.9	0.5
Spokesperson	56.7	56.2	17.8	20.6	13.1	13.6	7.6	6.4	4.8	3.3
Public office	94.8	96.5	2.6	1.7	1.6	1.0	0.3	0.2	0.6	0.5
Contact national gov't	24.7	24.8	26.0	27.0	23.9	24.8	14.7	13.7	10.7	9.7
Contact local gov't	29.4	28.0	27.7	28.3	23.2	24.3	11.9	11.3	7.7	8.1
Donate to political group	54.8	59.9	22.5	20.0	14.6	13.1	4.8	4.9	3.3	2.1

My interest is comparing, when possible, contemporary Pagans' environmental activism with that of other Americans as well as an internal comparison between solitary and group practitioners. This analysis indicates that contemporary Pagans are more environmentally involved than the typical American and those in groups more so than solitary practitioners.

TABLE 5.8. *Environmental Activism among Solitary and Group Practitioners (in percentages)*

	SOLO ONLY	GROUP
Self-define as environmentalist	74.6	81.7
Recycle	85.5	90.7
Participate in a demonstration for environmentalism	27.0	34.6
Give money to an environmental group	57.4	69.6
Signed a petition for environmental reform	74.8	82.6
Consider the environment when voting	90.4	93.8
Belong to an environmental group	18.0	26.6

Table 5.8 indicates that the majority of contemporary Pagans, whether they practice alone or in a group, consider themselves environmentalists, recycle, give money to environmental groups, sign petitions for environmental reform, and consider politicians' stance on environment issues when voting. But the majority does not participate in demonstrations for the environment or belong to an environmental group. Among all U.S. contemporary Pagans 29.7 percent have participated in a demonstration for the environment and 20.6 percent belong to an environmental group. If the criteria for being an environmentalist is belonging to an environmental group or participating in demonstrations for environmental issues, then the majority of contemporary Pagans are not environmentalists. However if one considers what Giddens referred to as life politics, they would be considered environmentalists; they self-define as environmentalists and recycle. They also consider environmental issues when voting and sign petitions and give money to environmental causes. What is more important, when compared to other Americans, contemporary Pagans are politically involved in environmental politics. Data from the GSS indicates that only 41.2 percent of Americans claim to have given money, 27.8 percent to have signed a petition, and 3.2 percent to have participated in a demonstration for the environment. Only 9.6 percent of the general American public belongs to an environmental group. Being a member of this religion does not make one an environmental activist; however, contemporary Pagans are more environmentally active than most other Americans.

Those who practice in a group are more involved in all environmental activities, including contributing money to environmental causes, protesting, and being members in environmental organizations, than solitary practitioners. This is true even for recycling, which in many neighborhoods has been made easy, by either curbside pickups or the local dump having on-site recycling. Nonetheless those who are in a group are more likely to recycle. Group members are also more likely to self-define as environmentalists than are solitaries. It is impossible to know whether or not individuals were drawn to contemporary Paganism because they were already interested in environmental issues or if their participation in rituals, readings, and the larger group of contemporary Pagans has influenced their beliefs and behaviors. However, the fact that those who practice in groups are more involved in environmental politics suggests that they may be encouraged to increase their participation because they are in greater contact with others who are also doing so and who celebrate those who participate in these activities.

AGE

As table 5.9 indicates age has a very small but noticeable effect on environmental activity, with the young being less active than their elders. This may in part be a generational difference, or it might be a matter of having time. As one respondent stated at the end of his answers to the long list of questions about political behaviors: "I plan to do many of these things once I have my life sorted out :)-." The young in the long run may be as active, or more active, than their elders. What is clear, however, is that those who work in groups are more active in environmental issues than those who are solitary. In fact the young who work in a group are more likely to participate in environmental actions than are solitaries regardless of age in every category except recycling and donating money to an environmental cause.

TABLE 5.9. *Young Solo and Group Members as Environmental Activists Compared with All Contemporary Pagans (in percentages)*

	SOLO ONLY	YOUNG SOLO ONLY	GROUP	YOUNG GROUP
Self-define as environmentalist	74.6	71.9	81.7	76.0
Recycle	85.5	81.6	90.7	84.5
Participate in a demonstration for environmentalism	27.0	21.4	34.6	30.2
Give money to an environmental group	57.4	44.3	69.6	57.1
Signed a petition for environmental reform	74.8	66.1	82.6	77.0
Consider the environment when voting	90.4	89.4	93.8	92.5
Belong to an environmental group	18.0	12.6	26.6	20.7

Gender

Like age gender has a small influence on political activity for environmental causes. As seen in table 5.10, women solitaries are somewhat more likely than male solitaries to do all the activities listed. The differences between solitary men and women are small, and clearly whether one practices alone or with others is the more important factor. On the whole women who work in groups tend to be more active in all areas than the men who work in groups, with the exception of demonstrating—which has virtually no gender difference—and belonging to an organization that works for environmental causes—which men are slightly more likely to do than women. Gender has a very small effect on environmental activism; form of practice, however, has a much larger effect.

TABLE 5.10. *Gender and Environmental Activism for Solitary and Group Practitioners (in percentages)*

	SOLO ONLY WOMEN	SOLO ONLY MEN	GROUP WOMEN	GROUP MEN
Self-define as environmentalist	74.8	73.6	82.2	79.8
Recycle	86.6	82.0	91.0	90.0
Participate in a demonstration for environmentalism	26.3	29.6	34.3	34.8
Give money to an environmental group	57.9	55.9	70.5	66.8
Signed a petition for environmental reform	75.6	72.5	82.3	82.6
Consider the environment when voting	91.2	87.8	94.4	92.2
Belong to an environmental group	18.6	16.2	26.1	27.2

Women's Rights

As noted in chapter 1 the worship of the Goddess has drawn women to contemporary Paganism. For some it is part of a larger commitment to women's rights; for others it is a way for them to see themselves in the divine. Historically and cross-culturally, worshipping a goddess or goddesses has not necessarily resulted in women being treated with greater respect. Wicca as first practiced by Gardner presented a romantic notion of womanhood, requiring the High Priestess to step down when she was no longer young, with no equivalent requirement for the High Priest (Neitz 1991). This has changed as the religion has aged and as it has been influenced by the women's movement and the feminists that have helped to transform it (Griffin 2005). The most important figure in this transformation is Starhawk, who as previously noted is the most read author among contemporary Pagans. Her books incorporate both environmentalism and feminism into the fabric of the religion. However not all contemporary Pagans would consider themselves feminist; in fact fewer would self-define as feminists than environmentalists. In part this is the result of the term being denigrated in the press—as Jennifer Baumgardner and Amy Richards (2000) describe it, feminism is the new F word.

Not all spiritual paths have been equally influenced by feminism. Nonetheless, as can be seen in table 5.11, the majority of American contemporary Pagans consider themselves to be feminists. As with environmentalism the percentage is higher for those who work in a group than solitaries. However regardless of form of practice a higher percentage of contemporary Pagans self-define as feminists than do members of the general American population. According to the GSS about 21 percent of the general American population self-identify as feminists. As with environmentalism it is unclear whether individuals join the religion because they are feminists or if being a member of the religion influences them to become feminists; however, again as with environmentalism, those who practice in groups are more likely to self-identify as feminists and are more politically active than solitary practitioners. This suggests that being with others who have similar views on a regular basis contributes to one's commitment to a cause or an issue.

TABLE 5.11. *Solo and Group Practitioners and Feminist Activism (in percentages)*

	SOLO ONLY	GROUP
Self-define as feminist	57.0	64.2
Participate in demonstration for women's rights	25.2	35.7
Sign petition for gender rights	58.5	70.3
Give money to a feminist group	35.4	50.0
Consider feminist issues when voting	86.5	90.8
Participate in an organization that advocates women's rights	11.2	17.3

As seen in table 5.11, group members are more likely to sign petitions, participate in demonstrations, give money, and join feminist organizations. Although slightly more group members than solitary practitioners consider a politician's stance on feminism when voting, the vast majority do think about the issue enough to include it in their decision of who to vote for. The majority of both forms of practice have also signed a petition for gender equity, although many more who work in a group than those who are solitary have signed petitions for this issue. Although more contemporary Pagans than the general population tend to consider themselves feminists and to be involved in feminist activities, those who work in groups tend to be the most committed in every category that was examined. Nonetheless there is less support for women's rights than for environmental issues among contemporary Pagans.

I repeated three questions from the first survey in the second to gauge attitudes toward women's rights. The survey asked on a seven-point scale whether the respondent agreed or disagreed with three propositions: (1) "women should not be included in the military"; (2) "to redress previous discrimination there should be preferential hiring of women at all levels of employment"; (3) "women in the military forces should be included in combat positions." I found that the majority disagreed with the first two proposition and supported the third. Of solitary practitioners 53.9 percent, and of group practitioners 58.4 percent, disagreed that women should be excluded from a military draft with 31.9 percent of solitaries and 33.5 percent of group members stating they strongly disagreed with the proposition. Unfortunately on these questions respondents could not write comments, as I suspect many of them would say that they were opposed to a draft or to wars and therefore were opposed to anyone being drafted. Most contemporary Pagans are opposed to the notion of affirmative action, with 56.8 percent of both those who practice as solos and those who practice in groups opposing it. Solitary practitioners are very slightly more likely to strongly oppose it than group practitioners (25.4 percent versus 23.4 percent), but the difference is small. Most contemporary Pagans consider themselves feminists but do not believe in affirmative action for women. In part this is because the media have presented the issue as being unfair to men, and in part because there is a libertarian bent within contemporary Paganism, with a sense that everyone should be treated fairly, without a deeper analysis of what fairly means in a society that is based on inequality.

The last issue is one that garners a stronger response, with 75.0 percent of solo practitioners and 76.6 percent of group practitioners stating that they agree with women already in the military being in combat roles, and with about half of those stating they strongly agree with the statement. Only 11.0 percent of solitary and 10.4 percent of those who work in a group disagreed with the statement to any degree. On all three issues there is very little difference between solitary and group practitioners.

The vast majority of contemporary Pagans support a women's right to choose an abortion. The question, which was phrased "do you believe there should be legal access to abortion," received support from 93.7 percent of solo practitioners and 97.3 percent of group practitioners. Although group practitioners are more likely than solo practitioners to support women's right to choose, the more important fact is the strength of support for reproductive rights has among contemporary Pagans. According to the 2014 GSS survey 43.9 percent of Americans support abortion with no restrictions. For contemporary Pagans this may be a feminist issue, or it may be an issue of individual autonomy, or it may be both.

GENDER

Not surprisingly female contemporary Pagans are more likely to support women's rights than their male counterparts. What is more interesting is the part played by the form of practice. As seen in table 5.12, whether practicing in a group or not, men are about equally likely to self-define as feminists. Less than half do, although this is higher than among Americans in general. According to the GSS, 17.7 percent of men and 26.5 percent of women self-identify as feminists. Women who practice in groups are more likely than those who are solitary practitioners to self-define as feminists, although even among women who are solitary practitioners 62 percent self-define as feminist, significantly more than American women in the general population. However, when focusing on behaviors, what is most interesting is that men who practice in a group are about as active for women's rights as women who practice alone. Women who practice alone are slightly more likely to participate in a demonstration than men who practice in a group but are slightly less likely to sign a petition or give money to a feminist group. A small percentage of contemporary Pagans are members of each of the political action groups I have included. This is true for feminist groups as well but, not surprisingly, women are more likely to be members than men regardless of form of practice. However, men who work in a group are more than twice as likely to be members of a feminist group than are men who practice alone; and women who practice in a group are more likely than women who practice alone to be members of a feminist political group. In all areas that I explored, women who practice in a group are the most active, and men who practice alone the least active for the feminist cause. Gender clearly has an effect on how involved an individual is in women's issues, but so does form of practice.

TABLE 5.12. *Feminism, Gender, and Form of Practice (in percentages)*

	SOLO WOMEN	SOLO MEN	GROUP WOMEN	GROUP MEN
Self-define as feminist	61.8	42.2	72.2	45.6
Participate in demonstration for women's rights	27.0	19.1	40.4	25.3
Sign petition for gender rights	61.2	49.3	73.5	62.5
Give money to a feminist group	37.9	26.9	53.6	40.0
Consider feminist issues when voting	88.2	81.0	93.3	85.2
Member of feminist group	12.1	4.9	20.6	10.0

Just as the gender of the respondent is a more important indicator of behaviors that support women's rights, it is also a more important indicator of attitudes to gendered issues than is form of practice. When asked about their attitudes toward women being excluded from the military draft, men regardless of form of practice were more strongly opposed than were women. Among solitary men 64.1 percent are opposed to women being excluded from the military draft, with 44.9 percent strongly opposed. Men who practice in groups are only slightly more opposed, with 67.5 percent opposed to any degree and 45.0 percent strongly opposed to women being excluded from the draft. Among women the sentiment is weaker; 49.8 percent of women who practice alone and 54.6 percent of those in groups oppose women being excluded from the draft. But more tellingly a much smaller percentage feels strongly about this issue; 26.6 percent of solitary women practitioners and 28.5 percent of female group practitioners feel strongly about women not being excluded.

The differences between men and women are less pronounced for the other two questions. When asked if preferential hiring should be encouraged to redress previous discrimination, the majority of both men and women were opposed to it regardless of form of practice, but a larger percentage of men were opposed; 67.5 percent of solitary male and 62.3 percent male group practitioners were opposed; with 36.2 percent of solitary male practitioners and 33.3 percent of the group male practitioners strongly opposing affirmative action. Among women 21.9 percent of solitary practitioners and 18.9 percent of group practitioners strongly oppose affirmative action. Approximately three quarters of contemporary Pagans oppose women who are in the military being excluded from combat positions. Men are somewhat more strongly opposed than women; among men who practice alone 38.8 percent and among those who practice in a group 39.9 percent feel strongly about this issue. Among women 32.4 percent who practice alone and 32.1 percent who practice in a group feel strongly about military women being excluded from combat positions. The differences are small, but it is still interesting that men feel more strongly about this issue than women. The data does not permit me to determine why this is the case, but I suspect that it is because they believe it unfair to men if women are excluded from situations that would put them in harm's way. For people in the military, being in combat positions may carry status and the possibility of promotion but it also involves risk.

AGE

As was previously noted in this chapter, the young tend to be less politically active than their elders. This is true for feminist activities too, although the difference is notable only in terms of signing petitions and giving money. On the whole the young have less discretionary money to make donations. More telling is that the young in groups are less likely than their elders to sign petitions for women's rights. The young are slightly less likely than their elders to consider themselves feminists although the majorities of the young—both those who are solitary and those who are group practitioners—are feminists, with those in groups slightly more likely to self-define as feminists than those who are not in groups. As table 5.13 indicates youth who work in groups are more active than those who are solitary in all areas except in considering a politician's stand on feminist issues when voting—87.4 percent of solitary practitioners and 85.3 percent of group practitioners claim to consider a politician's stand on feminist issues when voting. Youth who are group members are 62 percent more likely to participate in a demonstration for women's rights and 70 percent more likely to join a feminist group than those who are solitary. Although youth are less involved in political action, there is no difference when compared to their elders in their attitudes toward women being conscripted into the military if men are being conscripted, women in the military being permitted to participate in combat, or toward affirmative action.

TABLE 5.13. *Young Practitioners and Feminist Activities (in percentages)*

	YOUNG SOLO	YOUNG GROUP
Self-define as feminist	53.8	60.0
Participate in demonstration for women's rights	19.4	31.3
Sign petition for gender rights	54.4	58.8
Give money to a feminist group	25.4	33.9
Consider feminist issues when voting	87.4	85.2
Member women's rights group	9.2	13.2

Gay Rights

As noted in chapter 2, contemporary Paganism has drawn to it a disproportionate number of gay, lesbian, bisexual, and transgender, and those that consider themselves "other." This is in part because contemporary Paganism has been a welcoming community. Most contemporary Pagans strongly advocate for gay rights. This is true for both those who self-identify as heterosexual and those who do not. As seen in table 5.14, those who are members of a coven or other group are more active than solitary practitioners for gay rights. This is true for all areas of activity that were examined, but is most clearly seen in the percentage that have participated in a demonstration or given money for gay rights. As with the other areas of political activity, only a minority is a member of a gay rights organization, but those whose spiritual practice is in groups are also more likely to join a gay rights group than those who are solitary practitioners.

In comparing the data in table 5.14 with table 5.13, it is clear that more contemporary Pagans consider themselves gay rights activists and work for gay rights causes than consider themselves feminists or work for women's rights. This is consistent with data on the general U.S. population. In 2013, 58 percent of Americans stated they support general of acceptance for homosexuals (Pew 2013). As noted above fewer Americans consider themselves feminists. It is therefore not completely surprising that gay rights get greater support among contemporary Pagans than feminism gets. However, it does make clear that worshipping the Goddess or goddesses does not necessarily make one a feminist.

TABLE 5.14. *Gay Rights and Solo and Group Practitioners (in percentages)*

	SOLO	GROUP
Self-define as gay rights activist	69.6	76.0
Participate in demonstrations for gay rights	27.0	41.0
Sign petition for gay rights	63.2	74.9
Given money to a gay rights organization	26.9	40.6
Consider gay rights when voting	86.6	91.5
Belong to gay rights group	11.2	16.4

GENDER

As can be seen in table 5.15, unlike environmental activism where gender plays a very minor role in the level of contemporary Pagans' political engagement, it is a factor in political activity for gay rights, although not to the degree that it is for women's rights. Women are more likely to self-define as advocates for gay rights than men regardless of the form of practice, although men are more likely to be members of a gay rights group. As with all political action groups, only a minority of contemporary Pagans belong to gay rights groups. There are more gay men in my sample than lesbians, which may account for the difference in membership in gay rights organizations. Women are more likely to give money to gay rights organizations, but group members are more likely than solitary practitioners regardless of gender to participate in a demonstration for gay rights. Table 5.15 gives a mixed sense of the relationship between gender, form of practice, and gay rights advocacy. Gender plays a more important role in some behaviors and form of practice in others. For example both women who practice alone and those in groups are more likely to consider themselves gay rights activists than their male counterparts.

TABLE 5.15. *Gender, Form of Practice, and Gay Rights Advocacy (in percentages)*

	SOLO WOMEN	SOLO MEN	GROUP WOMEN	GROUP MEN
Self-define as gay rights activist	72.3	60.8	78.9	69.3
Participate in demonstrations for gay rights	26.7	25.7	40.6	40.6
Sign petition for gay rights	64.7	57.5	76.7	70.1
Given money to a gay rights organization	26.6	26.1	39.3	41.7
Consider gay rights when voting	87.9	82.1	94.0	85.7
Belong to a gay rights group	10.4	15.7	12.2	16.7

AGE

The young are very slightly more likely than their elders to consider themselves advocates of gay rights, to participate in demonstrations, and to belong to a gay rights group. This is one cause in which the young are somewhat more active than their elders. Consistent with the other data that I have examined, I find that those in groups are on whole more active than those who practice alone, except curiously for belonging to gay rights groups. This is the only case in all my U.S. data in which those who practice alone are more active than those in groups. It is unclear why this is the case. Consistent with all the other data, only a small number are in an advocacy group at all. I could find no data on the number of Americans in gay rights organizations and hence cannot reliably determine if contemporary Pagans are more active than the average American, although my sense is that they are.

TABLE 5.16. *Gay Rights Activities for Young Solo and Group Practitioners (in percentages)*

	SOLO	GROUP
Self-define as gay rights activist	75.5	81.7
Participate in demonstrations for gay rights	33.9	46.1
Sign petition for gay rights	64.1	74.8
Given money to a gay rights organization	24.8	33.0
Consider gay rights when voting	89.8	90.4
Belongs to gay rights group	16.7	14.8

Animal Rights

Animal rights is the last social movement that I will be exploring. As with the other three movements discussed, a concern with animal rights is consistent with contemporary Pagan theology. Animals are viewed as an integral part of the web of nature. All nature, whether animals or rocks or trees, are viewed as filled with energy that is linked in a web of life. There is a belief by many in an ability to communicate with animals and fairly typically to think of them as part of the larger family of life that humans are also a part of. Animals are associated with each of the four directions and are often seen as sacred. Only a minority of contemporary Pagans are vegetarian or vegan, but this is still larger than in the general American public, particularly for vegetarianism. Among contemporary Pagans 10.5 percent are vegetarian and 2.4 percent are vegan. This can be compared to the general American public in which Gallup finds that 5 percent are vegetarian and 2 percent vegan (Newport 2012). There is also a growing interest in animism among contemporary Pagans (Harvey 2005, 2015). Animal rights is the only area in which those who practice in groups and solitary practitioners have about the same level of political participation. Although fewer contemporary Pagans would consider themselves animal activists than environmentalist or gay rights activists, slightly more are interested in animal rights than women's rights, at least among solitary practitioners, who are less likely to be feminists than group practitioners. It is important to reiterate that contemporary Pagans are much more likely to be feminists than the general American population. Nonetheless other issues take precedence over women's rights for them. In part this might be because although the early writings, such as those by Starhawk, were clearly feminist, more current works emphasize contemporary Paganism as an earth-based religion and focus more on environmental issues, part of which is one's relationship to and with animals.

TABLE 5.17. *Gender Differences in Animal Rights Activism among Contemporary Pagans (in percentages)*

	FEMALE	MALE
Self-define as animal rights activist	69.6	54.8
Participate in demonstrations for animal rights	16.1	12.0
Donate money for animal rights	54.8	38.6
Sign petitions for animal rights	62.5	50.9
Belong to an animal rights group	20.5	12.8

Although there is not a difference between solitary and group practitioners there is, as table 5.17 indicates, a gender difference in response to animal rights. Women are more likely than men to consider themselves animal rights activists and to participate in every one of the activities listed. As with the other forms of political activity that were discussed, only a minority are members of an animal rights group. Among women 20.5 percent are members of an animal rights group, while among men it is only 12.8 percent. Women are more likely to sign a petition, demonstrate, and donate money to animal rights causes. This is consistent with gender differences in the larger American society. A Gallup poll found that while only a minority wanted to give animals the same rights as humans, almost twice as many women as men (33 percent vs. 17 percent) supported this proposition (Riffkin 2015). My survey did not ask the same question as the Gallup poll, and it is therefore impossible to compare the data, and none exists on how many American's consider themselves animal rights advocates, but it should be noted that even among male contemporary Pagans, more than half self-define as animal rights advocates.

Spiritual Paths

On the whole there is very little difference in political activities and positions among contemporary Pagans of different spiritual paths with the exception of Heathens, who tend to be more conservative than members of other spiritual paths that I am exploring. Although Heathens are less politically active in the four social movements that I have discussed in this chapter, they are less likely to view themselves as apolitical. When answering questions about the frequency with which they vote, sign petitions, participate in demonstrations, or do any of the other ten political activities listed in the survey, they were about as active as other contemporary Pagans, and in some instances slightly less active. Although Heathens do not appear from my data to be more politically active, they are more likely to have a political orientation. As noted in chapter 2, there is a small subset of Heathens who are part of the alt right and in some instances Neo-Nazis. My data reflects this in that 1.1 percent of Heathens identify as far right. This is a very small percentage of the entire group, but none of the other Pagan traditions has more than 0.2 percent of their members who state that they are far right. Of course not all those even in this small percentage are necessarily white supremacists, but the group is on the whole more conservative, with a larger percentage self-defining as right and libertarian than other spiritual paths. About a quarter (22.8 percent) of Heathens claim to be libertarian as compared to Wiccans, among whom only 9.9 percent are libertarian. In the United States libertarians tend to be liberal on social issues and conservative on economic issues, most typically voting Republican. Adding together conservative, right, and far right, I found that only 19.8 percent of Heathens self-define in one of these categories—certainly a minority, but when combined with those who are libertarian a healthy minority of 42.6 percent. This can be compared with only 3.1 percent of Wiccans who self-define as conservative, right, or far right, and only an additional 7.9 percent who state they are libertarian.

When asked directly about their attitudes toward Neo-Nazis and racialists, Heathens had a higher proportion both of members who had extremely negative and positive attitudes toward both of these than did the rest of contemporary Pagans. Among Heathens 77.2 percent had extremely negative attitudes toward Neo-Nazis as compared to 75.5 percent of all contemporary Pagans. Similarly when asked about their attitudes toward racialists 41.0 percent of Heathens and 38.6 percent of all contemporary Pagans have strong negative attitudes toward racialists. However, although the same percentage (92 percent) of Heathens and other contemporary Pagans have a negative or extremely negative attitude toward Neo-Nazis, Heathens are less likely to have a negative attitude toward racialists. Nonetheless approximately two-thirds of Heathens (66.7 percent) view racialism either negatively or extremely negatively as compared to over 70 percent of other contemporary Pagans. Looking at the other end of the scale, as can be seen in table 5.18, those with positive views of these two groups are a very small percentage, but Heathens are twice as likely to view Neo-Nazis positively than are other contemporary Pagans (1.2 percent versus 0.6 percent) and three times more likely to have positive views of racialists (9.6 percent versus 3.2 percent).

The greater likelihood of Heathens having extremely negatives views than other contemporary Pagans of Neo-Nazis is probably because those who are not alt-right members or sympathizers, which are clearly the vast majority, feel the need to protect themselves and their religion against Neo-Nazis who self-identify as Heathens. Although the majority also oppose racialist attitudes fewer do so strongly because of the strong pull within the religion of blood and blood ties. However when Heathens are compared with other Americans they appear much less supportive of Neo-Nazis and white identity politics than the general population. A survey done by Reuters, Ipsos, and the University of Virginia Center for Politics shortly after the Unite the Right march in Charlottesville found that 4 percent of American support or strongly support Neo-Nazis. This is more than three times as strongly as Heathens. Although no question was asked about support for racialists, 31 percent of respondents to the Reuters survey supported or supported strongly the notion that the United States needed to "protect and preserve its White European heritage" (Reuters et al. 2010). As Heathens were a very small percentage of my sample, it is possible that those on the extreme right were underrepresented. Nonetheless when the data from my survey is compared with that for other Americans, the group on the whole does not appear particularly racialist. Another survey completed shortly after the

Charlottesville march, conducted by the *Washington Post* and ABC news, that has received wide distribution, found that 9 percent of Americans supported Neo-Nazism or white supremacy (Washington Post and ABC 2017). The Reuters survey's question is closer to that which appeared in my survey as it specifically asked about Neo-Nazis. It also found that 8 percent of American's support white supremacists.

TABLE 5.18. *Attitudes of Heathens and All Contemporary Pagans toward Neo-Nazis and Racialists (in percentages)*

	HEATHEN		ALL CONTEMPORARY PAGANS	
	ATTITUDES TOWARD NEO-NAZIS		*ATTITUDES TOWARD RACIALISTS*	
	Heathens	All U.S. Pagans	Heathens	All U.S. Pagans
Extremely negative	77.2	75.5	41.0	38.6
Negative	15.2	17.7	26.7	31.7
Neutral	6.4	6.3	22.8	26.5
Positive	0.7	0.3	5.1	2.2
Extremely positive	0.5	0.3	4.4	1.0

Heathens are the least likely of all the spiritual paths I examined to demonstrate for any cause or to provide money to a social cause. They are also the least likely to state that they are advocates for any of the four causes that we examined. Although the difference is small for environmentalism, it is higher for the other three, particularly for women's rights and gay rights. Table 5.19 examines the difference between the Heathens and other contemporary Pagans in the two movements in which the difference is highest—gay and women's rights.

Although the majority of Heathens consider themselves advocates of gay rights, fewer Heathens are advocates than in the general contemporary Pagan population. Consistent with that they are less likely to do any of the other activities examined than are other contemporary Pagans, although the difference is small for demonstrating for gay rights, possibly because such a small percentage—less than a third of all contemporary Pagans—have demonstrated for gay rights. Feminism is less popular as a movement than gay rights in general among contemporary Pagans, but most do consider themselves feminists. This is not true of Heathens, among whom just under half consider themselves feminists. While noting the differences, it is important not to exaggerate them. Almost as many Heathens have signed a petition for women's rights as other contemporary Pagans. Furthermore, when compared to the general American public, Heathens are much more likely to claim to be feminists than non-Pagan Americans.

TABLE 5.19. *Heathens Compared to All U.S. Contemporary Pagans' Activism for Gay and Women's Rights (in percentages)*

	U.S. ALL PAGANS	HEATHENS
Belong to gay rights group	12.5	9.2
Gay rights advocate	71.4	64.6
Demonstrated for gay rights	31.6	27.9
Signed petition for gay rights	66.8	61.4
Given money to gay rights organization	31.1	24.7
Belong to a women's rights group	12.2	8.9
Self-define as feminist	58.9	48.3
Participate in a demonstration for women's rights	28.8	23.9
Sign a petition for women's rights	62.1	53.9
Give money to a women's right group	39.8	28.8

Heathens are the most conservative form of contemporary Paganism that I am exploring. As noted in chapter 2, there is a larger percentage of men in this spiritual path than in any other that is examined. Heathens have a more traditional view of the family and hence on the whole are less likely to celebrate homosexuality or bisexuality. However, American Heathens, like all the other spiritual paths, have been influenced by Wicca and the larger contemporary Pagan community (Snook 2015). Jennifer Snook (2015) contends that the rhetoric of American Heathens is often similar to that of the religious right, with the addition of a celebration of nature and the "folk"—a romanticized notion of a people of northern Europe. The reality, however, she notes is often more complex. She cites a survey in which 77 percent of Heathens state their support for marriage equality for gays and lesbians (Snook 2015:17–18). My survey showed even stronger support for gay marriage with 82.9 percent of Heathens supporting gay marriage and of those 71.9 percent doing so strongly. This is very slightly weaker support than in the general Pagan population but is clearly very high. This is also true for the other three questions I asked about gay rights: "should homosexuals be excluded from the military," "should homosexuals be permitted to adopt children," and "should non-discrimination based on sexual preference be part of any civil rights legislation"? In all instances the majority of Heathens support gay rights, but at a lower rate and less strongly than the general contemporary Pagan population. This is consistent with libertarianism with its focus on individual rights. It is also an indication that while there is a celebration of what Snook refers to as hypermasculinity—an emphasis on the man as warrior or protector of his family and community—that is tempered by an acceptance of alternatives.

As with all forms of contemporary Paganism, there is variation among the practitioners. However among Heathens this variation appears to be greater than in other spiritual paths. There is a minority of Heathens who are strongly antigay. In 2015 the Ásatrú Fellowship in Iceland, where the religion has had a substantial revival, received e-mails from German and American Ásatrú threatening to "re-consecrate" their church with animal blood because of the church's willingness to marry same-sex couples. The Ásatrú church is a popular wedding site among the LGBTQ Icelandic community because they were performing same-sex marriages years before these became legal in Iceland. Animal sacrifice is forbidden by the Icelandic group, and they were concerned that they might become the victims of vandalism. The church received overwhelming support from thousands of Heathens throughout the world, including from the United States and Germany, indicating that the antigay Heathens were a fringe group within the religion, but a vocal and organized one (Scott 2015).

The relationship between Heathens and gay, lesbian, bisexual, and transgender rights is a complicated one. For some transgender contemporary Pagans, the Heathen god Loki, the trickster god of Norse mythology, has become an icon of transgenderism. He is seen as bending gender because in one myth he transforms himself into a mare and is impregnated (Strmiska 2016). My data confirms not only a diversity of opinion on gay issues among Heathens, but also that the majority of Heathens are supportive of gay rights, even if that support is less robust than among other contemporary Pagan spiritual paths.

Heathens are also less supportive of women's equity than are other contemporary American Pagans. Snook presents a complicated picture of gender roles and performance within this spiritual path. She contends that Heathens claim to have gender equity, which is not based on shared or interchangeable roles, but on a celebration of each gender's role as important and worthy of respect. This is based on a traditional division of labor. Women are viewed as responsible for kin work, handicrafts, maintenance of the home, and raising good children for the tribe. Men's roles are that of warriors and protectors. There is an acceptance of women being outspoken and assertive; it is viewed as normative and part of their heritage. This is not a typical twenty-first-century notion of feminist women's roles. As with gay rights, Heathens have a complicated and convoluted relationship with feminism.

American Pagans and Political Activity

Contemporary Pagans, regardless of whether or not they practice in a group, are politically active when compared to other Americans. When the data was analyzed to determine what percentage belonged to any political action group—

whether for the environment, women's rights, gay rights, or animal rights—I discovered that 42.8 percent were members of at least one political action group. Of course there is always variation in the extent of activity even among those that belong to a political action group, but nonetheless it does indicate a fairly large commitment. This combined with the percentages that donate money, sign petitions, write to political leaders, and participate in protests suggests that on the whole contemporary Pagans are more politically active than other Americans. This is consistent with what we found in *Voices from the Pagan Census* (H. Berger et al. 2003). It is worth reiterating, as I have heard repeatedly at academic meetings other scholars of contemporary Paganism claim that Pagans are not active in emancipatory politics. But my data does not support that view. Certainly contemporary Paganism is not a political movement—it is a religion. Some scholars of contemporary Paganism seem to believe that as a religion that claims to be an earth-based spirituality, its members should be more active, at least in environmental causes, if not in any others.

At first glance it does appear that contemporary Pagans' strongest commitment is to environmental issues, as a larger percentage of those who practice alone or in a group claim to be environmentalists than to be advocates for any other political cause I examined. However, determining where their strongest commitment lies becomes murkier when one looks at other factors, such as their participation in demonstrations, joining groups, signing petitions, or giving money. American solitary practitioners for example are as likely to demonstrate for gay rights as they are for environmental rights. American group practitioners are more likely to participate in demonstrations for gay rights and are about as likely to attend a women's rights demonstration as an environmental one. Both solitary and group American practitioners are most likely to give money to environmental groups but are least likely to financially support gay rights. This raises an interesting question: Why do more American contemporary Pagans indicate that they are environmentalists than claim they are supporters of any other cause? I suspect that the growing dialogue both online and offline describing contemporary Paganism as a nature religion has resulted in their coming to self-define as environmentalists, recycling, and at least stating that they consider a politician's stand on this issue. This may contribute to some scholars of the religion coming to believe that contemporary Pagans are environmentalists in name only. But the level of political activity for environmental issues among contemporary Pagans is still greater than that of the average American.

American contemporary Pagans are active in both emancipatory and lifestyle politics, but those who work in groups are more active than those who are solitary. The differences between those in group and solitaries are more or less pronounced depending on the activity and social issue but, with the exception of animal rights, are consistent. Those who practice alone are less politically active.

Causation is of course difficult to determine. Are solitary practitioners less involved in activities in general including spiritual and political ones, because they tend to be loners while those who practice in a group are more socially oriented to begin with? Or is being solitary, in some way, causal in making individuals less politically and socially active? My data does not permit me to determine this for certain. However studies in social psychology have found that when people interact they influence each other's attitudes, beliefs, and behaviors. Recent research, which has been widely circulated, has shown that even the weight of one's friends' friends can influence weight gain or loss among members of social networks and that there is an increase in voting when individuals report on social media sites that they have voted on election day (Junge 2011; Bond et al. 2012). It seems most likely that those who practice in groups influence each other to be more active and help to determine which activities are most important or appropriate to participate in. Nonetheless those who are solitary are also influenced by their interactions with others on the Internet and social media, reading the same books, and in more occasional face-to-face interactions at a variety of venues discussed in the last two chapters. Group practitioners are more politically active than solitary practitioners, but it is important to remember that solitary practitioners are more active than the average American.

Canada and the United Kingdom

Similarly to the United States experience, those who practice in groups are more politically active than those who are solitary practitioners in the United Kingdom and Canada. Group practitioners are more likely to vote in local and national elections, participate in demonstrations, contact their elected officials, and vote more often than solitary practitioners. The only exception is solitary practitioners in the United Kingdom, who are about as likely as group practitioners to sign petitions.

Table 5.20 indicates that, on the whole, group practitioners in both nations are more politically active in the four social movements I have been exploring than their solitary counterparts, with the exception of animal rights activism in the United Kingdom. British group practitioners are less likely to self-describe as animal rights advocates and less likely to donate money or sign petition for animal rights than are those who practice alone. This is similar to the findings for the United States. But in the United Kingdom interestingly both group and solitary practitioners are about equally likely to participate in a demonstration for animal rights. Although less pronounced than in the United States, group practitioners are on whole more politically active in the four areas that I explored than are solitary practitioners. As in the United States, contemporary Pagans in other English-speaking nations are most likely to state they are advocates of environmentalism than any of the other three social movements I analyzed;

and group members are more likely than solitary practitioners to take this label. In the United Kingdom, animal rights is the next most important social cause, followed by gay rights. Of the four movements discussed, fewest contemporary Pagans state that they are feminists. Less than half of both solitary and group practitioners in the United Kingdom consider themselves feminists. The majority of group and solitary practitioners in Canada self-define as feminists. The difference between group and solitary practitioners is most pronounced in Canada, in which 71.8 percent of group practitioners and only 52.2 percent of solitary practitioners claim to be feminists. Because the percentage of women in group and solitary practices is about the same, the differences found cannot be attributed to gender differences. Across the board in all other areas of political activity for social causes, contemporary Pagans who practice in groups are more likely to participate in demonstrations and donate money than those who are solitary, with the exception of animal rights.

TABLE 5.20. *Political Activities of Solitary and Group Practitioners in the United Kingdom and Canada (in percentages)*

	U.K. SOLO	U.K. GROUP	CANADA SOLO	CANADA GROUP
Environmentalist	71.2	74.3	74.0	84.7
Recycle	93.9	95.5	97.0	98.2
Environmental demonstration	32.1	37.9	35.7	45.0
Donated for environmental cause	66.8	78.8	57.6	65.5
Signed an environmental petition	83.9	83.3	73.5	85.6
Environmentalism and voting	91.9	90.9	91.4	94.5
Feminist	41.0	48.5	52.2	71.8
Feminist demonstration	10.8	19.7	28.6	44.1
Signed feminist petition	39.2	51.1	48.7	70.3
Donate to feminist group	14.6	28.8	22.8	39.6
Feminism and voting	70.1	68.2	81.4	92.7
Gay rights supporter	47.2	50.0	62.3	68.5
Demonstrate for gay rights	20.8	25.8	33.8	38.7
Sign gay rights petition	45.3	51.5	56.5	66.7
Donated to gay rights	21.7	21.2	19.8	23.6
Gay rights and voting	67.3	72.3	16.7	89.1
Animal rights advocate	61.6	50.8	47.8	48.6
Demonstrate for animal rights	19.8	19.7	16.7	16.4
Donate to animal rights	61.8	50.8	47.8	48.6
Sign petition for animal rights	75.4	66.2	55.4	59.5

The greater activity of those who practice in a group is even more clearly seen when looking at participation in political action groups. With the one exception that about the same percentage of group and solitary practitioners in Canada are members of an animal rights group, and group members in both countries are more likely to be members of a political action group. More Canadian and British contemporary Pagans participate in alternative political groups and environmental groups than American contemporary Pagans. In turn American contemporary Pagans are more likely than their British or Canadian counterparts to be members of gay or women's rights groups. There is a greater consistency in the United Kingdom and Canada between stated advocacy and actual political behavior. A higher percentage of contemporary Pagans in those nations claim to be advocates of environmentalism, and it is the movement they are most likely to involved in, as can be seen through their participation in political action groups, attendance at demonstrations, donations, and willingness to sign petitions for this cause.

TABLE 5.21. *Participation in Political Action Groups among Solitary and Group Practitioners in the United Kingdom and Canada (in percentages)*

	U.K. SOLO	U.K. GROUP	CANADA SOLO	CANADA GROUP
Alternative political group	25.3	29.7	17.7	26.4
Environmental group	33.3	33.8	18.3	26.4
Women's rights group	6.3	9.4	7.8	16.2
Gay rights	8.6	9.1	7.5	8.1
Animal rights	20.0	23.1	14.7	14.5

Contemporary Pagans in the United Kingdom are more active in environmental groups than those in the United States or Canada. There is clearly an international difference in how important each of the movements is within local contemporary Pagan communities and a difference in the level of political activity. But in all instances contemporary Pagans appear to be politically engaged. The vast majority of contemporary Pagans in all English-speaking nations consider themselves environmentalist. It is the cause that most claim as part of their identity. In Canada and the United Kingdom it is also consistently the cause that contemporary Pagans are most likely to work for, demonstrate for, and donate money to. The emphasis on contemporary Paganism being an earth-based religion appears to have influenced people's behavior in all three nations but more so in the United Kingdom and Canada.

Conclusion

In *Voices from the Pagan Census* (H. Berger et al. 2003) we found that contemporary Pagans were about as politically active as Unitarian Universalists. In the fifteen years between surveys, that has not changed. We had not included questions about participation in the environmental and feminist, gay, and animal rights movements in the first survey. The addition of these questions in "The Pagan Census Revisited" was prompted by concerns raised in the literature that when participants worship the Goddess they withdraw from emancipatory politics for women's rights (Eller 2000) and that contemporary Pagans were environmentalists in name only (Clifton 2006; Oboler 2004). The animal rights and gay rights movements were included as they too are related to contemporary Pagan rituals and mythology, and many of the same issues could be raised about them. All four of these movements are what Woodhead has referred to as feeder projects that are related to contemporary Pagan spirituality.

My research indicates that contemporary American Pagans are active in all four of these movements, although the majority of contemporary Pagans are not members of a political action group. However, they do on the whole consider themselves advocates for these movements to varying degrees, and a number have signed petitions or attended rallies and demonstrations. Furthermore more than 40 percent are members of a political action group for at least one of these causes. When data has been available, I have compared my results with data on the political activity of the general American population. In all instances contemporary Pagans are more politically active than other Americans.

Although more identify with environmentalism than any other social movement, it is not necessarily the movement for which American contemporary Pagans are most likely to actually do political work. This disparity may be an indication that contemporary Pagans believe they should self-define as environmentalists or it may have to do with some other factor, such as the ease of signing a petition for some other cause, or being drawn along with other friends to a rally. The vast majority of contemporary Pagans recycle. The level of commitment of this activity varies by locality; in some areas it is mandatory to recycle, in some areas curbside recycling is provided, and in still others an effort is required to find a recycling center. It is therefore impossible for me to determine if the large percentage of contemporary Pagans who recycle is or is not an indication of a strong commitment to at least this environmental activity. More interestingly American contemporary Pagans are somewhat more likely to a sign petition or attend a rally in support of one of the other issues for which I tested than for environmentalism. This is different for contemporary Pagans in the United Kingdom and Canada, who are more consistent in their commitment to environmentalism, as it is the social movement the largest percentage stating they support and the one for which they are most likely to do political work. The majority of American contemporary Pagans consider themselves feminists, gay rights advocates, and animal right advocates as well as environmentalists. However fewer participate in demonstrations for any of these causes, give money, or sign petitions than self-define as advocates of the movement. This raises the question of what it means to be an advocate for these movements. Is it in name only? To some degree even taking the name feminist or gay rights activist is a political act. What is more important, contemporary Pagans are more politically active for each of the four movements discussed than Americans in general.

It is impossible to determine causation from my data. Are contemporary Pagans more politically active because people who are concerned about these issues join the religion, or does the religion foster these concerns? Social psychology studies indicate that being in a network influences one's views and behavior. Even those contemporary Pagans who have little contact with others in their religion read the same books and visit the same Internet sites and, at least some of the time, participate in open rituals, festivals, and metaphysical classes. What is more important, my data indicates that being a member of a group as opposed to being a solitary practitioner results in people being more active and more likely to self-identify as environmentalists, feminists, and advocates for gay and animal rights. In other words those who interact in a religious or spiritual group (and as we saw in chapter 3, socially) with other contemporary Pagans are more politically active than those who do not.

I began this chapter discussing the debate about whether spiritual or religious isolation results in individuals becoming apolitical or results in their politics moving from emancipatory to lifestyle politics. My data suggests that neither is correct. Those who work in groups are more active in emancipatory politics than solitary practitioners. However, solitary practitioners are not on the whole apolitical or involved only in lifestyle politics. To the contrary, although I did see an effect of group practice, on the whole contemporary Pagans are politically active regardless of their form of practice. Although group practitioners are more politically active, solitaries are not withdrawn from political action.

Solitary practitioners, who as previously noted are the vast majority of this religion, are part of the larger phenomenon in the West of people who are unaffiliated, who are often described as spiritual even if not traditionally religious. My research findings, therefore, have implications for a growing segment of American society. Kelly Besecke (2007:197), in her discussion of *Habits of the Heart* (Bellah et al. 1985) on the twentieth anniversary of its publication, defends religious individualism. She describes her own research as indicating that for her subjects "religion became more compelling, and . . . religious commitments became more solid, once they adopted a mode of religiosity that prioritizes individual reflection, discernment, and authority." She notes that this can result in greater political commitment as well. Berghuijs, Pieper, and Bakker (2013) in their study of New Age participants in Holland found that members of this group are not disengaged. Although less engaged than those in their sample who attended traditional churches, New Agers are more engaged than those who are secular. My research similarly finds that those who practice alone are engaged, particularly on issues of social justice, environmentalism, and animal rights.

Putnam argued that withdrawal from groups would result in less social and civic engagement. Indeed those who are solitary practitioners in my sample have a somewhat lower rate of political engagement than those in groups, although the difference is not as large as he found between the churched and unchurched. Group participation does matter. However, what is more important, this form of spirituality results in individuals being more engaged than the average American. They are particularly engaged in causes that in some way are reflective of their spirituality—the feeder projects mentioned by Woodhead—but these are not the only political activities they do. They vote, they write letters to the elected representatives, they join alternative political organizations, and they attend marches in much larger numbers than the average American. This political activity may be lost from view because they are not joining political groups or activities as members of a church or other religious organization—but their spiritual or religious beliefs, rituals, mythology, readings, and possibly self-reflection and self-authority that Besecke notes may nonetheless be influencing their political activities. Their participation, even in a very loose community that may occur more often online than face to face, appears to influence their behavior in much the same way that recording that one voted on social media influences the behavior of one's social network. Religion, whether practiced alone or in groups, can have a powerful effect on political engagement. This is true of this metaphysical religion and I suspect others as well.

Conclusion

Most contemporary Pagans are solitary practitioners. I found this to be true when I completed my first survey, "The Pagan Census," but at that time just over half of my sample was solitary. Groups still appeared to be the center of contemporary Pagan practice as they were the social norm, even if they were barely no longer the statistical norm. For example Linda Woodhead (2013) contends that most contemporary Pagans work in groups, citing the number of ethnographies that have been written on group practices. Both because groups are easier to study than single practitioners and because at one point they were the only way to learn about the religion, they have been viewed as the cultural norm, even as they have increasingly not been the statistical norm.

In the more recent survey, "The Pagan Census Revisited," the trend toward solitary Paganism has become clearer. Over three-quarters of contemporary Pagans are solitary practitioners; and even a higher percentage of the young practice alone. Internationally, as in the United States, most contemporary Pagans are solitary practitioners. The trend is toward the growth of solitary practice, although I doubt that group practice will ever completely fade away.

The majority of solitary practitioners has worked at some point in a group. Some, although a minority, have been trained in groups, and most will join a group for the celebration of sabbats or for other spiritual events from time to time. Although some contemporary Pagans enjoy working alone or live in an area where there is little choice but to work alone and will never join a group, others will be in a group on and off throughout their lives. Some of the young who are now solitary may in the future become members of a group. The increase in the percentage of young who practice alone, in and of itself, does not suggest a trend as it may be a passing phase in their spiritual practice. However when it is combined with the data that shows a sharp increase in the percentage of solitary practitioners between the two surveys, it is indicative that the primary face of contemporary Paganism is that of those who practice alone.

Solitary and group practitioners are not completely "birds of a different feather," but part of the same growing phenomenon. About 10 percent of those who claim to be solitary practitioners also claim to practice in a group. This is not an oxymoron but instead is a difference in how they define practicing alone. For them it is not spiritual isolation but a belief that they are completely in control of their own spirituality, and even while joining with others, are creating something unique to themselves. Of course believing one is and actually producing something completely different is not the same thing. We are all influenced by those we interact with, the books, magazine, journals, and blogs we read, and Internet sites we visit. Given the criteria I used, those who claimed to be simultaneously solitary and in a group are more similar to those who work in a group than those who claimed not to work in a group at all—that is, those who are completely solitary.

My data indicate that almost no contemporary Pagans are completely isolated. They interact with others in person, on the Internet, and on the phone. They participate in festivals and workshops and at times attend classes with others. Some contemporary Pagans move back and forth between being group practitioners and solitaries. The groups are often unstable, falling apart either because of internal conflicts or because too many members have moved away to continue. They may be re-created with some of the same people and some new ones. Some individuals who began in one spiritual path within contemporary Paganism move to another and in so doing leave their original group. Nonetheless there are some clear differences between those who practice alone and those who do not. Some of these differences are demographic; others are social, political, or spiritual.

Solitary practitioners are on the whole somewhat younger, less likely to be married or in a long term relationship, slightly less likely to be queer, and more likely to live in a rural area and to be female than those who work in groups. However, both solitary and group practitioners are in most ways very similar—they are disproportionately well educated and female, live in urban and suburban neighborhoods, and are either small business owners or in the helping professions. The professional affiliation of contemporary Pagans has changed between surveys. In "The Pagan Census" the most likely profession was computer programmer. Currently contemporary Pagans are more likely to major in the humanities or social sciences than in the STEM fields that I found in the first survey. Data from the second survey indicates that contemporary Pagans have become more similar to typical American college graduates than they had been.

As did my first survey, my second finds that contemporary Pagans live throughout the United States. In the second survey, unlike the first, the distribution of contemporary Pagans throughout the United States is more or less consistent with that of other Americans—states with larger populations have a larger number of contemporary Pagans. Contemporary Pagans have somewhat bucked the trend toward greater urbanization, as a larger proportion of contemporary Pagans are now living in rural areas than in the first survey, at the same time that fewer Americans in general are living in those areas. Contemporary

Pagans who are rural dwellers are still a small minority, and they are most likely to be solitary practitioners. It is, nonetheless, indicative that contemporary Pagans do not just see the divine in nature or their religion as earth based while avoiding the natural world. Most are urban or suburban dwellers, just as most Americans are; nonetheless more than the national average of contemporary Pagans are living in rural areas.

Although contemporary Pagans have become more similar to other middle-class Americans between surveys, they have not completely blended in. They remain on the whole better educated than most of their neighbors and more liberal, and what is most important, they are following what is still a controversial religious practice. The majority of contemporary Pagans does not belong to or attend a church. The growth of the Covenant of Unitarian Universalist Pagans has given some contemporary Pagans a church, albeit a minority and somewhat unconventional one to be members of, while continuing to practice contemporary Paganism. A minority still practices in groups, which vary in size but are normally small enough to meet in members' living rooms or basements. When possible contemporary Pagans prefer to do their rituals, particularly their sabbat rituals, outside, in state or local parks or in their backyards. Mother Nature is more likely to be viewed as consecrated space than is a church or other building.

Wicca still remains the most popular spiritual path for group practitioners, but not for solitaries. They favor eclectic Paganism, followed by Witchcraft, with Wicca being the third most popular spiritual path. It is unclear what this will ultimately mean for the religion. Wicca has influenced almost all other spiritual paths within contemporary Paganism. There are more how-to books about Wicca than any of the other spiritual paths. Nonetheless it is unclear whether it will continue to be as important in the future. The focus on ritual, the celebration of the seasonal wheel of the year, and the use of magic as a way of connecting to the universe or the divine all have come from Wiccan practice. Will those effects remain as Wicca itself becomes less popular? It is possible that Wicca has been so absorbed into all contemporary Pagan practices and most spiritual paths that its influence will remain largely untouched; alternatively ethnic or regional forms of Paganism, with their own sets of rituals and mythology, may become more important. The growth of solitary practice is clearly changing the place of Wicca in the larger religion.

Solitary practitioners are less likely to share their spiritual path with their romantic partner or spouse or with their children than are group practitioners. Nonetheless over three-quarters of all contemporary Pagans, regardless of form of practice, do share their spiritual path with their children, but it is higher among group practitioners than solitaries. Most do not insist that their children participate as there is a strong individualistic ethic and a belief that everyone should choose the spiritual path that speaks to her or him. There are currently some families that include three, and in a few instances four, generations of contemporary Pagans. Will this become the norm? Only 10 percent of my survey is composed of those who were raised in a contemporary Pagan home.

Traditionally to survive over generations religions have depended on the young remaining in the religion. More research is needed to determine the extent to which the young from contemporary Pagan families are remaining in the religion, and to determine whether metaphysical religions more generally can maintain themselves without most of their own young remaining in the religion. Some early research suggests that most of the adult children of contemporary Pagans are remaining in the religion, at least vaguely, by continuing to practice a bit and by having absorbed their parents' magical and mystical worldview. The research is still too preliminary to be certain of the degree to which it is accurate across the country, let alone across the globe.

On the whole solitary practitioners are less involved on every level than those in groups: socially, politically, and even in participation in metaphysical practices. Predictably they have less contact with other contemporary Pagans for spiritual reasons, but they also have less social contact. They are less likely to participate in online contemporary Pagan Internet forums or websites, to have phone conversations or share e-mails with others in their religion, or to attend a festival or moot. They are not isolated. Most do have regular contact with others in their religion but it is less frequent than for group members. Those in groups are more likely to participate in workshops, take classes, and use alternative medical or health practices. They also practice magic more often.

Age and gender are also factors. Women, particularly those who practice in groups, are most likely to participate in metaphysical workshops and, classes, and to pay for alternative health services. They are more likely to believe in the efficacy of astrology and to use divination as a way of planning their future than men are. Although contemporary Pagans are more likely to do any of these activities than non-Pagan Americans, the gender difference exists across American society. Women in general are more religious than men, and contemporary Pagan women tend to participate in more metaphysical activities than their male counterparts, with one exception: men are more likely to claim that they practice magic frequently than women are. However, a larger percentage of men than women also claim that they never practice magic. Nonetheless on the whole the most active spiritually are women who practice in a group; the least are men who practice alone.

There are very few differences in belief between solitary and group practitioners, at least on the criteria I examined. Contemporary Pagans read many of the same books and blogs and visit the same Internet sites. This has resulted in a good deal of homogeneity in views and in determining in which spiritual practices they participate. "The Pagan Census Revisited." received responses from fifty-nine nations from around the globe. Although my data internationally is less robust than that for the United States, it does suggest that there is a growing similarity among members of this religion globally. Contemporary Pagans internationally share many of the same views and appear more similar to one another than they do to others in their home countries.

The Contemporary Paganism and the New Metaphysicals

Contemporary Paganism shares much with what Bender (2010) refers to as the New Metaphysicals, and earlier Paul Heelas and his coauthors (2005) referred to as holistic spirituality, and prior to them James Beckford (1984) called the New Religious and Healing Movements. Contemporary Pagans attend many of the same workshops on topics like meditation, astral projection, and lucid dreaming. They use many of the same alternative medical practices, such as Reiki or the Alexander Technique as the New Metaphysicals, and they share a holistic view of the world in which one can influence events by changing one's thoughts and attitudes. Change is seen as beginning with the individual. In "New Forms of Public Religion," Linda Woodhead (2013) lays out six components of holistic spirituality: (1) each individual is the final arbitrator of spiritual truth; (2) there is an open and tolerant attitude to other truths and forms of religion and spirituality; (3) the universe is viewed as an interconnected whole; (4) the body is important for reaching spiritual enlightenment, such as through meditation; (5) morality is linked to progressive causes, such as fighting inequality; (6) spirituality is viewed as separate from, and more valued than, religion. Although Woodhead's is the most comprehensive list of characteristics, it is similar to those provided by Beckford (1984) and Bender (2010) in describing the individuals they are studying.

Woodhead demarcates three different varieties of New Metaphysicals, to use Bender's term. These are the New Age; Mind, Body, and Spirit groups; and contemporary Pagans. Although she believes they share the characteristics discussed above, they have some distinct aspects. Woodhead is cognizant that most of those who practice the New Age do not take the label, but she nonetheless uses it as a heuristic to distinguish them from the other two subgroups. She describes the New Age as based on belief in the "dawning of a new era of heightened consciousness, which it believes will supplant the narrow, egoistic, materialism of modern times, and transform those who are able to realize their destiny into enlightened, empowered, fully spiritual beings." She notes that Mind, Body, and Spirit practitioners have become more popular than the New Age. She describes them as cultivating "personal 'wellbeing' by way of a range of holistic body-conscious practices—including Yoga, Reiki, and Tai Chi." Individuals participate in these practices both to improve personal health and well-being and to improve their relationship with "self, others, and the whole ecological order."

She describes contemporary Paganism as differing from these two by "insisting on its greater respect for tradition; rooted in time and place; lesser focus on the self at the expense of community; recognition of the reality of death, destruction, and evil; and the affirmation not only of 'Oneness' but of plurality and difference" (Woodhead 2013:31). I would add to Woodhead's list the emphasis within contemporary Paganism on rituals, particularly those of the seasonal cycles of year; the veneration of nature as divine or the site of divinity; and the practice of magic as simultaneously a form of empowerment and a conduit for connecting to the divine.

The differences between contemporary Pagans and the other forms of metaphysical practitioners mean that the six components that Woodhead uses to define this group are not equally applicable to them. The first four I listed are ones that contemporary Pagans comfortably embrace. They believe that each person is responsible for his or her own spiritual truth. This is even more clearly the case for solitary practitioners than for those in a group. They celebrate difference, including different paths to the divine or to enlightenment. They are holistic, viewing the universe as an interconnected web, and participate in an embodied form of spirituality. They speak of experiencing the divine, not of believing in it. Although they do on the whole support progressive causes, it as an expression of their morality of radical empathy—which is based on their notion of all living things, and, for some, nonliving things, being in an interconnected web. One's empathy with the other makes one concerned for their well-being and encourages one to put oneself in their place.

When I began my study of contemporary Pagans they, like other of the New Metaphysicals, eschewed the term "religion," favoring instead "spirituality." Religion was seen as institutional, unresponsive to individuals' spiritual needs, hierarchical, and patriarchal. Spirituality to the contrary was viewed as connecting an individual to the divine, of being personal and therefore more meaningful. Although most contemporary Pagans continue to see themselves as spiritual, and many as spiritual but not religious, it is becoming more common to hear them refer to their spiritual practice as a religion. At least among leaders of contemporary Pagan umbrella groups, as well as some participants, there is a realization that the label of religion comes with legal and social protections that are not afforded spirituality.

I have referred to contemporary Paganism as a disorganized religion. This suggests not only that there is little clear organization or accepted hierarchy but that there is a desire not to have any. Most contemporary Pagans pride themselves on their differences, on their individualism, and on their lack of organized religion. The lack of boundaries makes it impossible to exclude anyone. Everyone who claims to be a contemporary Pagan or to practice a particular spiritual path is accepted as a member of the religion. There is in fact no authority or hierarchy to exclude or excommunicate anyone or any subgroup as there is no organizational structure that is recognized to have that power. There are, at times, snide remarks made about a particular individual's training or magical power, or whether a particular group really is practicing contemporary Paganism, but on the whole there is an acceptance of many different paths all equally enabling a connection with the divine or the universe.

Courtney Bender (2010) has objected to the New Metaphysicals being called unorganized or disorganized, in part because she is responding to theorists like Bruce (1996) who argue that the lack of organization will ultimately mean that these movements are evanescent and will have no lasting effect on the society or culture. She, more than anyone else, has shown the underlying social networks that help to support this form of spirituality. My use of the term disorganized religion is not to suggest that there are no underlying cultural or social networks and institutions that support and maintain the religion. It is to acknowledge that this is a very different type of religious practice than mainstream religions, one whose borders are more open and vague, but not completely missing.

The lack of a traditional organizational structure makes these forms of spirituality more open to personal interpretation and change, more flexible and harder to define and pin down. The New Metaphysicals, in all its forms including contemporary Paganism, is a religion of late modernity (Beckford 1992a 1992b; Woodhead 2009b, 2013; H. Berger 1999). It celebrates the individual and her or his relationship to the divine. This does not make the practitioners narcissists, or social or political isolates, or their religious practices ethereal or amoral, as has been suggested by theorists such as Christopher Lasch (1979), Roy Wallis (1984), Steve Bruce (1996), Robert Bellah et al. (1985) or Robert Putnam (2001). But it does suggest that the way in which the religion is practiced and influences its members is different, as are the ways in which members of the religion interact with the larger social and political world.

Woodhead (2009b) has argued that religions like contemporary Paganism are part of a new religious paradigm, in which spiritual practices are at once individual and influenced by global cultural forces. Each practitioner is ultimately responsible for her or his own spirituality. However, it is never completely individual. As Paul DiMaggio and Walter Powell (1983) argue, the ambiguity of hierarchy and the lack of clear lines of authority in late modern organizations result in a greater homogenization, as each actor attempts to find a comfortable knowledge base on which to anchor his or her actions. For contemporary Pagans this has resulted in certain authors becoming particularly important in the formation of their spiritual practice. Five authors stand out in the popularity: Starhawk, Scott Cunningham, Margot Adler, Silver RavenWolf, and Ronald Hutton. Websites are also of importance for most of those in my sample; two in particular, Witchvox and the Wild Hunt, were cited by more contemporary

Pagans than any other. Both Woodhead and Bender (2010) describe the connections created among practitioners through shared workshops. These forms of spirituality are not completely privatized and should therefore not be trivialized.

As Eeva Sointu and Linda Woodhead (2008) have noted the trivialization of these religions has a gender bias. Like contemporary Paganism all the New Metaphysics have drawn more women than men to their ranks. These religions or spiritualities celebrate the self and its development. They advocate for individuals taking time for themselves, which they view as important for spiritual development and ultimately to repair the world. This brings to mind, for many, pampered middle-class women who are selfishly focusing on themselves. Disproportionately these spiritualities are appealing to the white middle class, the group that is most likely to have the time and resources to attend workshops, to meditate, and to want to develop themselves. The class status of contemporary Pagans is varied. Although most do have college degrees they are not on the whole in high-paying professions. Training, at least in groups, has traditionally been free, and therefore no money is required to learn the techniques, rituals, and magical practices of the religion. Like other forms of the New Metaphysicals, most are composed of women. For women, even privileged women, there is always a pull between the cultural injunction to take care of others and finding time for oneself. These spiritualities provide a legitimation for women to carve out time, much as men have always done, for themselves and their own development (Woodhead 2009a). This is a counterbalance to the societal pressures for women to put their own needs aside and care for others, not to avoid those responsibilities, but to place them within a context of responsibility to oneself and to the larger community.

Globalization has influenced every aspect of contemporary life from economics and politics to social, family, and gender relationships. It has disrupted traditional ways of living, opening opportunities for some people, such as women, those who are not heterosexually normative, and minorities, but has also resulted in a growing sense of uncertainty. This uncertainty has resulted in some individuals joining fundamentalist churches that provide clear directives on how to live (Bauman 1993). Contemporary Paganism and other metaphysical religions provide an alternative response. Bellah and his coauthors (1985) believe that these religions provide no more than a balm for the psychological wounds of late modernity. Since Karl Marx religion has often been viewed as nothing more than a social opiate. Certainly all religions provide an explanation and solace for life's vicissitudes. However, as all the research on religion in the past hundred years has demonstrated, religions clearly do much more. Among other things they provide a worldview, ethical system, and social network.

Among Bruce's criticisms of the New Metaphysicals is that their lack of clear boundaries will make them unable to survive as a religion or social force for any length of time. This lack of boundaries, he argues, will also make it difficult to respond to moral issues, as there is no clear "us" and "them." The boundaries of contemporary Paganism are somewhat fuzzy; as previously noted there is no one in a position of authority to throw anyone else out. Nonetheless these boundaries are not completely missing. The ethical system of contemporary Paganism is consistent with the condition of late modernity. It does not provide a set of clear precepts but instead a method for making ethical decisions in a pluralistic world that is based on a sense of connection to the other. This is a morality that has been associated with women. It is an ethic of caring and connection. This does not, of course, result in every contemporary Pagan acting morally or even faithfully following the ethical methods of radical empathy, no more than the precepts laid out in Christianity result in all its adherents acting in a manner that appears consistent with the teachings of Christ.

Contemporary Paganism and Politics

Politically most contemporary Pagans are more liberal than their compatriots. My research shows that contemporary Pagans are more politically and socially engaged than the typical American. This is true not only for life politics but in all areas of political life. Contemporary Pagans are more likely to vote in national and local elections, to contact their representatives about an issue important to them, and to join a political action group. This was true in both my first and second surveys. However in the second survey what has become clear is that solitary practitioners are less engaged than their counterparts who practice in groups. Although the differences are not on the whole large, they are consistent. In almost every category of political activity solitary practitioners are less engaged than those in groups; this includes voting, protesting, signing petitions, calling one's elected officials, and joining political action groups.

Causation is always difficult to determine. It is possible that those who practice alone are by their nature less political, and joining a coven or other group would not change that. However, social psychological studies are consistent in showing that being part of a group influences one's views and behaviors even if the participants believe they do not (Junge 2011). It is therefore reasonable to presume that group practice does increase political activity. Members of a coven or other group encourage each other in their actions. Social media have been shown to also be effective in helping individuals influence each other. As previously noted just posting on Facebook that one has voted in a local or national election increases the probability that others the person knows will also vote (Bond et al. 2012). My data, nonetheless, suggests that while social media is effective, it is still not as effective as face-to-face interactions in encouraging actual political activities, although it appears to be as effective in influencing attitudes.

Contemporary Pagans support the "feeder projects" mentioned by Woodhead. More than 40 percent of contemporary Pagans belong to at least one action group, most commonly an environmental group. They also support women's rights, gay rights, and animal rights in smaller numbers. More would consider themselves environmentalists than feminists, or gay or animal rights activists. This is true for solitary and group practitioners. However this advocacy does not always translate into environmentalism garnering the most political activity from contemporary Pagans.

Contemporary Pagan men and women are about equally politically active. Age has some effect on level of political involvement as young Americans, whether contemporary Pagans or not, tend to less politically active than their elders. However, form of practice is more important than age in determining the level of political activity. Being a group member results in the young, as well as their seniors, being more politically active.

There is a small group of contemporary Pagans who are ultraright. These most commonly self-define as Ásatrú or Odinists. It is important to note that the majority of those who self-define as Ásatrú or Odinist are not ultraright. But the religion's celebration of Nordic deities and culture has made them appealing to some in the alt right. Just as the majority of contemporary Pagans participate in feeder projects that reflect liberal concerns, those in the alt right are joining other global movements that are xenophobic and anti–minority groups (Boggs 2002).

The Ásatrú is the spiritual path that has changed the most between my two surveys. In "The Pagan Census" the Ásatrú were disproportionately male. This was and is unusual in contemporary Paganism as all other spiritual paths have a larger proportion of women to men. In "The Pagan Census Revisited," the Ásatrú are now almost gender balanced with only slightly more women than men. They still stand out within the larger religion as most spiritual paths have, if anything, become more disproportionately female.

Throughout I have used the term Heathen for the combined data on Ásatrú and Odinist, as there was no statistical difference between the two groups and they were a very small part of my sample. The term Heathen is now a more commonly used designation for those that worship the northern deities. Although most are not ultraright, Heathens are more conservative than other contemporary Pagans; they are less likely to march for a cause or donate money, and less likely to support gay or women's rights than those in other spiritual paths. Of all spiritual paths, a smaller percentage of Heathens are advocates for gay rights than any other. They are the only spiritual path that does not have a majority who are advocates for women's rights. They are, however, as likely as any other spiritual path to sign a petition for women's rights, which suggests the need for caution in how they are characterized. Nonetheless they are the spiritual path that stands out as having the strongest differences with other contemporary Pagans.

They are also the group that has the youngest members both in groups and among solitary practitioners. Young men and women are joining this religion. Some are doing so because of the links of Heathenry to the Germanic or Nordic culture. Of these there are those who are part of the alt right. Gardell's (2003) research indicates that many of the young among the alt-right in the United States self-identify as Heathens. The older white supremacists, like the members of the KKK, are more likely to self-identify as Christian. This has created a problem for contemporary Pagans on the whole and for nonracist Heathens (Samuel 2017).

The response to the white supremacist marchers on August 12, 2017, in Charlottesville, Virginia, who carried shields with Odinist symbols is telling. There were several symbols that I noticed as I looked at the pictures from the marches. The most common was the use of one of the runes, the Othala, "ᛟ," which was seen on many of the flags and shields. Writing shortly after the events in Charlottesville on a Heathen blog, Stella Helasdottir (2017) states:

> As I absorbed articles and scrolled past images of the Charlottesville Racists this week, I was more than disturbed. I was one angry Heathen. . . . Once again, white supremacists and neo-Nazis have seized our spiritual identity and twisted our hearth culture for their nefarious purposes. . . . My personal practice, the way I live my Heathenry, is firmly opposed to racism. . . . We are duty-bound to call out injustice when we see it. . . . As Heathens or even just descendants of the peoples of Northern Europe, we must reject these attempts to claim our heritage for fascist propaganda

Stella Helasdottir begins her remarks by stating that her personal practice is opposed to racism but then goes further and makes a moral claim about what she believes all in her community must do in the face of Neo-Nazis claiming Heathenry. She is not alone among contemporary Pagans in speaking out against racist Heathens. Internationally, Heathen organizations were quick to condemn these individuals and their use of Heathen imagery. It is unclear how many of those who carried the rune symbol are actually Heathens. Patrik Hermansson, a Swedish graduate student who has infiltrated the American alt right for his master's thesis, found that Odinist symbols were used by some of these individuals and groups, but they were not practicing Odinism (Singal 2017).

Contemporary Paganism has prided itself on the acceptance of difference and openness to alternative ways of living and seeking the divine. Like Helasdottir, Pagans have focused on their personal moral standing, and at least in theory, been laissez-faire about others. There have been concerns raised within the contemporary Pagan community since I first began my fieldwork in 1986 that not all Heathens be tarred with the same brush. However, the current growth of the alt-right, and its links to Odinism, is testing the elasticity of contemporary Pagans' borders and boundaries. Among the more liberal fractions of Heathens as well as some other contemporary Pagans there is at least the beginning of an attempt to draw clearer boundaries that exclude those who are racists, antigay, and clearly misogynist. They are doing this without there being a structure in place that privileges any group or individual as the one that has the final say. Through conversations online and offline, the limits of openness and acceptance are being defined. Time will tell how effective this will be in stemming the growth of Neo-Nazis in one strand of Heathenry. However even religions with clearer boundaries, for example traditional Christian churches, have welcomed members of the KKK to their pews, possibly denying knowledge of the congregants' other identity or not thinking it relevant to their practice of the faith.

Contemporary Pagans tend not to do political activities as a religious or spiritual group, although there are contemporary Pagan groups that have marched against racism, the alt-right, or participated in the Parliament of World Religions as members of their religious group. The individual nature of their activities hides the way in which their spiritual and religious affiliation may be influencing their beliefs and behaviors. They may march, for example, for an environmental cause as an individual or as a member of a political action group, such as Earth Now, and not as contemporary Pagans. The extent to which their participation in the religion has influenced their choices is hidden, often from them as well as from researchers. Nonetheless these political and social choices at least in part have grown from their sense of the world as an interconnected web, which magically and spiritually connects them to all other living (and at times nonliving) beings and makes them responsible for them.

Solitary practitioners share a similar view of magic and a relationship to the divine and are committed to the same political and social issues as group members but as already noted are somewhat less active. This raises issues about other forms of the New Metaphysicals. Putnam has argued that face-to-face groups bestow social capital on their members, by which he means the benefits accrued from social interactions. These are both personal, in terms of things like job referrals that one might gain from someone in one's social circle, and civic, in that he found that those less socially integrated are less civically and politically motivated. My data does not permit me to discuss those personal forms of social capital, although in my earlier ethnographic work I did find that contemporary Pagans share leads about job opportunities and the availability of apartments and help one another when they became ill or have other problems. These are now sometimes shared on Facebook or other online venues too. However, as Putnam himself notes, personal forms of social capital have a downside societally as they tend to reinforce race and class advantages that are reflected in our social circles. A decrease in personal capital might ultimately be beneficial for a more egalitarian society.

Putnam shares with other theorists, such as Bruce (1996 2003) and Bellah and colleagues (1985), a belief that the withdrawal from groups result in a corresponding withdrawal from the civic and political arena. For Putnam this is the result of a decrease in their social capital; for others like Bellah and colleagues, it stems from the growth of self-absorption. Although at first glance my data seems to give sustenance to their claims, the fact that solitary practitioners are so much more politically engaged than the average American suggests otherwise. Yes, group membership can be seen to increase engagement over others that are also members of the religion, but the religion itself is supportive of social engagement. Some of this engagement is, as noted above, for feeder projects that grow directly out the spiritual expression of contemporary Pagans, but they are also engaged in what Giddens referred to as emancipatory politics—voting, writing letters to elected officials, and demonstrating. It is unclear if this increased political activity is a result of the spiritual practices, mythology, and rituals of this religion, as people who are drawn to the religion may also be more socially engaged. However, it is an indication that participation in this religion, even as a solitary practitioner, does not result in withdrawal from political activity.

Future Research

This book offers a first overview of a growing trend—contemporary Pagan solitary practitioners—but I hope will not be the last to explore it. The growth of solitary practice is subtly changing contemporary Paganism. Eclecticism is now the overall most popular spiritual path. Most solitaries still have some contact with groups: they have trained in them, have been a member at some time, or join with others for celebrations. But they are less involved in the larger amorphous community. The extent of this change is still in the process of being felt, and more research is required on this growing phenomenon.

More surveys are needed, particularly throughout the world written in the native tongues of those areas. We also need ethnographies of those who practice alone. It would be useful to do a longitudinal study of approximately twenty solitary practitioners over a decade or more to follow how many remained in the religion, how many joined groups, whether or not they remain in them or return to solitary practice, and how their practice changes over time. More research is needed on different spiritual paths; as eclectic is now the most common spiritual path it is important that more research is directed at better understanding what that practice is, and how it does or does not differ among group and solitary practitioners. Ethnic and regionally specific forms of contemporary Paganism are being studied now—but more again is needed here on those who practice an ethnic form of contemporary Paganism as solitaries.

I have become particularly concerned about those who are worshipping the northern gods—who are called Heathen, Ásatrú, or Odinists. There are differences among these three appellations, but they often blend together. In my survey, for example, I found no statistical differences between Odinists and Ásatrú. As I have already noted a very small group within this spiritual path is part of the alt-right. Although this is a minority within a minority spiritual path of a minority religion, it is nonetheless having, and I suspect will have, a long-term impact on this religion and politics both nationally and globally. Disproportionately those who become Heathens are young. Without condemning an entire religion or spiritual path for what a minority of their adherents do, it is important to understand how and why these young people—mostly young men—who are members of the alt-right are joining this religion. How is it supporting their views and actions or guarding against them? And to what degree is there a difference between being a member of a group—a kindred or hearth—and being a solitary Odinist? Do groups encourage this form of political action or thwart it?

My research, as is often the case, raises as many questions as it answers, if not more. My hope is to begin the dialogue about solitary practitioners who, although the majority of the religion, appear absent from most of the discussion about the religion. A study of this religion will, I believe, contribute to the larger dialogue about other forms of the New Metaphysicals. As this form of religion or spirituality becomes more popular it is important to understand how it may offer avenues for civic engagement and politics and provide an ethical system, which is different from that which has come to seem normative, but which nonetheless provides its own forms of social cohesion and social tensions.

Works Cited

Adler, Margot. 1978. *Drawing Down the Moon.* Boston: Beacon.

———. 1986. *Drawing Down the Moon.* Revised and expanded ed. Boston: Beacon.

Almendrala, Anna. 2016. "Nearly 90 Percent of Americans Have Prayed for Healing." *Huffington Post,* April 25. http://www.huffingtonpost.com/entry/healing-prayer-most-americans-pray-for-healing_us_571e4e52e4b0d912d5ff42dc.

Ammerman, Nancy. 2013. "Spiritual But Not Religious? beyond Binary Choices." *Journal for the Scientific Study of Religion* 52 (2): 258–78.

Bauman, Zygmunt. 1993. *Postmodern Ethics* Oxford, UK, and Cambridge, MA: Blackwell.

Barker, Eileen. 1984. *The Making of a Moonie: Choice or Brainwashing.* Oxford: Blackwell.

———. 2005. "Crossing the Boundary: New Challenges to Religious Authority and Control As a Consequence of Access to the Internet." In *Religion and Cyberspace,* edited by Morten Hojsgaard and Margit Warburg, 67–85. London: Routledge.

Baumgardner, Jennifer, and Amy Richards. 2000. *Manifesta: Young Women, Feminism, and the Future.* New York: Farrar, Straus, and Giroux.

BBC News. 2009. "Most Britons 'Believe in Heaven.'" April 12. http://news.bbc.co.uk/2/hi/uk_news/7996187.stm.

Beckford, James. 1984. "Holistic Imagery and Ethics in New Religious and Healing Movements." *Social Compass* 31:259–72.

———. 1992a. *Religion and Advanced Industrial Society.* London: Routledge.

———. 1992b. "Religion and Modernity, Post-Modernity." In *Religion: Contemporary Issues,* edited by Bryan Wilson, 11–23. London: Bellew.

Bellah, Robert N., Richard Madsen, William M. Sullivan, Ann Swidler, and Steven M. Tipton. 1985. *Habits of the Heart: Individualism and Commitment in American Life.* New York: Harper and Row.

Bender, Courtney. 2010. *The New Metaphysicals: Spirituality and the American Religious Imagination.* Chicago: University of Chicago Press.

Berger, Helen A., Andras Corban Arthen, Evan A. Leach, and Leigh S. Shaffer. 1993–95. "the Pagan Census." Murray Institute, Harvard University. http://dvn.iq.harvard.edu/dvn/dv/haberger/faces/study/StudyPage.xhtml?studyId=18826&studyListingIndex=24_f99b89fcf82af878c307a83e09db.

Berger, Helen A. 1994. "Witches and Scientists." *Sociological Viewpoints* 10:56–65.

———. 1999. *A Community of Witches: Contemporary Neo-Paganism and Witchcraft in the United States.* Columbia: University of South Carolina Press.

Berger, Helen A., and Douglas Ezzy. 2007. *Teenage Witches: Magical Youth and the Search for the Self.* New Brunswick, N.J.: Rutgers University Press.

Berger, Helen A., Evan A. Leach, and Leigh S. Shaffer. 2003. *Voices from the Pagan Census: Contemporary; A National Survey of Witches and Neo-Pagans in the United States.* Columbia: University of South Carolina Press.

Berger, Peter L. 1967. *The Sacred Canopy: Elements of Sociological Theory of Religion.* Garden City, N.Y.: Doubleday.

Berghuijs, Joantine, Jos Pieper, Cok Bakker. 2013. "New Spirituality and Social Engagement." *Journal for the Scientific Study of Religion* 52 (4): 775–92.

Besecke, Kelly. 2005. "Seeing Invisible Religion: Religion as a Societal Conversation about Transcendent Meaning." *Sociological Theory* 23 (2): 179–96.

———. 2007. "Not Just Individualism: Studying American Culture and Religion after *Habits of the Heart.*" *Sociology of Religion* 68 (2): 195–200.

Boggs, Carl. 2002. "Social Capital as Political Fantasy." *In Social Capital: Critical Perspective on Community and Bowling Alone,* edited by Scott L. McLean, David A. Schultz, and Manfred B. Steger, 183–200. New York: New York University Press.

Bond, Robert, Christopher J. Fariss, Jason J. Jones, and Adam D. I. Kramer. 2012. "A 61-Million-Person Experiment in Social Influence and Political Mobilization." *Nature* 489: 295–98.

Bonewits, Isaac. 2006. *Bonewits's Essential Guide to Druidism.* New York: Citadel.

Boyer, Paul, and Stephen Nissenbaum. 1976. *Salem Possessed: The Social Origins of Witchcraft.* Cambridge, Mass.: Harvard University Press.

Bruce, Steve. 1996. *Religion in the Modern World: From Cathedrals to Cults.* Oxford: Oxford University Press.

———. 2003. "The Demise of Christianity in Britain." In *Predicting Religion: Christian, Secular and Alternative Futures,* edited by Grace Davie, Paul Heelas, and Linda Woodhead, 53–63. Aldershot: Ashgate.

Buckland, Raymond. 1986. *Buckland's Complete Book of Witchcraft.* St. Paul, Minn.: Llewellyn.

Budapest, Zuzanna. 1986. *The Holy Book of Women's Mysteries.* Vol. 1, rev. ed. Oakland, Calif.: Susan B. Anthony Coven Number One.

Campbell, Heidi A. 2013. "Community." In *Digital Religion: Understanding Religious Practice in New Media Worlds,* edited by Heidi A. Campbell, 57–71. London: Routledge.

Clifton, Chas S. 2006. *Her Hidden Children: The Rise of Wicca and Paganism in America.* Lanham, Md.: AltaMira.

Cooper, Michael T. 2010. *Contemporary Druidry: A Historic Ethnographic Study.* Salt Lake City: Sacred Tribes.

Cowan, Douglas E. 2005. *Cyberhenge: Modern Pagans on the Internet.* New York: Routledge.

Crowley, Vivianne. 2000. "Healing in Wicca." In *Daughters of the Goddess: Studies of Healing, Identity, and Empowerment,* edited by Wendy Griffin, 151–65. Walnut Creek, Calif.: AltaMira.

———. 2014. "Standing Up to Be Counted: Understanding Pagan Responses in the 2011 British Censuses." *Religion,* May, 483–501.

Cunningham, Scott. 1988. *Wicca: A Guide for the Solitary Practitioner.* St. Paul, Minn.: Llewellyn.

———. 1994. *Living Wicca: A Further Guide for the Solitary Practitioner.* St. Paul, Minn.: Llewellyn.

Curott, Phyllis. 2001. *Witch Crafting: A Spiritual Guide to Making Magic.* New York: Broadway Books.

Davidsen, Marcus A. 2012. "What's with Pagan Studies." *Method and Theory in the Study of Religion* 24:183–99.

Davy, Barbara Jane. 2005. "Being at Home in Nature: A Levinasian Approach to Pagan Environmental Ethics." *Pomegranate: The International Journal of Pagan Studies* 7 (2): 157–72.

DiMaggio, Paul, and Walter Powell. 1983. "The Iron Cage Revisited: Institutional Isomorphism and Collective Rationality in Organizational Fields." *American Sociological Review* 48 (April): 147–60.

Doyle, Arthur Conan. 2010. *The Hound of the Baskervilles.* London: Penguin.

Doyle White, Ethan. 2016. *Wicca: History, Belief, and Community in Modern Pagan Witchcraft.* Brighton, U.K.: Sussex Academic.

Duck, Steve, and Paul H. Wright. 1993. "Reexamining Gender Differences in Same-Gender Friendships: A Close Look at Two Kinds of Data." *Sex Roles* 28 (11/12): 709–27.

Durkheim, Emile. 1964 [1893]. *The Division of Labor in Society.* New York: Free Press.

———. 1965 [1912]. *The Elementary Forms of the Religious Life.* New York: Free Press.

Ehrenreich, Barbara, and Deirdre English. 1973. *Witches, Midwives, and Nurses: A History of Women Healers.* New York: Feminist.

Eller, Cynthia. 2000. *The Myth of Matriarchal Prehistory: Why an Invented Past Won't Give Women a Future.* Boston: Beacon.

Evans-Pritchard, E. E. 1937. *Witchcraft, Oracles, and Magic among the Azande.* Oxford: Clarendon.

Ezzy, Douglas, and Helen A. Berger. 2009. "Witchcraft: Changing Patterns of Participation in the Early Twenty-First Century." *Pomegranate: The International Journal of Pagan Studies* 11 (2): 165–80.

Fennell, Julie and Laura A. Wildman-Hanlon. 2017. "Children of Converts: Beyond the First Generation of Contemporary Pagans." *Social Compass* April 28. https://journals.sagepub.com/doi/abs/10.1177/0037768617704165

Gardell, Mattias. 2003. *Gods of Blood: The Pagan Revival and White Separatism.* Durham, NC: Duke University Press.

Giddens, Anthony. 1991. *Modernity and Self Identity: Self and Society in the Late Modern Age.* Stanford, Calif.: Stanford University Press.

Gilligan, Carol. 1982. *In A Different Voice: Psychological Theory and Women's Development.* Cambridge, Mass.: Harvard University Press.

Gray, Thomas. 1990. "Gender differences in belief in scientifically unsubstantiated phenomena." *Canadian Journal of Behavioural Science / Revue canadienne des sciences du comportement* 22 (2): 181–90.

Greenwood, Susan. 2000. *Magic, Witchcraft and the Otherworld: An Anthropology.* Oxford: Berg.

Griffin, Wendy. 2005. "Web of Women: Feminist Spiritualities." In *Witchcraft and Magic: Contemporary North America,* edited by Helen A. Berger, 55–80. Philadelphia: University of Pennsylvania Press.

Hammer, Olaf. 2010. "I Did It My Way: Individual Choice and Social Conformity in New Age Religion." In *Religions of Modernity Relocating the Sacred to the Self and the Digital,* edited by Stef Auper and Dick Houtman, 49–67 Leiden: Brill.

Hampton, Keith, Lauren Sessions Goulet, Eun Ja Her, and Lee Rainie. 2009. "Social Isolation and New Technology: How the Internet and Mobile Phones Impact Americans' Social Networks." Pew Internet and American Life Project. http://www.pewinternet.org/2009/11/04/social-isolation-and-new-technology.

Harrington, Melissa. 2007. "The Perennial Teen Witch: A Discussion of Teenage Interest in Modern Pagan Witchcraft." In *The New Generation of Witches: Teenage Witchcraft in Contemporary Culture,* edited by Peg Aloi and Hannah E. Johnston, 25–40. Hampshire, U.K.: Ashgate.

Harvey, Graham. 1997. *Contemporary Paganism: Listening People, Speaking Earth.* New York: New York University Press.

———. 2005. *Animism: Respecting the Living World.* New York: Columbia University Press.

———. 2015. *The Handbook of Contemporary Animism.* London: Routledge.

Heelas, Paul. 1996. *The New Age Movement.* Blackwell, Oxford.

Heelas, Paul, et al. 2005. *The Spiritual Revolution: Why Religion Is Giving Way to Spirituality.* Oxford: Blackwell.

Helasdottir, Stella. 2017. "No Frið for Charlottesville Racists." Huggin's Heathen Hof. Blog, August 15. http://www.heathenhof.com/no-frith-charlottesville-racists/.

Heselton, Philip. 2000. *Wiccan Roots: Gerald Gardner and the Modern Witchcraft Revival.* Chieveley: Capall Bann.

Hoffman, Jan. 2016. "Estimate of U.S. Transgender Population Doubles to 1.4 Million Adults." *New York Times,* June 30. míhttps://www.nytimes.com/2016/07/01/health/transgender-population.html.

Houtman, Dick, and Stef Aupers. 2010. "Religions of Modernity: Relocating the Sacred to the Self and the Digital." In *Religions of Modernity: Relocating the Sacred to the Self and the Digital,* edited by Stef Auper and Dick Houtman, 1–29. Leiden: Brill.

Howard, Robert Glenn. 2011. *Digital Jesus: Making of a New Christian Fundamentalist Community on the Internet.* New York: New York University Press.

Hutton, Ronald. 1999. *The Triumph of the Moon: A History of Modern Pagan Witchcraft.* Oxford: Oxford University Press.

———. 2009. *Blood and Mistletoe: The History of the Druids in Britain.* New Haven, Conn.: Yale University Press.

Johnson, Fern. 1996. "Friendships among Women: Closeness in Dialogue." In *Gendered Relationships,* edited by Julia Wood, 79–94. Mountain View, Calif.: Mayfield.

Jorgensen, Danny L., and Scott E. Russell. 1999. "American Neo-Paganism: The Participants' Social Identities." *Journal for the Scientific Study of Religion* 38 (September): 325–38.

Junge, Christine. 2011. "How Your Friends Make You Fat: The Social Network of Weight." In *Harvard Health Publications*. http://www.health.harvard.edu/blog/how-your-friends-make-you-fat%E2%80%94the-social-network-of-weight-201105242666.

Kaplan, Jeffrey. 1996. "The Reconstruction of the Ásatrú and Odinist Traditions." In *Magical Religion and Modern Witchcraft*, edited by James R. Lewis, 193–236. Albany, N.Y.: State University of New York Press.

———. 1997. *Radical Religion in America: Millenarian Movements from the Far Right to Children of Noah*. Syracuse, N.Y.: Syracuse University Press.

Kermani, S. Zohreh. 2013. *Pagan Family Values: Childhood and the Religious Imagination in Contemporary American Paganism*. New York: New York University Press.

Kuhn, Thomas S. 1962. *The Structure of Scientific Revolutions*. Chicago: University of Chicago Press.

Lasch, Christopher. 1979. *The Culture of Narcissism*. New York: Norton.

———. 1984. *The Minimal Self*. New York: Norton.

Letcher, Andrew. 2000. "Virtual Paganism or Direct Action?" *Diskus* 6. http://www.uni-marburg.de/religionswissenschaft/journal/diskus.

Lewis, James R. 1996. Introduction. In *Magical Religion and Modern Witchcraft*, edited by James R. Lewis, 1–5. Albany: State University of New York Press.

———. 2007. "The Pagan Explosion: An Overview of Select Census and Survey Data." In *The New Generation Witches: Teenage Witchcraft in Contemporary Culture*, edited by Hannah E. Johnston and Peggy Aloi, 13–23. Hampshire, U.K.: Ashgate.

———. 2011. Personal communication. September.

———. 2012. "The Pagan Explosion Revisited: A Statistical Postmortem on the Teen Witch Fad." *Pomegranate: The International Journal of Pagan Studies* 14:1.

Lipka, Michael. 2016. "Five Facts about Religion." Pew Research Center, May 4. http://www.pewresearch.org/fact-tank/2016/05/04/5-facts-about-prayer/.

Lövheim, Mia. 2013. "Identity." In *Digital Religion: Understanding Religious Practice in New Media Worlds*, edited by Heidi A. Campbell, 41–56. London: Routledge.

Luhrmann, Tanya M. 1989. *Persuasions of the Witch's Craft*. Oxford: Blackwell.

———. 2012. *When God Talks Back: Understanding the American Evangelical Relationship with God*. New York: Alfred A. Knopf.

Lyons, Linda. 2005. "Paranormal Beliefs Come (Super) Naturally to Some." Gallup. http://www.gallup.com/poll/19558/paranormal-beliefs-come-supernaturally-some.aspx.

Mania Greg. 2018. "The Olsen Twins Have Some New Boutique Witchy Products for You to Buy." *Out Magazine*. March 7. https://www.out.com/popnography/2018/3/07/first-look-olsen-twins-release-line-wiccan-supplies-accessories.

Martí, Gerardo. 2017. "New Concepts for New Dynamics: Generating Theory for the Study of Religious Innovation and Social Change" *Journal for the Scientific Study of Religion* 56 (1): 6–18.

McDowell, Amy D. "'Christian but Not Religious: Being Church as Christian Hardcore Punk." *Sociology of Religion* 79 (1) 58–77.

McGraw, Barbara. 2004. "The Witch's Will: Magick as a Religious Social Ethic." Presented at the Annual Meeting of the Association for the Sociology of Religion. San Francisco, August 14–17.

McGuire, Meredith B. 2008. *Lived Religion: Faith and Practice in Everyday Life.* Oxford: Oxford University Press.

Mears, Daniel, and Christopher Ellison. 2000. "Who Buys New Age Materials? Exploring Sociodemographic, Religious, Network and Contextual Correlates of New Age Consumption." *Sociology of Religion* 61 (3): 289–313.

Moore, David W. 2005. "Three in Four Americans Believe in Paranormal." Gallup News, June 16. http://news.gallup.com/poll/16915/three-four-americans-believe-paranormal.aspx.

Murray, Margaret A. 1971 [1921]. *The Witch-Cult in Western Europe.* Oxford: Clarendon. http://www.gallup.com/poll/19558/paranormal-beliefs-come-supernaturally-some.aspx.

Neitz, Mary-Jo. 1991. "In Goddess We Trust." In *In Gods We Trust,* edited by Thomas Robbins and Dick Anthony, 353–72. New Brunswick, N.J.: Transaction.

Newport, Frank. 2012. "In the U.S., 5% Consider Themselves Vegetarians." Gallup. https://news.gallup.com/poll/156215/consider-themselves-vegetarians.aspx, accessed November 30, 2018.

Oboler, Regina S. 2004. "Nature Religion as a Cultural System?" *Pomegranate: The International Journal of Pagan Studies* 6 (1): 86–106.

Orion, Loretta. 1995. *Never Again the Burning Times: Paganism Revived.* Prospect Heights, Ill.: Waveland Press.

Orsi, Robert. 1995. *Thank You St. Jude: Women's Devotion to the Patron Saint of Hopeless Causes.* New York: Citadel, 1996.

Paxon, Diana L. 2006. *Essential* Ásatrú*: Walking the Path of Norse Paganism.* New York: Citadel.

Pearson, Jo. 2003. "'Witchcraft Will Not Soon Vanish from This Earth': Wicca in the 21st Century." In *Predicting Religion: Christian, Secular, and Alternative Futures,* edited by Grace Davies, Paul Heelas, and Linda Woodhead, 170–83. Hampshire, U.K.: Ashgate.

Pew. 2009. "Many Americans Mixed Multiple Faiths." http://www.pewforum.org/2009/12/09/many-americans-mix-multiple-faiths.

———. 2013. "Growing Public Support for Same Sex Marriage: Changed Minds and Changed Demographics. http://www.people-press.org/2013/03/20/growing-support-for-gay-marriage-changed-minds-and-changing-demographics.

———. 2014. "Religious Landscape Study" http://www.pewforum.org/religious-landscape-study, accessed November 30, 2018.

———. 2018 "Americans are far more religious than adults in other wealthy nations. July 31. http://www.pewresearch.org/fact-tank/2018/07/31/americans-are-far-more-religious-than-adults-in-other-wealthy-nations.

Pike, Sarah M. 2001. *Earthly Bodies, Magical Selves: Contemporary Pagans and the Search for Community.* Berkeley: University of California Press.

———. 2004. *New Age and Neopagan Religions in America.* New York: Columbia University Press.

Putnam, Robert. 2001. *Bowling Alone: The Collapse and Revival of American Community.* New York: Simon and Shuster.

Putnam, Robert, and David E. Campbell. 2010. *American Grace: How Religion Divides and Unites Us.* New York: Simon and Shuster.

RavenWolf, Silver. 1993. *To Ride a Silver Broomstick: New Generation Witchcraft.* St. Paul, Minn.: Llewellyn.

———. 1999. *Teen Witch: Wicca for a New Generation.* St. Paul, Minn.: Llewellyn.

Reuters, Ipsos, and the University of Virginia Center for Politics. 2017. "Race Poll" http://www.centerforpolitics.org/crystalball/wp-content/uploads/2017/09/2017-Reuters-UVA-Ipsos-Race-Poll-9–11–2017.pdf.

Riffkin, Rebecca. 2015. "In U.S. More Say Animals Should Have Same Rights as People" *Social and Policy Issues,* May 18. https://news.gallup.com/poll/183275/say-animals-rights-people.aspx.

Rubin, Lillian B. 1985. *Just Friends: The Role of Friendship in Our Lives.* New York: Harper and Row.

Ryan, Camille L. and Kurt Bauman. 2016. "Educational Attainment in United States: 2015" *The United States Census Bureau. https://www.census.gov/content/dam/Census/library/publications/2016/demo/p20–578.pdf,* accessed November 30, 2018.

Saiving-Goldstein, Valerie. 1960. "The Human Situation: A Feminine View." *Journal of Religion* 40 (2): 100–12.

Salomonsen, Jone. 2002. *Enchanted Feminism: The Reclaiming Witches of San Francisco.* London: Routledge.

Samuel, Sigal. 2017. "What to Do When Racists Try to Hijack Your Religion." Atlantic, November 2. https://www.theatlantic.com/international/archive/2017/11/Ásatrú-heathenry-racism/543864.

Scott, Eric O. 2015. "Ásatrúarfélagið Threatened with Vandalism over LGBTQ Support." Wild Hunt. http://wildhunt.org/2015/07/Ásatrúarfelagid-threatened-with-vandalism-over-lgbtq-support.html, accessed July 19, 2015.

Sennett, Richard. 2011. "Review of *Age of Fracture* by Daniel T. Rogers." *Contemporary Sociology: A Journal of Review* 41 (2): 164–66.

Shumaker, Wayne. 1979. *Occult Science in the Renaissance: A Study in Intellectual Patterns.* Berkeley: University of California Press.

Singal, Jesse. 2017. "Undercover with the Alt-Right." *New York Times,* September 19. https://www.nytimes.com/2017/09/19/opinion/alt-right-white-supremacy-under cover.html?smid=fb-share&_r=0.

Snook, Jennifer. 2015. *American Heathens: The Politics of Identity in a Pagan Religious Movement.* Philadelphia: Temple University Press.

Sointu, Eeva, and Linda Woodhead. 2008. "Spirituality, Gender, and Expressive Selfhood." *Journal for the Scientific Study of Religion* 47 (2): 259–76.

Starhawk. 1979. *The Spiral Dance.* San Francisco: Harper and Row.

———. 1982. *Dreaming the Dark.* Boston: Beacon.

———. 1994. *The Fifth Sacred Thing.* New York: Bantam.

Stark, Rodney. 2001. "Reconceptualizing Religion, Magic, and Science." *Review of Religious Research* 43 (2): 101–20.

Stoller, Paul, and Cheryl Olkes. 1987. *In Sorcery's Shadow.* Chicago: University of Chicago Press.

Strmiska, Michael F. 2016. "Playfully Religious: Paganesque in Popular Culture." *Lithuanian Journal of Anthropology.*

Taylor, Charles. 1989. *Ethics of Authenticity.* Cambridge, Mass.: Harvard University Press.

———. 1992. *Sources of the Self.* Cambridge: Cambridge University Press.

Troeltsch, Ernst. 1992 [1912]. *The Social Teachings of the Christian Churches.* Louisville, Ky.: Westminster John Knox.

Wallis, Roy. 1976. *The Road to Total Freedom: A Sociological Analysis of Scientology.* London: Heinemann.

Samuel, Sigal. 2017. "What to Do When Racists Try to Hijack Your Religion." *Atlantic,* November 2. https://www.theatlantic.com/international/archive/2017/11/Ásatrú-heathenry-racism/543864/

Warner, R. Stephen. 1993. "Work in Progress: Toward a New Paradigm for the Sociological Study of Religion in the United States." *American Journal of Sociology* 98:1044–93.

Washington Post and ABC. 2017. Poll. http://apps.washingtonpost.com/g/page/politics/washington-post-abc-news-poll-aug-16-20-2017/2235.

Wildman-Hanlon, Laura. 2009. "Generational Retention within the New Religious Movement of Neo-Paganism." In *Paganism: Critical Concepts in Religion,* edited by Barbara J. Davy, 350–66. New York: Routledge.

Wilson, Bryan. 1990. *The Social Dimensions of Sectarianism: Sects and Social Movements in Contemporary Society.* Oxford: Clarendon.

Woodhead, Linda. 2013. "New Forms of Public Religion: Spirituality in Global Civil Society." In *Religion beyond Its Private Role in Modern Society,* edited by Wim Hofstee and Arie van der Kooij, 29–52. Leiden: Brill.

———. 2009a. "'Because I'm Worth It': Religion and Women's Changing Lives in the West." In *Women and Secularisation,* edited by Kristin Aune, Sonya Sharma, and Giselle Vincett, 145–67. Aldershot: Ashgate.

———. 2009b. "Old, New, and Emerging Paradigms in the Sociological Study of Religion." *Nordic Journal of Religion and Society* 22:103–21.

———. 2010. "Real Religion and Fuzzy Spirituality? Taking Sides in the Sociology of Religion." In *Relocating the Sacred to the Self and the Digital,* edited by Stef Auper and Dick Houtman, 31–48. Leiden: Brill.

York, Michael. 1995. *The Emerging Network: A Sociology of the New Age and Neo-Pagan Movements.* London: Rowman and Littlefield.

———. 2004 "Pagan Ethics" Presented at the Annual Meeting of the Association for the Sociology of Religion San Francisco, CA August 14-17.

———. 2016. *Pagan Ethics: Paganism as a World Religion.* Cham, Switzerland: Springer.

Index

Page numbers in *italics* refer to tables.